YANKEE
GO
HOME?

J.L. GRANATSTEIN

YANKEE GO HOME?

CANADIANS AND ANTI-AMERICANISM

A Phyllis Bruce Book
HarperCollins*PublishersLtd*

YANKEE GO HOME? CANADIANS AND ANTI-AMERICANISM
Copyright © 1996 by J.L. Granatstein.
All rights reserved. No part of this book may be used or reproduced
in any manner whatsoever without prior written permission
except in the case of brief quotations embodied in reviews.
For information address HarperCollins Publishers Ltd,
Suite 2900, Hazelton Lanes, 55 Avenue Road,
Toronto, Canada M5R 3L2.

http://www.harpercollins.com/canada

All effort has been made to obtain copyright permission
for the cartoons reprinted in this book.

The excerpt from "Civil Elegies" by Dennis Lee is used with permission of Stoddart
Publishing Co. Limited, Don Mills, Ont.

First edition

Canadian Cataloguing in Publication Data

Granatstein, J.L., 1939-
Yankee go home? : Canadians and anti-Americanism

"A Phyllis Bruce book."
Includes bibliographical references and index.
ISBN 0-00-255301-5

1. Canada - Relations - United States.   2. United States - Relations - Canada.
3. Nationalism - Canada.   I. Title.

FC249.G73 1996   327.71073   C96-933309-6
F1029.5.U6G73 1996

96 97 98 99 ❖ HC 10 9 8 7 6 5 4 3 2 1

Printed and bound in the United States

For Carole and Eric

CONTENTS

PREFACE

Macdonald, Diefenbaker, Mulroney . . .
what a difference a prime minister makes.

T his book is not the book I expected to write when I began it several years ago. As a devout anti-American for as long as I can remember, I antici- pated producing a justification that would be a rationale for what I believed and knew to be true: the United States was and remained a threat to Canada's independence, and anti-Americanism was a rational defence against the takeover of Canada by American money, ideas, and culture. To my surprise, the research and writing of this book began to alter my views. From the Loyalists through to the reciprocity elections of 1891 and 1911 and beyond, I decided, anti-Americanism was almost always employed as a tool by Canadian political and economic élites bent on preserving or enhancing their power. It was largely the Tory way of keeping pro-British attitudes uppermost in the Canadian psyche. After the Second World War, anti-Americanism gradually became an ever more feeble and defensive response to the increasing American economic, military, and political suzerainty over Canada and the world. I can identify with that aspect of rational anti-Americanism, which has an honourable tradition on the social-democratic left, in Red Toryism, and in other areas of Canadian life, but many of its most virulent expressions since the 1950s have been either overtly Marxist or just plain silly. Groucho Marxism, in other words, was not for me, and the conclusions of this book will certainly surprise my friends and may puzzle some of those who have always disagreed with me.

By focusing on some key figures and some representative events, I attempt to indicate the roots of Canadian attitudes to the United States, to show how they have evolved, and to assess the past and present force of anti-Americanism in Canadian life. My emphasis is on English Canada, though francophone attitudes appear throughout the work.

I have also discovered in writing *Yankee Go Home?* that each Canadian has his or her own definition of anti-Americanism, strong views on its merits or demerits, and firm convictions that it either does or does not flourish in the Maritimes, Quebec, the Prairies, or British Columbia. (Everyone insists that anti-Americanism flourishes in Ontario.) We are all experts on the various Canadian attitudes to the Americans. Perhaps that is why, despite the widespread interest in the subject, few Canadians have tried to write about it. This book is the first that surveys the history of Canadian anti-Americanism from the Loyalists to yesterday. To those who disagree with my argument, I can understand, sympathize, and even concede that they may be right. At the same time, they should know that every other Canadian will disagree with them in some manner.

The text is lightly referenced, but there is a note on sources for each chapter that provides the key books and manuscript collections used. If the source of any quotation is wanted, full citations can be provided on request.

*   *   *

As always, I have benefited from the assistance and advice of many people. I owe much to researchers Bettina Steinhauser, James D'Ombrain, Patrick

Nugent, Chris Moore, Xavier Gélinas, Richard Lund, Milena Ivkovic, Daniel Robinson, Jamie Glazov, and especially Graham Rawlinson; to York University and the Social Science and Humanities Research Council of Canada, which helped pay for their work and my own research travel; and to my friends Michael Bliss, Norman Hillmer, Robert Bothwell, William Kaplan, and Paul Grayson, who commented on the manuscript in whole or in part to my great benefit, as did Phyllis Bruce and Rosemary Shipton, the best of editors. Dr Jonathan Vance kindly shared some of his own important research, and the staff of the United States Consulate General in Toronto secured access for me to United States Information Agency opinion polls, and (although he will greatly dislike being linked to the USIA even in a sentence) Professor Robin Mathews engaged me in a long, contentious correspondence that was most helpful to my work. To all of them I am grateful and pronounce them completely responsible for this book and for any errors that have persisted.

JLG
Toronto

INTRODUCTION

The American Dream

1891: The old man looked out over the audience of cheering partisans gathered to greet him in Toronto. Now seventy-six, his face deeply lined and showing the effects of his regular heavy drinking, the Prime Minister could still stir a crowd, his soft Scottish burr hypnotizing his listeners until, reaching his emotional peroration, he could bring the people out of their chairs, shouting and stamping their feet. Yes, Sir John A. Macdonald told the country, his government had desired reciprocity with the United States, but the idea could not be sold in the American capital.

INTRODUCTION

Why? Because Canadian traitors had gone to Washington to tell the people there that if they did not try to obstruct Canada's trade, they would never annex Canada. It was a deliberate conspiracy, a conspiracy "by force, by fraud or by both to force Canada into the American union." In the circumstances, he cried, for the Liberals to call for Unrestricted Reciprocity—complete free trade—with the United States was treason, a betrayal of Canada's British destiny. "We had a free Queen over a free people—governed by the principles of equity, the principles of religion, the principles of morality—which a fierce democracy never had and never would have. Would the people of Canada submit to such a change?" Wilfrid Laurier and the Liberals were readying themselves to sell out Canada to the Yankees, but he would not permit this to happen. The Americans could use their gold to try to buy Laurier an election victory, but "we prize our country as much as they do . . . we would fight for our existence." Then, in the greatest lines in Canadian political oratory, Macdonald smashed the Liberal campaign for Unrestricted Reciprocity: "A British subject I was born, and a British subject I will die. With my utmost effort, with my last breath, will I oppose the 'veiled treason' which attempts by sordid means and mercenary proffers to lure our people from their allegiance."

1991: Edmonton publisher Mel Hurtig lashed out in his book, *The Betrayal of Canada*, at those Canadian business and corporate leaders who had supported the Free Trade Agreement of 1988 and, with their contributions, helped Brian Mulroney's Progressive Conservatives win re-election that year. "The FTA means the Americanization of Canada," he wrote, and "the supporters of the FTA approve of this." It was time for blunt talk, Hurtig added. "The time has come to stop using muddy terms like 'continentalism'" which are far too weak. "So many of the voices heard from Canada's élite today are not the voices of continentalism; they are the voices of those who advocate the Americanization of Canada, though they never have the courage to say so. As much as separatists in Quebec," he went on, "they are the anti-Canadians. They are the harmonizers, the integrationists, the capitulators, the abandoners of a nation. They are the 'Canada-lasters.' It seems as if many of them don't give a damn for our country, its welfare or its survival."

Made exactly one hundred years apart, the two statements had much in common. To Macdonald, just as to Hurtig, those who wanted free trade with the United States were willing, indeed eager, to see Canada

2

absorbed. The stench of treason, explicit in Macdonald, implicit in Hurtig, hung over the free trade forces. Free trade would seduce Canadians from their allegiance, and lead to the physical or the psychological absorption of the country by the United States. For Hurtig, the maxim laid down by philosopher George Grant in his 1965 *Lament for a Nation* remained all too true: "No small country can depend for its existence upon the loyalty of its capitalists." Anti-Americanism for him was a powerful weapon in 1991, just as it had been for Sir John A. in 1891.

But there were differences, too. In 1891 the power and money of Canada's business leaders was firmly behind Macdonald and his Conservative Party, the creators and defencers of the National Policy of high tariffs behind which Canadian manufacturers sought protection from cheaper American goods. In 1991 corporate Canada supported the Free Trade Agreement that the Progressive Conservative Party had negotiated and put into place. Business was delighted to see tariffs abolished, and they applauded every government effort to harmonize Canadian policies with those of the United States.

In the course of a century, the Conservative Party had changed from a fierce opponent of free trade into its advocate. Business had made the same transition. What had not changed was the anti-Americanism that so many Canadians shouted at all those who tried to bring the two North American nations closer together. But there was an important difference. In 1891 the anti-American campaign had been brilliantly successful, giving Macdonald a smashing victory as Canadians rallied around the Old Man, the Old Flag, and the Old Policy. In the election of 1988, anti-Americanism failed to carry the country, and Mulroney won a substantial majority for his Free Trade Agreement. Intended as a call to action, Hurtig's book was only an angry lament for what had already and irreversibly come to pass.

*　　*　　*

Canadians are used to being ignored by their neighbours, and it will come as no surprise to discover that two American political scientists studying the Third World in 1985 wrote that anti-Americanism "is a new phenomenon, differing markedly from the anti-British, anti-French or anti-Dutch sentiments" that arose under colonial rule. The authors clearly had never heard or read anything of Canada. More to the point, they contended that the tendency towards anti-Americanism is "most intense" among the intellectual élite, "and the political élite, like the intellectuals, frequently function on the basis of the connection between anti-Americanism and nationalism."[1] That rings true to Canadian ears.

There is some resonance, too, in the definitions of anti-Americanism employed by other writers to explain the phenomenon. Paul Hollander, a leading scholar of the subject, defines anti-Americanism as "a particular mind-set, an attitude of distaste, aversion or intense hostility the roots of which may be found in matters unrelated to the actual qualities or attributes of American society or the foreign policies of the United States." To Hollander and to British author Paul Johnson anti-Americanism, whether found among Americans or foreigners, is much like racism, sexism, or anti-Semitism.[2] Two more American scholars, Alvin Rubinstein and Donald Smith, break down the definition even further as an "undifferentiated attack on the foreign policy, society, culture and values of the United States." They see it as issue-oriented, ideological, instrumental (by which they mean the manipulation of anti-American feelings by a government for ulterior purposes), or revolutionary (in which anti-Americanism arises in groups seeking to topple a pro-US government).[3]

None of these definitions completely captures the unique nature of Canadian anti-Americanism. How could they when the Canadian variant is far older than any other? How could non-Canadians understand the central place that anti-Americanism has played in all our history? Who else could believe that Canadian anti-Americanism, just as much as the country's French–English duality, has for two centuries been a central buttress of the national identity?

I believe that Canadian anti-Americanism is both more simple and more complex to define. It is a distaste for and a fear of American military, political, cultural, and economic activities that, while widespread in the population, is usually benign unless and until it is exploited by business, political, or cultural groups for their own ends. Added to this is a snippet—and sometimes more—of envy at the greatness, wealth, and power of the Republic and its citizens, and a dash of discomfort at the excesses that mar American life.

In Canada, anti-Americanism began with the understandable hostility that develops when imperial powers and their colonies go to war. It existed in New France, and it flourished when the rebellious Americans invaded British North America in 1776. It became a conservative phenomenon as

NEWS ITEM: U.S. ARMS SALES
(100 BILLION) EQUAL TO THOSE
OF ALL THE REST OF THE WORLD.

Macpherson/Reprinted with permission—The Toronto Star
Syndicate/National Archives of Canada C-113099

.the Loyalists and their supporters, not least the relatively recent immigrants from the British Isles, employed hatred of the Yankees to justify their detestation of democractic forms and republicanism, a tactic that was reinforced by the War of 1812 and the Rebellions of 1837. The Loyalist epic was bolstered by historians and turned into a folk myth, and, once the Dominion of Canada came together, anti-Americanism became the key tool in the maintenance of the established political and economic order, as Sir John A. Macdonald demonstrated in the reciprocity election of 1891. But the power of anti-Americanism could never remain constant and unvarying. Over the years, thanks largely to the devastating and debilitating impact of the world wars on Britain's economic and military power, the Canadian governing and business classes adjusted themselves to the presence and enormous power of the United States, though pockets of protectionism relied, in part, on anti-American sentiments to keep them safe. Anti-Americanism remained for the left to exploit, and Communists and social democrats both tried their hand at it. So, too, did elements within Walter Gordon's wing of the Liberal Party, where Mel Hurtig first made his mark. Then there were the Red Tories, that curious Canadian amalgam of social progressivism and conservativism whose anti-Americanism, embedded in the writings of George Grant and historian Donald Creighton, among others, was arguably the fiercest of any in the last half of the twentieth century.

Anti-Americanism has been found, at differing periods and in differing intensities, across the entire spectrum of Canadian politics and in all segments of Canadian life. All these groupings in Canadian society—the right, the protectionist centre, the Red Tories, and the Liberal, Marxist, and social-democratic left—now have largely succumbed to the homogenizing forces of continentalism. Only among the literati, in the cultural industries, and in academe does anti-Americanism remain alive and well in contemporary Canada.

In some ways, then, Canada today is unique in its anti-Americanism, or the absence of it. Although Canadian intellectuals and artists remain largely opposed to Americanization, the élites in society no longer resist it. This is not true elsewhere.Virtually all who look at anti-Americanism around the globe pinpoint its greatest strength among the élites *and* the cultural professions, a curious combination of what British writer Kenneth Minogue labelled "snobbery and socialism."[4] The élites of Europe and Asia fear and respect American military and economic power, but they dismiss the Americans themselves as uncultured cowboys or loud tourists festooned with cameras.

The intellectuals take a different tack. Anti-Americanism is, as a Dutch commentator said, "a disease of the intellectuals," a symptom of their "revulsion against Western society"[5] and, in some cases, until the collapse of Soviet Communism, of their foolish admiration for Moscow and all its works. Above all, for both élites and intellectuals, to be anti-American, as one German journalist noted, "is to defend one's right to protect one's own tradition against the presumptiveness of the marketplace psychology, the insistence on selling and reselling one's cultural values as if they were so many washing machines." The world recognizes that it is being Americanized, and it worries about the process. It also recognizes that the process of seduction is not wholly unpleasant.

Americanization, in other words, is much like the curate's egg—parts of it are good and parts are not. Most people outside the United States admire American dynamism, modernism, democracy, and labour-saving devices. Many of them fear the sometimes misguided energy of the United States and worry about the impact of American popular culture on their own—the elimination of the croissant by the donut. No one should be surprised that people worry about this process that continues to sweep all before it.[6] "Always blame the Americans," advises one of the characters in Costa-Gavras's political film Z. "Even when you're wrong, you're right."[7]

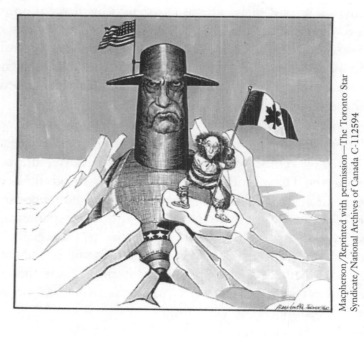

Macpherson/Reprinted with permission—The Toronto Star Syndicate/National Archives of Canada C-112594

*   *   *

Canadians recognize that they are being Americanized, fret about the process (while grasping eagerly for the rewards), and readily blame the Americans for foisting Americanization upon them.[8] These sentiments are usually latent. They combine with and merge into a sense that the line dividing Canadians from Americans is small, that, in fact, Canadians really *are* Americans. It is a sense that Canadians conceal from others and also, most vigorously, from themselves. Perhaps that is why their expressions of anti-Americanism have sometimes been so strong.

As North Americans, Canadians have tried to create their own distinctive society on the continent they share with the United States. As Canadians, they have been obliged to wrestle with their vastly richer and more powerful neighbour, so much so that they have come to define themselves not as they were and are, but in contradistinction from that great and grasping neighbour. Novelist Hugh MacLennan put it well in 1946: "It took me a long time to accept the fact that in the eyes of the average American this whole continent—at least all of it that is worth much—belongs to him."[9] Canadian views of the United States are informed by the American presence—so big, so familiar. That is what MacLennan saw, and many Canadians shared his perception, more than enough to demonstrate the fundamental truth of the definitive comment on this country's tradition of anti-Americanism. The Canadian, wrote historian Frank Underhill, "is the first anti-American, the model anti-American, the archetypal anti-American, the ideal anti-American as he exists in the mind of God."

The Canadians were the first and the model anti-Americans because the *habitants* and the Loyalists both wanted to remain free of the United States. They were the ideal anti-Americans because, unlike many in Europe and the Third World, they actually understood the United States and appreciated its idealism and passion while simultaneously rejecting much of the American ethos. They were the archetypal anti-Americans because, even if the world has failed to realize it, Canadians had set the terms of the debate—virtually everything that is said of the crassness and violence of American society today, for example, was first uttered by nineteenth-century British North Americans who looked down their noses at the mobocracy to the south.

All this is certainly true. Yet, given the enormous influence of the United States on every aspect of Canadian life, I find myself asking, along with political writer Rick Salutin, why Canada is today "probably the least anti-American country around, around the Free World anyway, those countries which fall under direct US influence."[10] Certainly Salutin is right if the global definitions of anti-Americanism are applied to Canada. Moreover, as Canadians regularly write, say, and apparently believe that they define themselves against the United States, why is it that they have never produced any sustained critiques or appreciations of the United States? Why is it that the French, their culture protected by history, language, and the Atlantic Ocean, have defined, written about, and devoutly practised anti-Americanism in this century, and not Canadians?[11] Why is it that, since the reciprocity election of 1911, anti-Americanism has never been victorious in political warfare in this country and, Robin Mathews's campaign against the Americanization of Canadian universities aside, scarcely won triumphs of any kind?

INTRODUCTION

In the circumstances, is Canada's anti-Americanism anything more than a defensive reaction from a people who, in fact, are not simply North Americans but Americans in all but name? The Canadian, I might argue in this vein, is only an American with medicare and without a President, a Congress, a foreign policy that mixes violence and altruism, and a domestic policy that fosters murder, ghettoes, and widespread illegitimacy among blacks and whites. A kinder, gentler American, a different American, in other words.

Perhaps this similarity explains why Canadian anti-Americanism always was so much milder than the virulent varieties that afflicted Europe, Latin America, Africa, and Asia. "Yankee Go Home?" the title of this book, is deliberately used in an ironic way, as the question mark suggests. Yet in the parts of the world exploited by American corporations, and where regimes owed their survival to Washington's military support, it remained the epithet of choice until very recently. Even so, the characteristics of anti-Americanism in the world at large have their variants here. John Diefenbaker, like John A. Macdonald and Robert Borden before him, used anti-Americanism for instrumental and electoral purposes. Canadian Communists and fellow-travellers like Reverend James Endicott were every bit as ideological in their denunciations of American imperialism as their Soviet masters. George Grant was intellectually and philosophically anti-American, and Walter Gordon, determined to control the inflow of American capital and to foster domestic investment, was the very model of an issue-oriented anti-American. Strange bed-fellows indeed.

But Canadians have never been revolutionary anti-Americans, nor have they ever been given to burning United States Information Agency libraries, killing American diplomats and tourists or taking them hostage, or storming Washington's embassy and consulates on their soil. Even during the Vietnam War, when crowds demonstrated in front of the United States Embassy in Ottawa and the consulates in Montreal, Toronto, and Vancouver, Canadian responses were so bland that American draft resisters complained about the unrelenting passivity of their hosts.

Although Canadian anti-Americanism often shared the distaste, aversion, and unreasoning hostility to all things American that characterized anti-Americanism generally, proximity and a shared heritage made the Canadian variant more understanding of the United States than that practised abroad. Sixty-five years ago, Percy Corbett of McGill University noted that Canadians had "a network of intimate friendships" with

Americans, but at the same time "a widespread distaste for Americans in general."[12] More recently, Charles Doran and James Sewell characterized anti-Americanism in Canada as mixing derision and affection.[13] Canadian economist Harry Johnson was more scathing in his condemnation of the "genteel hypocrisy" and immaturity with which Canadians practised their anti-Americanism. He pointed to the "eminent Canadians loudly expressing their admiration and warm friendship for the American people while advocating schemes for depriving some of them of control of their property, and professional-explainers of Canada to the Americans begging the Americans not to be offended by the nasty anti-American remarks they are about to hear, because we're just having a friendly argument among ourselves, and really we love them."[14] Some of our best friends are Americans, in other words, but we wouldn't want our sons and daughters to marry them—though they do!

These comments precisely reflect the contradictory nature of Canadian attitudes to the United States. Even as we revel in the differences between our societies (or, at least, those that we assume favour us), we continue to observe the Americans with a sympathetic if dubious gaze. Canadians, even the Loyalists, Britannic imperialists of the late nineteenth-century, and the crusaders of the Committee for an Independent Canada in the 1970s, have always been ready to listen to on-going American debates and to take the best American ideas to put into practice. Canada's federal system, for example, was designed during the American Civil War to be a more perfect form of the structure created by Washington, Jefferson, Hamilton, and Adams. Our national parks were modelled on those established by the United States. Prairie Progressives in the 1920s, like Ontario populists thirty years earlier, modelled their policy prescriptions on American thinking. Our schools regularly followed American trends, for good and often for ill, and Pierre Trudeau's Charter of Rights and Freedoms introduced what many consider to be American concepts of individual rights and litigiousness into our hitherto more ordered society. Should we be surprised? Canadians are Americans, after all, shaped by and shaping the North American environment, so that the lives we enjoy are much like those of our cousins to the more prosperous south.

Historians and politicians have naturally focused on the difficult periods in Canadian–American relations, the years in which anti-Americanism flourished. The barometer of public opinion measured the recurring storms that troubled relations along the border and, whenever the mercury dropped, the threats from Washington invariably produced expressions of Canadian determination to resist the damn Yankees to the last man—or to strike a special deal with the United States by reminding Washington that the dominion really was its best friend in the world. There were always enough genuine grievances and irritants on both sides of the line to keep the weather, for those who worried about the climate, unstable in good times and bad. In general, however, despite the efforts of those who wanted to keep the border closed, most Canadians and Americans have got on better than almost any two peoples anywhere.

Even at its periods of greatest intensity, anti-Americanism in Canada tended to be limited to plucking the occasional feather from the eagle's tail. It has always been more defensive than offensive. It also has been much more of a chimera than Canadians have been led to believe, a useful political, economic, and cultural tool at times but one whose power has faded into insignificance in the era of the Free Trade Agreement, the North American Free Trade Agreement, and massive cultural domination by New York and Hollywood.

Anti-Americanism in the mid-1990s is at its lowest ebb ever. It was never an idea or an attitude that could bear the weight assigned to it by genera-tions of Canadians. Hating the Americans was a fundamentally unworthy attitude, a barren, soul-destroying conceit that Canadians employed to explain to themselves their slower growth and lesser power. Today, with Confederation threatened, with separatist sentiments waxing, Canadians need a new unifying and positive national mythos. We need to shed the habit of seeking unity by letting politicians and cultural leaders denounce our neighbours. Instead, we must begin to understand what makes Canada unique. That is easier to say than to do, of course. What is certain, how-ever, is that anti-Americanism now cannot, indeed never could, provide the glue to hold the nation together.

In the chapters that follow, I will try to demonstrate the centrality of anti-Americanism in Canadian history and life, how it developed, how those who espoused it shifted over the decades, and how, finally, it waned and became increasingly inconsequential.

1

BLIND HATRED?
THE LOYALIST INHERITANCE

National Archives of Canada C-78568

A Pertinent Question

Mrs. Britannia: "Is it possible, my dear, that you have ever given
your cousin Jonathan any encouragement?"

Miss Canada: "Encouragement! Certainly not, Mamma.
I have told him we can *never* be united."

The American Revolution was a war for the minds of the people, a
struggle to establish a new vision of the liberties of men. The winners
created their founding myths out of this struggle, their triumph over
adversity, their victory against the odds, the ascendency of their ideals.
Today, thanks to American dominance over popular culture, the entire

world knows that life, liberty, and the pursuit of happiness were and remain the United States' lodestar.

And what of the losers? The American Revolution was a civil war producing bloody fighting, shocking atrocities of neighbour against neighbour, and torn allegiances. The United Empire Loyalists, the supporters of King George III against George Washington and the Continental Congress, were left in a cruel limbo by the British surrender. They believed in constitutional order and the rule of law; they respected authority and the monarchical principle; but their cause had been defeated. Should they stay in their homes and risk the certain retaliation of the victors? Should they flee to the remaining British territories in North America, the cold, inhospitable, and largely unsettled territories to the north of the victors' territory? As every Canadian schoolchild knows, the Loyalists chose to come north, many leaving substantial fortunes behind to be confiscated by the new states of the American union, to carve homes out of the wilderness, and to create one of the two founding myths of Canada. Just as the *habitants* fended off the Iroquois to build a society, a story known to every Québécois, so too did the Loyalists sacrifice everything for principle, creating out of the ashes and despair of defeat and dislocation a new and better society in the wilderness: a society motivated by loyalty to the Crown, to Britain, to order; a society different from and better than the United States; a society anti-American to the very roots.

Like most myths, the image of the self-sacrificing loyal colonist is greatly oversimplified. The situation was more complex, the motivations more complicated. Douglas Glover's splendid 1993 novel about the effect of the Revolutionary War on Loyalists and Rebels alike, *The Life and Times of Captain N*, captures the psychic dislocations of the war. One of his principal characters rails against "the five thousand Republicans seething up the trail behind us" as "the shape of a grand new idea, which I abhor. They destroy everything in their path. . . . They watch the forest itself with suspicion, measuring it with a cold, acquisitive eye. It is this measured, yet total, destructiveness which unnerves me. They are the future. I am against the future." Another character is described as "a tangle of confusion, atrocity, and mixed allegiances [who] cannot abide the great split amongst her people." Yet a third thinks of his son, "who is a Republican and a sorry person more worried about what the neighbors think than the state of his own soul or the debt he owes his father."

Glover's novel brilliantly captures the ambivalence of the Loyalists towards the British with whom and for whom they are ostensibly fighting. "It is astonishing to note the alteration in our attitudes toward the English," Glover has one of his characters say, as the Revolutionary War seems lost and the militarily incompetent British seem to be preparing themselves to abandon the colonists who have fought with them.

> I have grown to despise [the British] except for one or two. . . .
> But others, as their fear of abandonment enlarges, become fiercely
> attached to the King. They are afraid of the new and unknown.
> They think that by good behavior and proper fealty they can influ-
> ence the Redcoat generals to save them. It never enters their minds
> that they have already been forgotten, that the light of the royal
> eye has passed on, that the will of old England has already been
> broken by self-doubt and a new idea, that they cannot be saved,
> their farms redeemed, their families restored.

After yet another British defeat far to the south in the Carolinas, word of the débâcle filtered north to the Loyalists fighting on the Niagara frontier. "Once more all our blood and terror have gone for nothing, cancelled out by events a thousand miles away. When they hear it, the men grow silent or scoff or begin to whisper of farming in Canada."[1]

The ambivalence of the Loyalist soldiers was genuine, their hushed fear of a cold future "farming in Canada" real. They had stood against the revolutionary republican mobs and the revolutionists' professed ideals, and they had lost. Condemned by their neighbours for their apostasy, they would be forced to flee their native land for the inhospitable forests and bush of Canada. Their resentment and humiliation were palpable, but their hatred was never so uniformly focused on the victorious United States as Canadian legend has it. It was also directed at the London politicians and planners who had led them to defeat by failing to understand North American conditions. The Yankees had pride of place on the Loyalists' hate list, to be sure, but there were other names inscribed too.

*   *   *

Loyalism has had a mixed press in Canada in this century, though its anti-American component has survived for more than two centuries.

For too many Canadians, the United Empire Loyalists and their descendants either were or aspired to be a part of a natural ruling élite, an anti-democratic Family Compact, and élitism ran against the Canadian grain. The descendants of the forty or fifty thousand Loyalists who had fled to British North America after the conclusion of the Revolutionary War claimed that their forebears were "the very cream of the Thirteen Colonies." They argued that the Loyalists had "represented in very large measure the learning, the piety, the gentle birth, the wealth and good citizenship of the British race in America, as well as its devotion to law and order [and] British institutions." Such claims were offensive to later arrivals.

In fact, they were not even remotely true, especially of the Upper Canadian settlers. The Loyalists in their diversity were far more representative of the population of the revolting colonies than most United Empire Loyalist proponents could admit. Historian S.F. Wise, for example, noted that most Loyalists

> were not wealthy, well-born, well-educated Americans. Most were frontier farmers, skilled and semi-skilled artisans and small tradesmen. A high proportion were illiterate. Most were not Anglican but represented that broad band of Protestant denominationalism typical of colonial America; many were Catholic and a few were Jews. Though it is probable that a majority could trace their origins to Britain, many were Dutch or German or French-Canadian, some were American blacks and others were Six Nations Iroquois.[2]

What united the Loyalists was not just their devotion to the Crown and the British Empire or their shared sense of grievance against the United States. To be sure, they had the deep hatreds of those who had lost property, family, and homeland, who had been abused and defeated in war. But the Loyalists, the educated and the illiterate, the lawyers and the artisans, were also North Americans, citizens of the New World, men and women who, their political beliefs aside, were in every way the same as those who had driven them off their lands. Their exile to British North America at the end of the American Revolution was a testimony to their determination to have the best of both worlds—loyalty to the empire *and* a place in the New World that was so full of opportunity.

The Loyalists wanted to recreate what they believed they had lost—"a conservative, deferential, loyal society, especially suited to the conditions of the land and the people"—and for this the monarchy was of great symbolic importance. Although many of the Loyalist élite had little admiration for particular British policies towards the Thirteen Colonies, and still more carped at London's lack of reward for their devotion to the empire, they refused to accept the symbolic regicide practised by their American kin. George III may have been barking mad a good part of the time, but his was the figure that linked the Loyalists to the empire, that spurred his subjects to noble and benevolent deeds. Under his "influence and example," religion and virtue would find a "steady support" and "vice, immorality and profaneness" would be suppressed.[3] Above all, their devotion to monarchy gave the Loyalists a unique identity that was critical to a people suddenly flung into the midst of a great wilderness.[4*]

The society the Loyalist leaders sought to create was different from that of the new United States. South of the line, the Americans professed democracy, a belief that, to the Loyalists, meant turning over control of government to mob rule. After all, many of them had experienced directly the fury of that mob both before and after the triumph of the revolution in 1783. Democracy was anarchy, a rejection of the rule of law, a turning away from the ideas of order needed in any civilized society. Society, much like nature, had a natural order, where those of birth and talent had the right to rule. The American Revolution had rejected this order, tearing down the symbols of the past and putting in its place . . . what? A new order where money ruled. A country where the strongest could enforce their will. A nation whose leaders catered to the demands of the mob and manipulated it in too-frequent elections. A political system that was violent in the extreme. And a press that regularly exercised its licence in scurrilous fashion. Democracy was the tyranny of the majority at its worst. Such statements were always presented as fact and were psychologically vital to the Loyalist population of British North America. How else could they justify

---

* These sentiments sound not unlike the fervent pro-monarchical writings of a few present-day columnists, but if the phrases are all but meaningless to late twentieth-century Canadians who giggle at the front-page adulteries of princes, princesses, and duchesses, they had undoubted meaning to the refugee Loyalists, who sought desperately for ways to make clear and permanent the differences between themselves and the Yankees.

the hard choice they had made? British North America was different from the democracy to the south; for its governing few, it was an explicitly counter-revolutionary and deeply conservative society.

Yet the Loyalists were North Americans at heart. Their lives had been shaped by the land on which they lived and farmed, and its conditions had determined their lives. They had all been subjected to ideas of the equality of men,* freedom of religion, and hostility to special privilege. They were North Americans despite their being on the losing side in the revolution. No one of sense, therefore, should have hoped to create a "little England" in Nova Scotia, New Brunswick, the Eastern Townships of Quebec, or the southern portions of Upper Canada, where the Loyalists came to clear the land or live in the small towns. Many tried, however, aiming to make New Brunswick, which like Nova Scotia already had some viable English-speaking settlements, "a country fit for gentlemen," and seeking to use the 1791 Constitutional Act's provisions for a hereditary aristocracy in both the Canadas. When Lieutenant Governor John Graves Simcoe tried to create this caste system in Upper Canada by erecting the three pillars of monarchy, aristocracy, and an established Church of England, many of the King's loyal subjects objected strenuously. They were wiser than the Governor and his pathetic little group of British-born courtiers; such a situation would sow "the seeds of Civil disorder [by] perhaps laying the Foundation for Future Revolution." Simcoe, though he considered the Anglican Church established as the "national church," failed in his efforts to make it the controlling religious force in the country. Happily, he also failed to find enough gentlemen of quality in Upper Canada to create an aristocracy with "an Hereditary Right of being summoned to the Legislative Council." The Americanness of British North America made a colonial aristocracy almost laughable, though the idea drew the allegiance of all, especially those who had arrived in the Canadas directly from Britain, who thought they belonged within its ranks.

---

* But not the equality of women. In the new United States, historian (and Saskatchewan's NDP Finance Minister) Janice Potter-MacKinnon noted, the "anti-patriarchal aspects of the Revolution changed the status of women within the family and the society" for the better. But for Loyalist women, on the contrary, "the power structure they lived under was more, not less, authoritarian and patriarchal than that in the former American colonies." *While the Women Only Wept: Loyalist Refugee Women* (Montreal 1993), xv–xvi.

Evil though the republican United States might be in the eyes of those who clustered around Simcoe, sensible Upper Canadians realized that they were to a substantial extent economically dependent on their neighbour and even more reliant on the United States for creative ideas. New England Loyalists had grown up with town meetings and representative government, and they wanted something similar in their new homeland. The Loyalists watched American economic and social practices with interest across a border that ordinarily remained wide open to the flow of ideas. For example, Americans understood the agricultural methods best suited to the new societies the Loyalists were carving out of the "howling wilderness" that was British North America. If they were to turn their lands into productive farms, they needed American expertise. Roads and towns, schools, banks, and social institutions could be and were modelled on the practices to the south. It followed, therefore, that "late Loyalists," the influx of American settlers who came north in the years after the Loyalist migration for myriad reasons ranging from a desire for free land to disillusion with the fruits of the revolution, were welcomed because they helped to open up the country. The influx quickly diluted the Loyalist nature of the Upper Canadian settlements, and by 1800 there were more latecomers than original settlers. In its early years, Upper Canada was as demographically American as any community in the United States, and in Oxford County, it was said, nine of ten inhabitants celebrated the Fourth of July.

Despite their avowed anti-Americanism and the frequent upsets in Anglo-American relations after 1784 that disrupted trade and aroused concern of renewed warfare, many Loyalists had no qualms whatsoever about continuing business and social links with former associates in the United States. Some even advocated free trade and the complete elimination of the boundary for commercial purposes. Many prospered because of their ties to the south. Americans, too, had little difficulty accepting the situation after the Revolutionary War. The Burlington, Vermont, tavern-keeper whose sign, pointing north, showed Admiral Horatio Nelson and, pointing south, featured George Washington was typical in not wanting to alienate any passing customers.

In fact, once the immediate shock of defeat and dispossession began to ease, many in the British North American communities came to accept that there were good and bad Americans. The good, Federalists like Alexander Hamilton, generally wanted a conservative society of authority and order, much like that desired by the Loyalists. The bad, Republicans like Thomas Jefferson, were the democratic creators of the stereotypical Loyalist view of the United States as a land of wild anarchy. The whole of the United States could not be condemned, therefore, for to do so would be to attack friends and relatives and to condemn the North American inheritance the Loyalists shared. Perhaps the shared heritage and the tugs from home, as much as the hardships the Loyalists endured, explain why thousands returned to the United States. Shelburne, Nova Scotia, a once-thriving Loyalist capital of eight thousand in 1789, for example, was all but denuded of its population by the return to the south; by 1815 its residents numbered a mere six hundred. "Nova Scarcity," the Americans sneered. In Saint John, New Brunswick, at least one in ten returned home. It was the same in the Canadas, too, where the magistrates recorded many names under the heading "Quitted his land and gone off."

The vast majority of those who had come north remained in British North America. Some stayed because of their principled refusal to accept the idea that revolution should prevail. For others, almost certainly for most, the new land became home, a land of substantial promise where secure and satisfying lives could be made, where roots could be put down. British North America did have possibilities, but as the United States thrived and prospered, it soon became clear that the Loyalists had ended up in a lesser land. Good as British North America was, great as it might yet become, it was all too evident that it was never going to be anything more than second best. Envy was added to the list of principled grievances that Loyalists still held against the United States.

*   *   *

The makings of the Loyalist myth that mid-nineteenth-century Canadians would create were in place by the end of the eighteenth century. The War of 1812, a savage conflict that saw the United States try to seize the Canadas, reinforced the myth with battlefield martyrs and victory against high odds. That the Americans were genuinely provoked was overlooked.

The United States of President James Madison had real grievances against Great Britain. Fighting a war against Napoleon's French Empire, the Royal Navy used its control of the sea in ways that interfered with American rights of free passage. Moreover, the British did their best with money and arms to support Indian tribes such as the Wyandots, the Shawnee, and the Miami in their attempts to block American westward expansion and create a satellite native nation that would give Upper Canada a friendly neighbour to its southwest—a key aim of London's policy. To add to American resentment, British North America was seen as a repository of European values and institutions, by definition evil, in the New World. In 1775 one of the first acts of the Continental Congress had been to launch an invasion of Canada to drive out those values and institutions and to offer the *habitants* and the small number of British merchants in Quebec the blessings of republicanism at the point of a bayonet. Now, in 1812, the same aggressive offer would be made again. Whether or not Britain's sins justified an American declaration of war, Canadians did not want one, and most were unable to fathom why their neighbours would attack them.

Ready explanations could be found for American aggressive expansionism by those who sought them. To those Loyalists who had continued to cherish their anti-American sentiments for thirty years in the new lands, a second Anglo-American war was proof positive of the evils inherent in the American political system. "The characteristic evil of their democratic system," said the *Kingston Gazette* in January 1811, "is its tendency to foster an uncontrollable spirit of party. Their frequent popular elections of all branches of their government . . . fuel and fan the flame." The United States was a society where justice and stability had been lost. The Republic was a nation bitterly divided, led by a venal and corrupt Democratic Party oligarchy that would not hesitate to wage war to advance its interests. Democracy had corrupted the United States.* Federalists in the United States themselves uttered the same complaints.

The democratic evil was also loose in Upper Canada, most of its settlements huddled cheek by jowl against the international border or a short water voyage away. The cozy practices of the governing élite in dividing up offices and allocating land grants among themselves had begun to be denounced by aspiring democratic politicians as tyrannical. In response, office-holders grumbled about the way political partyism complicated their lives and obliged them to defend their actions. The critics were dis-

---

* Clergyman and educator Egerton Ryerson later characterized the War of 1812 as "a purely partizan war—the carrying out of the intrigue between the American Democratic President and the French despoiler of Europe [Napoleon]—a war against the intelligence and patriotism of the American people, as well as against the independence and liberties of nations." Egerton Ryerson, *The Loyalists of America and Their Times* (Toronto 1880), vol. 2, 332.

loyal, the élites maintained, and war with the United States would put down this rabble.

As war drew close in early 1812, Upper Canadian military and political leaders worried that the evil principles that had found their way into this country had begun to corrupt the loyalty of the people. They were greatly outnumbered even if everyone in Upper Canada had been united under the Union Jack: against 8 million Americans, there were 80,000 Upper Canadians, mostly American by birth, and 225,000 Lower Canadians, mostly French Canadians thought to be of dubious loyalty. Many in the Canadas looked nervously over their shoulder at the British and forward at the advancing Yankees. Where did self-interest lie? In neutrality? In resistance? Or in collaboration? It was not only recent American settlers who were uncertain. The Loyalists and their offspring were similarly affected by doubts, and some, at least, by the insidious democratic ideas that had spread northwards. Many in the colonial government feared massive defections.*

At first it was a war of words. The Americans, the colonial authorities declared, were "an Army of Banditti whose sole object was cowardly Plunder." For their part, the Republic's commanders claimed that the American armies had come to liberate the Canadas from British tyranny, and none expected much difficulty in carrying out the task. It would be "a mere matter of marching," as former President Thomas Jefferson put it delicately. Canadians were urged by their leaders to fight not only for their homes but also for the liberties enshrined in the British constitution. The rhetoric on both sides must have seemed grandiloquent to those who simply wished to be left alone as they eked out a living in the bush.

Major-General Sir Isaac Brock, the British military and civil commander in Upper Canada, had no illusions about the problems he faced. He had only 1600 British regulars in the province. Most of the disparate, fragmented population in western Upper Canada was of doubtful loyalty: "The greater part are either indifferent to what is passing, or so completely

* In 1816 the Executive Council of Upper Canada decreed that no petitions for land from the children of United Empire Loyalists would be granted unless proof was provided that the parent or the adult son or daughter had maintained loyalty during the War of 1812 and was under no suspicion of having aided the invaders. That decree suggested very strongly that some Loyalists had not maintained their allegiances. J.J. Talman, "The United Empire Loyalists," in Edith Firth, ed., *Profiles of a Province* (Toronto 1967), 5–6.

American as to rejoice in the prospects of a change of Government," he said in 1812. To fight this defeatism, Brock understood that he needed quick victories to rally the troops, military and civil, in the opening days of war. With bluff, guile, and clever tactics, his forces took Michilimackinac in July and Detroit in August 1812, forcing the surrender of a large, ill-led American army; in October his regulars defeated the invading Americans at Queenston Heights on the Niagara frontier, though at the cost of heavy casualties, including Brock himself. Cautious optimism replaced the hopelessness that hung over the colony, pro-American sentiments waned (though some American settlers apparently joined the invaders or returned to the United States with them), and British Canadians had some reason to believe they might survive. Their resistance to the United States, their anti-Americanism, increased exponentially with the triumphs of British arms.

Reverend John Strachan's letters traced the course of the war from his vantage point at York, the tiny, raw, and muddy Upper Canadian capital set on the Lake Ontario shore like an oasis of demi-civilization in the midst of the forest. Intelligent, shrewd, and innately conservative, the Anglican Strachan was thirty-four years old in 1812, a Scots-born teacher and preacher who had lived in Upper Canada since 1799. Like many of the Britishers who emigrated to Canada after the Loyalists had arrived, he was sharply anti-American, and he instinctively reacted against the Americanization that he saw infecting Upper Canada's politics. The "character of the Americans is generally speaking bad," he wrote; they are a people of "little or no religion . . . prone to low cunning." Moreover, the House of Assembly was "composed of ignorant clowns, for the spirit of levelling seems to pervade the province." Strachan was convinced that northern nations, Britain and Canada, were inherently superior to southern countries, where governments were despotic and slavery rampant. Monarchy was by definition superior to republicanism, and the type of government under which citizens lived had a direct influence on the manner of the people.

The American-born Loyalists and their Canadian offspring had to be bucked up to their task, Strachan believed. Already the rector of York, he did his best to encourage loyalty. In a sermon in August 1812, he denounced the United States for its *de facto* alliance with the cruel tyrant Napoleon and for its war against Britain, the pillar of freedom and happiness in the world. Upper Canada was "environed almost with our enemies, and mixed with doubtful characters and secret Traitors," so strong measures were necessary to combat the invading Americans and their supporters within the colony.[5] There would be executions of the disloyal to encourage the others.

Strachan initially had doubts about the languid manner with which General Brock was prosecuting the war: "Forbearance will never answer with our present enemy; it is founded upon a most fallacious idea of the American character, and the situation of parties in that country." The war, Strachan knew, was not popular with large and influential sections of American opinion, and "a successful attack, instead of irritating the federalists, will produce the contrary effect by furnishing them with additional proofs of the incapacity of their present rulers." But Strachan's hopes were high after Brock's initial moves met success. "The province is wonderfully animated," he wrote on November 1, 1812. The same month, he assessed the true cause of the war in the American aims for the conquest of Upper Canada: "The importance of this country to them is incalculable—the possession of it would give them the complete command of the Indians who must either submit or starve . . . and thus leave all the western frontier clear and unmolested. The Americans are systematically employed in exterminating the savages, but they can never succeed while we keep possession of this country."

Strachan remained in York in April 1813 when the Americans captured the town and, with the surviving defenders having abandoned the field to the invaders, he played a crucial role in arranging for the capitulation and worked mightily to persuade the Americans to restrain their looting. Strachan, one historian wrote with some irony, "had stood up to the Americans; he had been British."[6]* Strachan performed the same task when the Yankees returned in July to finish the job at York, though he noted on the second occasion that the Americans, "while on shore, behaved themselves, and no private house was entered or disturbed." Still, "should they be able to make us a third visit, every house will be in flames and what we shall say of York as was said of Troy, *Fuimus*."

---

* The war, while viciously fought, saw the usual military courtesies of the day shown by both sides. One young British officer, sent under a white flag to parley with the Yankees (and to spy), dined with an officer, saw American senior officers, and chatted about hunting. The same officer's regiment, largely raised in New Brunswick, captured American officers later in the war and provided them with dinner and comfortable beds. See Donald E. Graves, ed., *Merry Hearts Make Light Days: The War of 1812 Journal of Lieutenant John Le Couteur, 104th Foot* (Ottawa 1993), 133ff., 202.

York was spared a third time, though discouragement in the colony between the two attacks ran rampant. Militiamen deserted, some politicians defected to the invaders, and many feared that all was lost. Strachan blamed the British, denouncing them for what he saw as their incompetence in fighting the war. General Prevost in 1812 was inexcusably blind and had "abandoned the Loyalists to be bound hand and foot to their fate." The next year, Upper Canada stood to be "more injured by the bad arrangements and absurd conduct of the head of the Commissariat" than by the enemy. Perhaps that was unfair: "The imbecility" of Prevost continued to hurt the cause, and his successor, he wrote in 1814, "seems to be destitute of that military fire and vigour of decision, which the principal commander in this country must possess in order to preserve it." Cleric that he was, Strachan had no compunction about playing the role of strategist and military critic. More often than not his judgments were correct.

Strachan's bitterness towards Britain's generals was almost as great as that he directed at the Americans. If Canada had been saved from the rapacious Yankees, the victory was due not to bumbling British regulars and their officers but to the "astonishing exertions of the militia,"[7] Strachan wrote in the winter of 1814. Untrained, ill-equipped, useless in the pitched battles that decided early nineteenth-century warfare, and formed of companies of local settlers who, obliged to serve, at every opportunity sought to return home, the militiamen were occasionally of worth as auxiliaries and skirmishers in situations where local knowledge could be of value. But almost nowhere else. The militia's efforts did not justify Strachan's hosannas, but his praise largely created the "militia myth" that has bedevilled Canadian defence ever since—the idea that professional soldiers are unneeded because the people, with minimal training, can defend the country.

Strachan believed what he wrote and, in the midst of war, a feeling of community had begun to take form in his mind. This Old Country man who became heart and soul of the Family Compact, and whose every effort was directed towards the retention of the British connection, also had stirrings that we can recognize as nationalism. The combined strains of resentment at Britain and the United States that had animated the Loyalists of the American Revolution had been reinforced anew in Strachan and in others by the War of 1812. He and his compatriots had fought for survival and for their homes and families, and those had mattered at least as much as the right to live under the Union Jack. So, too, had many *Canadiens* in Lower Canada, who were just as anxious as their

Upper Canadian compatriots to resist the United States' attempt to "Yankifier le Canada." For two centuries, French Canadians had demonstrated their attachment to their land. Now, home and family were beginning to have as much power as king and empire to motivate resistance in Upper Canada.

The war had checked the Americanization of Canada and intensified the resentment against the United States. A second layer of anti-Americanism had been put in place, and later historians would mine that resentment to serve Canadian needs. The War of 1812 had been won—if surviving can be counted as victory. Victory meant that the second chapter of British North America's history of rejection of republicanism had a happier ending than the first. The American Revolution had created the United States' myth of triumph against the odds, of good over evil; the War of 1812 created Canada's.

*   *   *

There was yet more anti-Americanism to come a generation later. The lesson that Strachan and other leading figures drew from the War of 1812 was that reformist ideals were a continuing threat to a colony situated so perilously as Upper Canada. Britain was the strong right arm of the Canadas, and conservatism, modelled on their ideas of what existed—or should have existed—in England, was the true basis of loyalty to the Crown. The link to Britain, in other words, depended on the creation and maintenance of a social order, a conservative social order, as distinct as possible from that of the United States. Inherently anti-American, conservatism and loyalty became interchangeable and intertwined, and reformers who advocated changes in the special character of Upper Canadian life were by definition pro-American and ultimately disloyal.* The syllogism went like this: reformers were at base republicans; republicans were disloyal; therefore, reformers were disloyal. The seeds of confrontation between those who hoped to democratize the Canadas and

* Times change, of course. As we shall see, the loyal and conservative anti-republican Canadians epitomized by Strachan eventually became the Progressive Conservative party of Brian Mulroney which took Canada into the Free Trade Agreement with the United States of Republican Ronald Reagan. Strachan, no doubt, would have attributed this betrayal to Mulroney's dubious Irish origins and Catholic religion.

those who resisted change, between anti-Americans and those who sought to give the Canadas some of the characteristics of the United States, were well planted.

Resentment soon grew up over the rights of "aliens," the American settlers in Upper Canada to whom the British government extended full naturalization rights after seven-years' residence. Some in the tightly knit Tory élite wanted to keep the Americans out, and had immigration from the south curtailed after 1815; Americans already in Upper Canada were to be kept in their place and deprived of the rights accorded Loyalists. It was "a disgrace," one Tory said, that Americans were on an equal footing with the loyal. Another, harking back to the 1780s, felt betrayed that any would consider giving civil and political rights to those "by whom I was driven from my patrimony." Still a third ranted that he "would suffer death before he would consent to a measure that would confer the rights of a subject on men who, but a few years ago, had *invaded our country—ransacked our villages—burnt our houses—and murdered our wives and children*." "This is a *British* province," a "True-Born Canadian" maintained, while yet another observed that Loyalist principles had been inculcated "into the minds of their descendants so . . . they form a most valuable and immovable mass of faithful and loyal adherents to the British Crown."

Simply put, John Strachan and the Family Compact, that self-selected agglomeration of bureaucrats and professional men who stood for all that was good and true in Upper Canada, believed that the goal of the American-born was to see Upper Canada, indeed all British North America, absorbed by the United States. The only way that unhappy fate could be resisted was by maintaining and strengthening links with Britain, while also forcing the province, now numbering some 400,000 people, into a conservative, Loyalist mould. A corollary was that those who had been educated in republican principles could never become attached to British principles. Seldom has the anti-American and ideological basis of Loyalism been stated so bluntly, though its force was diluted by the inefficiency, arbitrary behaviour, and occasional corruption of the Compact members who bellowed forth their views.

Not surprisingly, the class-conscious British-born reacted the most strongly to the Americans and American-born living in Upper Canada. Susanna Moodie and her husband initially purchased a cleared farm near Cobourg when they arrived in Upper Canada in 1832, and Mrs Moodie quickly found herself horrified by the pretensions, familiarity, and slyness of the neighbouring Yankees. "Don't pass off your English airs on us," one girl said hotly to Moodie, as recounted in *Roughing It In The Bush*. "We are *genuine* Yankees, and I think ourselves as good—yes, a great deal better than you." The "thin, weasel-faced," and "semi-barbarous" Americans, "loose in [their] lower joints," hated the new arrivals from England, borrowed and never returned their goods, stole from them, and lied to them with abandon. Moreover, their sexual morality was questionable. Even the Loyalists were untrustworthy, their "doubtful attachment to the British government" repaid by generous land grants. All the lower orders, in the eyes of the Moodies, went wild in Canada, their "unrestrained liberty" turning quickly into an "ultra-republican spirit."

The Reformers had no such fears of the American settlers. These settlers had resisted the invaders in 1812, so why fear their loyalty now? If they had come to the Canadas, could it not be because democracy in the United States was much less palatable in practice than it was in theory? Would education not turn the children of Americans into good British subjects? "Will they not feel a warm affection for the land in which they are reared?" one Reformer asked. If "they are taught by proper instructors, will they not love our institutions and never rebel against them?" To Reform supporters, including many of Loyalist heritage, the American-born could be assimilated into British and Loyalist ideals if they were treated fairly. But would they be so treated by those in the Family Compact who prattled on about "loyalty" on every occasion? One British half-pay officer in Middlesex County doubted it: "Loyalty, loyalty is all the cry now a-days, but analyze the term as it is now used, and you will find that it is loyalty to the Attorney General which is meant, because he is able to give away a great many good things."

The divisions between anti-American conservatives and moderate reformers were not confined to Upper Canada. New Brunswick saw a struggle for power and place between Loyalists and their descendants much like that in Upper Canada, but the relative neutrality of the province during the War of 1812 had not renewed the anti-Americanism of the Revolutionary War years with the fresh blood of additional martyrs to the British cause. It took boundary disputes between 1839 and 1841 with Maine and the abandonment of New Brunswick's claims in the Webster-Ashburton Treaty of 1842 to spur anti-Americanism anew. In Nova Scotia, conservatives pointed to the excesses of the United States, a land wracked by sectionalism, states' rights, slavery and other ills. Reform leader Joseph Howe would have none of these complaints. Where else, he asked, "excepting the British isles," could one find "an equal amount of freedom, prosperity and happiness?" But Howe was no republican. British government for him represented the summit of political evolution.

There was a pervasive suspicion of the United States in the Maritimes, nonetheless, a sense that tricky, grasping Americans were always ready to take advantage of naive and gullible Nova Scotians. Thomas Haliburton's inventive, vain, and very American clockmaker, Sam Slick, whose timepieces were guaranteed to last from "July to Etarnity," would allow "that the Bluenoses are the most gullible folks on the face of the airth—rigular soft horns; that's a fact." Though Haliburton was a good Nova Scotia nationalist, Sam's energy and drive stand out in sharp contrast to the inertia of the author's slower compatriots, hankering after Yankee prosperity and aware of the advantages of life in the United States, but not wanting to work very hard to achieve it and fearing what prosperity might do to their British North American values.

In Lower Canada, however, where Louis-Joseph Papineau fought against the ruling Château Clique that allied politicians, business, and government officials, anti-American views seemed to be softening. By the 1830s Papineau himself, who had earlier scorned the United States, had come to have substantial sympathy with its system of government, and he now greatly admired the "practical republicanism" of the old American colonies. French Canadians, he said, thinking clearly of the need to have a government responsible to the electorate with its majority of francophones, ought to accept American democratic political institutions as "notre modèle et notre étude."[8] Since the *habitants* had traditionally feared and despised the Anglo-American settlers who had posed a continuing military threat to French outposts for more than two hundred years, this was an amazing change in attitude. Later, Papineau even persuaded himself that annexation would be good for Quebec and that its linguistic and religious distinctiveness would be guaranteed by the doctrine of state's rights. His stunning naivety would find its modern parallel in the assumptions of easy relations between a separate Quebec and Washington, espoused by the Parti Québécois and Bloc Québécois.

As the separate but interconnected Rebellions of 1837 in the Canadas drew near, the division between reformers, increasingly radical in their exhortations and beliefs, and the conservative oligarchy hardened into a chasm. Mrs Anna Jameson, wife of the attorney general, noted after a dinner attended by the local élite in Toronto in 1837 that "the cold narrow minds,

the confused ideas, the by-gone prejudices of the society, are hardly conceivable."[9] In the southwestern part of the province, Tories in Middlesex
County put the situation with stark simplicity. Upper Canada was divided in
two parts: "The one will be composed of Loyal men—the other of
Disaffected men, of Republicans, of Revolutionists, and of Rebels. Shall I
stand up on the same side with these Revolutionary Republicans—on the
same side with these Rebels—or shall I stand up on the side of Loyalty?"[10]

For his part, publisher and politician William Lyon Mackenzie of the
Town of York knew where he stood. The American system was far from
perfect, but it was superior to that under which British North Americans
laboured. "I do admire their course as a nation," he wrote, "and glory in
their success, as affording a proof of the practical utility of the representative system of government." Most of all, the popularly elected executive
enjoyed by Americans was a great improvement over "a half pay officer a
stranger to our customs, and whose interest often would be opposite of
ours" under which Upper Canada usually laboured.[11] Mackenzie's
repeated advocacy of measures derived from American models naturally
infuriated the Family Compact. When a few radical Reformers rose in arms
against the government, the "Loyal men" had most of the population with
them, as well as the full power of duly constituted authority at their service. The militia turned out in large numbers, many more rallying to order
and authority than the few hundred who stood with Mackenzie at
Montgomery's Tavern. Still, those of Loyalist origins did not line up
wholly against Mackenzie—his followers included some of that heritage.

In Lower Canada, the democratic, anti-clerical, and revolutionary
patriotes staged a rebellion that involved pitched battles and at least 250
fatal casualties, and was not definitively put down until November 1838.
Although there were serious grievances against the administration, and a
democratic and "popular republicanism" drove the anti-government
campaign, the issue, as Lord Durham, sent from London to investigate
the causes of the unrest, put it, "has been a question of nationality . . .
the distinction of races."[12]

The rebellion in Upper Canada, by contrast, was a small-bore affair.
Mackenzie's attempt to topple the government at York failed completely, as
did the subsidiary uprising by largely American-born or American-
descended rebels in the London District and the "Patriot" invasions from
the United States in eastern and western Upper Canada. These events aside,
the Upper Canadian rebellion was notable primarily for its government-led

repression that saw hundreds of arrests, militia raids on dissidents, and an increase in popular anti-Americanism after the militia entered New York to burn the *Caroline*, a vessel used by the rebels. The Americans professed outrage, and relations became ever more strained after Washington's "connivance" in the Patriot invasions. Among the loyal majority, there was only scorn for Mackenzie and the "American" freedoms he offered. The recent British immigrant Catherine Parr Traill, homesteading in the isolated wilderness near Peterborough, wrote on Christmas Day 1837:

> We hear that Mackenzie is trying to stir up the Americans on the other side, and promises them large rewards for their services in endeavouring to tear us from our Government and laws, and force us to become a free and independent people. Surely our freedom would be a blessed gift so obtained! And with the traitor Mackenzie for our President our independence were most honourable and admirable! God forbid we should change our dependance on a gracious Sovereign to become the tools and victims of the most despicable of rebels.

To Mrs Traill and the thousands who thought like her, Mackenzie was a patent fraud, "obliged only to republican neighbours for men and the munitions of war" and the leader of "the factious cry of the discontented few. And shall we allow a few traitors to impose new laws and change the form of government? And shall we allow the Americans to force their republican form of government upon us against our inclinations? The Canadians are not oppressed."[13]

The rebellion and the subsequent Patriot raids across the border in 1838 had important and lasting effects on Canadian attitudes to the United States. The inheritance of anti-American feeling from the revolution, increased and perpetuated by the War of 1812, received a new infusion of venom from the aid and sympathy offered to Mackenzie. American attitudes to Canada did not help the situation. Many Americans—"the Sovereign mob" of "the Greatest Republic in the world," one Essex County newspaper sneeringly called them—seemed to believe that their neighbours lived in chains and waited only for the right moment to throw them off. The flood of emigrants from Upper Canada to the United States after the failure of the rebellions must have confirmed Americans in their view. The numbers leaving, not all rebel sympathizers fleeing to escape punishment by any means, were impressive enough for Lieutenant Governor Sir George Arthur to call it "astonishing."

Surely British North America was ripe for the taking. Some on both sides of the boundary believed that the seizure of the Canadas by the United States was all but inevitable. Lord Durham, the Governor-in-Chief of British North America fresh from England, worried that the United States might take Canada, just as the Americans had wrested Texas away from the Mexicans, to form, for a time, an independent republic. In his famous 1839 *Report on the Affairs of British North America*, he wrote that the only way to prevent annexation was "by raising up for the North American colonist some nationality of his own; by elevating these small and unimportant communities into a society having some objects of a national importance; and thus by giving their inhabitants a country which they will be unwilling to see absorbed even into one more powerful."

*   *   *

It would take a generation more to establish the Dominion of Canada and to elevate the small and insignificant British North American colonies into a nation. It would take still more time, particularly in English-speaking Canada, to develop the sense of the past and the ideas that could be used to tie the country together, though the Loyalist inheritance had begun to be turned into a "usable past" even before Confederation. The Loyalist myth, not always literally true but more than mere symbols and images, began to take shape in the 1850s and was fixed into concrete form in the 1880s.[14] One of the many aims of those who created the tradition was to argue that there had been, and still were, important distinctions between Canadians and Americans.

The Loyalist myth stressed a pattern of defeat and exile, followed by victory in a just cause. The Loyalists had been persecuted by the vindictive Americans, driven from their comfortable homes into the wilderness of British North America,* but they persevered to create a moral and

---

* Robertson Davies wrote in *Harper's* in January 1989 of the Loyalists as persecuted refugees and maintained that their sufferings still resonate in Canada: "Modern Canada is a prosperous country, but the miseries of its earliest white inhabitants [sic] are bred in the bone, and cannot, even now, be rooted out of the flesh."

political society which rejected the doctrines and practices that had turned the United States into a land of vicious politics, racial unrest, greed, and aggressiveness. The ideology of Loyalism meant loyalty to monarch and empire and adherence to the beliefs and institutions essential to the preservation of a way of life different from that in the United States. The Loyalists stood for law and order, not rebellion; for the British constitution, not republicanism; and for a hierarchical society in which rank had its recognized privileges, not democratic egalitarianism. Peace, order, and good government, in other words; not life, liberty, and the pursuit of happiness. This was myth, not reality, but the descendants of the United Empire Loyalists needed and wanted myth to serve their purposes.

The Loyalist myth had obvious utility in the years preceding and following Confederation. In New Brunswick, Loyalist sentiment flowered in the 1840s when the repeal of the Corn Laws in the United Kingdom threatened the colonies' long-established markets and when boundary disputes with the United States flared up. In the Canadas, the annexation crisis of 1849 demonstrated that it was important to remind Canadians of their roots, as a means of opposing the efforts of "loathed and execrated" traitors. Loyalism provided a balance to the economic growth accompanying the Reciprocity Treaty of 1854 and the near-panic that the North, victorious in the Civil War, might seek renewed unity with the defeated Confederacy in a quick conquest of British North America. Lincoln's Secretary of State, William Seward, had gloated that "Nature designs that this whole continent . . . shall be, sooner or later, within the magic circle of the American Union." The Loyalist heritage was also a comfort during the years of slow growth after the creation of the dominion, when the prospects of the new country seemed limited, not least by comparison with the extraordinary boom under way in the United States. In an unpromising present, a glorious past was all the more necessary.

Above all, the memory of the disputes and the differences that had existed with the Americans was essential precisely because Canadians seemed so very like their neighbours. A British observer shrewdly noted that "the typical Canadian tells you that he is not, but he *is* a Yankee—a Yankee in the sense that we use the term at home, as synonymous with everything that smacks of democracy."[15] That comment greatly exaggerated matters. Canadian democracy was much more constrained than American, as the British North America Act of 1867 would show, but the essential point was likely correct then—and is even more so now.

Artificial barriers had to be erected against the American tide. Monuments to celebrate the hallowed past were one roadblock to Americanization. The interest in the Loyalist inheritance in the 1850s could be seen in the re-erection of Brock's Monument on Queenston Heights in 1859. A monument towering above the Niagara escarpment, in full view of the American side of the Niagara River, had been built in 1827, and Brock's remains were reinterred beneath. It was destroyed by a bomb planted by "cowardly miscreants," believed to be Irish-Canadian supporters of Mackenzie's rebellion, thirteen years later. One of the resolutions of the committee struck to plan a replacement memorial observed that "there could scarcely have been found in any country individuals wicked and reckless enough to have violated by so atrocious an act the sanctuary of the illustrious dead, if it were not for the extraordinary and deplorable fact that from some alleged defect in the constitution of the U.S. of A., persons committing the most revolting crimes within the territory of their neighbours are sure of finding protection [in the United States]."[16] A competition for a new monument was held soon after, but construction did not begin until 1853. The work was completed in 1856, and the forty acres of grounds around the 185-foot-high fluted column, surmounted by its 31-foot-high statue of Brock, were landscaped for official inauguration in 1859.[17]

It was important, as well, to affirm the Loyalist myth in the history books. The Americans either maligned or, worse yet, ignored the Loyalists in their textbooks and ceremonies. As almost no one in British North America had written about the Loyalists, in part because the records were so thin, the American slanders "created a powerful stimulus toward the recovery of the Loyalist past." Of course, the relative absence of records itself created the ideal conditions in which a much-enhanced Loyalist tradition could flourish. The seventy-fifth anniversary of the arrival of the Loyalists in Upper Canada occurred in 1859 and that very year, urged by friends and the press, Egerton Ryerson, Chief Superintendent of Education in Canada West, began collecting material for a great Loyalist history. French Canadians, too, seemed much more conscious of their past and more interested in commemorating and embellishing it.

English Canada could not lag behind. By the 1860s, ritual incantations of the Loyalist past were included in most celebrations, as the American Civil War continued and Confederation drew near. The act of Confederation itself was the denial of American supremacy in North

America.* The "dangerous nature of 'Americanism,'" one student of Canadian opinion in the years before Confederation observed, "made that political complex still unacceptable. . . . The United States, with its full-blown belief in Manifest Destiny, its saturation with a master-mentality, and the instability of democratic-republican government certainly aided in the production of anti-American sentiment in Canada West, from which Confederation in large part resulted."[18] Moreover, the abortive, frequently farcical, Fenian invasions of 1866 and after, when Irish-Americans sought to free Ireland by attacking British North America, the closest imperial colonies, reinforced the image of the Loyalists fending off the American menace yet again—and, in this case, the disloyal Irish as well.** In New Brunswick and the Eastern Townships, too, the Fenian experience produced a similar resurgence of Loyalist values.

The Loyalist myth played a central role in creating English-Canadian nationalism, as the new Dominion of Canada tried to rise above the narrow provincialism that had characterized the separate colonies and to shape itself into a nation. Ryerson's massive history, appearing in 1880, immediately became one of the major sources on which the myth was based. Another was the simultaneous growth in support for the ideal of Imperial Federation, an attempt to unite Britain with its self-governing colonies and to formulate a distinctive British-Canadian identity, then winning converts among intellectuals in Britain and Canada. Imperial Federation was a colonial idea, not a British one, Canadians argued. Had

* Confederation may have denied American supremacy, but Canadian federalism was a new doctrine, and jurisprudence was lacking on how it should be interpreted. As a result, judges inevitably looked to American precedents as a guide for their first contacts with a federal system of government. Even before Confederation, in fact, the law library of the Law Society of Upper Canada carefully collected American case law and studies, simply because the United States' experience was, in so many ways, closer to the Canadian than any other.

** The Fenian invasions, aimed at New Brunswick and Canada East before Confederation and at Quebec after 1867, spawned some wonderful doggerel, such as Alex. Glendenning's "A Word to the Finnigans": "Draw a tight bead on them/ Crack at the head o' them;/ Down wi' the ruffians, and pound them like snakes:/ Base tatterdemalions,/ Rips, roughs and rapscallions,/ What business have they on this side of the lakes?" In F.R. Scott and A.J.M. Smith, eds., *The Blasted Pine* (Toronto 1967), 17.

Walker, Gunchuche/National Archives of Canada C-78572

the Loyalists not stood for imperial unity in 1776, there would have been no empire in 1880. The Loyalist ideal of fealty to the Crown existed still, and the imperial revival in Britain after the late 1870s was, to Canadians, nothing so much as a return to the ideals of the Loyalists.

When New Brunswick marked the centennial of the Loyalists' arrival in 1883, the commemoration was lavish and expensive, a celebration of the narcissism of small differences between Canadians and Americans. Confronted by growing American influence in every aspect of life—political, commercial, social, intellectual, and cultural—New Brunswickers seized the opportunity afforded by the centennial to assert their distinctiveness and to parade what many saw as their intrinsic moral superiority.[19] Notable for their absence from the celebrations, however, were overt anti-American sentiments, a trend others observed generally throughout the dominion in the 1880s. Popular literature, in the Maritimes as elsewhere in Canada, pointed to the differences between the two countries, invariably concluding that Canada was superior, but, while the tone could be sharp, there was little malice. The parliamentary librarian and intellectual Alphaeus Todd noted in 1881 that "the hostility and estrangement between Canadians and the citizens of the American Republic . . . has wholly died out, and is replaced by sentiments of mutual esteem and good-will."[20] The Myth of the Undefended Frontier, that celebration of Canadian–American friendship, was taking shape even as the United Empire Loyalists celebrated their ancestors.

In Ontario, the Loyalist centennial celebrations were more open in their anti-American sentiments. At Adolphustown, near Kingston, the centennial was marked by a grand fête and by speeches galore.* Dr William Canniff, an amateur Loyalist historian, spoke of how Canada, having built on the Loyalist legacy, had more liberty and a more democratic government, accomplished without revolution and with law and order, with the rights of Indians and blacks respected. How different from the United States, he cried, though he hoped that "their destiny may be as great as we believe ours is sure to be."[21] Reverend D.V. Lucas, a Methodist of Loyalist origins, spoke of the spirit that had brought the Loyalists into exile as one of allegiance to empire and to the British constitution. The American Revolution had been an unjustifiable rebellion, and the Loyalists had "honoured the flag of England and the principles that flag represented." Some still talked of annexation, of the absorption of Canada into and by the United States, Lucas said, referring to the address by Sir Richard Cartwright, the Kingston Liberal politician and supporter of Commercial Union or free trade between Canada and the United States. This was impossible, for British—and Canadian—loyalty was too strong "to admit any action which implies dismemberment of that mighty empire." Another orator picked up Lucas's theme and trashed the idea of annexation: "If our forefathers for their fervent loyalty to Britain, lost everything but their honour," A.L. Morden of the local organizing committee

* Loyalist Day is still celebrated in nearby Prince Edward County, Ontario, and, since 1984, the bicentennial of Ontario, Highway 33 has been dubbed the "Loyalist Parkway," its route marked with attractive signs showing a sturdy Loyalist couple, the man holding a long rifle. Every conceivable historic site along the parkway features its government-erected plaque.

said, "what feelings should animate our breasts today when with our attachment to British laws, institutions, rights, and liberties there is added the intensity of our attachment to the sovereign." Morden concluded proudly: "I am a British subject" who "did not want to be joined" to the republic to the south.[22] No one wanted such a fate, Canadians of Loyalist bent said proudly.

Three times Canadians had been tested, three times they had prevailed. The American Revolution had first tried the faith of the Loyalists by sending them, defeated and humiliated, into the wilderness. They had turned Canada into a garden, and during the War of 1812 they had been called upon to defend their lands yet again against the Americans. Against the odds, they had won. Then came attempted subversion from within, the efforts by Yankee sympathizers in the guise of Reformers to subvert the British traditions that the founders had instilled in the breasts of British North Americans. The rebels had been routed, and now the great Dominion of Canada, a British dominion in every respect, stretched from sea to sea. It was a story of triumph.

ACROSS THE LINE

Willson/Rare Book Collection, National Library of Canada/Collection des livres rares, Bibliothèque nationale du Canada C-076928

UNCLE SAM: "National Policy! British Connection! Protective Tariff! Canadian Pacific Railway! Colonization! And this is your 'friendship', Sir John! Pshaw!"

Just as Americans could use the myth of their Manifest Destiny to justify their appropriation of the western half of the continent, so Canadian conservatives could use the Loyalist myth as a weapon in the domestic political and social wars against French Canadians, Métis, immigrants, Americans, and all others who might object to Anglo–Canadian unity as the wave of the Canadian future. Against the Loyalist view of Canada stood nothing more than reality. F.H. Underhill, the contrarian historian, put it well two generations later. "It was not the Declaration of Independence which made the Americans a separate people, it was the Atlantic Ocean; and Canada is on the same side of the Atlantic."[23]* So it was, though for many years most Canadians would forget that essential fact. Anti-Americanism would prosper in the decades to come.

---

* Alberta entrepreneur Peter Pocklington would not agree. To him, Canadians had neglected the virtues of the United States. "Without Americans, the world would probably be back in the caves. They're the only people with the patriotism and courage to stand up for what they believe in. The United Empire Loyalists on this side of the border—they're more into: 'What can we get from government.'" Quoted in Marci McDonald, *Yankee Doodle Dandy: Brian Mulroney and the American Agenda* (Toronto 1995), 64.

2

UNDER WHICH FLAG?

THE FREE TRADE FOLLIES OF 1891 AND 1911

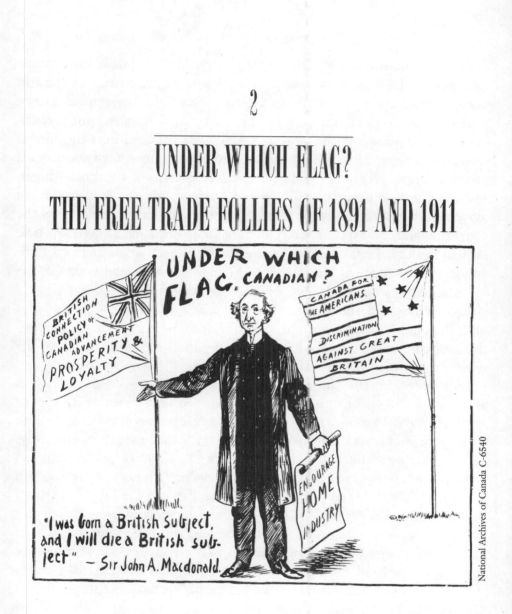

The country was stunned when the Reciprocity Agreement negotiated by Sir Wilfrid Laurier's Liberal government with President William Howard Taft's administration was announced in Parliament on January 26, 1911. Free trade had been a national goal ever since the United States had cancelled the Reciprocity Agreement of 1854 in 1866, and now Laurier, the old wizard of Canadian politics, had pulled it off. Remarkably, the new agreement protected Canadian manufacturing, and the removal of tariffs was essentially confined to agricultural products. Not even business could complain.

But it did. On February 20, newspapers published a manifesto by eighteen powerful Toronto men, all Liberals, damning reciprocity upside and down. Hundreds of millions of dollars, they argued, had been spent to give Canada the finest "railways, canals, steamships and other means of transportation between east and west and west and east," and now this investment was threatened by the proposal to divert trade into north-south lines. Worse yet, once reciprocity had been in effect for a few years, "the channels of Canada's trade would have become so changed that a termination of the agreement and a return by the United States to a protective tariff as against Canada would cause a disturbance of trade to an unparalleled extent." After all, had the Americans not done just this in 1866? The merest threat of abrogation, the manifesto of the "Toronto Eighteen" said, would force Canada "to extend the scope of the agreement so as to include manufactures."

Free trade with the United States would also weaken Canada's ties with the empire "and make it more difficult to avert political union with the United States." It would increase annexationist sentiment. It threatened Canada with an unenviable choice between "disruption of her channels of trade with the United States or political union with them." All in all, the voices of Toronto business cried, "Canadian nationality is now threatened with a more serious blow than any it has heretofore met." The message was clear: all who placed the interests of Canada "before those of any party or section" had a duty to fight the Reciprocity Agreement.[1]

It was only a matter of days before the monetary support of the Toronto Eighteen was transferred to the Conservative Party; it was only a matter of months before Laurier's Liberals, in power for fifteen years, were driven into defeat in the most extraordinary and expensive anti-American campaign in Canada's history—until business donations, this time in support of free trade, won the 1988 election for Brian Mulroney and eclipsed that record.

Whatever the cost, it was all worth it to the Toronto Eighteen. British Canada had been saved. Profits were secure. Anti-Americanism had triumphed yet again.

* * *

Trade had always meant money for businessmen and farmers alike, but trade and tariffs went hand in hand. While other nations' tariffs restrained trade, your own country's tariffs protected the development of industry. These were truisms, especially in a society struggling to diversify its economy and produce its own goods, a nation determined to be free of the foreign bankers and international terms of trade that always seemed to favour the old and established over the new and weak. Colonies trading in staple goods like lumber and wheat seemed particularly vulnerable. For a colony like Canada, the business of trade was complicated further by genuine loyalty to Britain and historical antipathy to the United States, combined with a fear that Britain might retreat across the North Atlantic and leave Canada defenceless against the grasping Yankees.

These issues had surfaced for the first time in 1846 when Britain, confident in its industrial strength and prepared to trade on an equal footing with every country, moved to eliminate the tariffs that had protected its manufacturers and the preferences given to Canadian exports of wheat, lumber, and natural products. For Canada, London's new trade gospel was a threat. Britain's desire to secure the cheapest foodstuffs and raw materials exposed British North American goods to direct competition with the exports of other nations. With no tariff advantage, critics demanded, why should Canada offer any preference to British goods? The Canadian legislature agreed, raising the tariff on British imports and lowering it on goods from the United States. By 1849, with a depression stifling business, the Canadas offered free trade to the United States in return for reciprocal treatment, an offer that met no response. Could the colony survive? Hotheads in the business community, their fortunes threatened by the loss of the British market and their political power jeopardized in Lower Canada by the grant of responsible government that gave control to the French-Canadian majority, began calling for annexation to the United States. The Annexation Manifesto printed in the Montreal *Gazette* was blunt:

> The proposed union would render Canada a field for American capital, into which it would enter as freely for the prosecution of public works and private enterprise as into any of the present States. . . . It would also introduce manufactures into Canada as rapidly as they have been introduced into the northern states . . . and [give] remunerative employment to what is at present a comparatively non-producing population.

Annexation would teach Britain a lesson, cut the rising power of the French Canadians, and, by opening access to the great American market, end the "ruin and decay" throughout the Canadas. For a brief time, the idea of annexation crackled like a summer thunderstorm among the leaders of the Montreal anglo bourgeoisie, with petitions being signed and riots splitting heads and families. So much for hatred of the Americans, so much for Loyalism, so much for the British connection. The lure of the Yankee dollar, as in the free trade election debate of 1988, was more powerful, especially when it was coupled with fear that perfidious Albion would place its interests ahead of those of the colonies.

The annexation panic died when business began to pick up in 1850. Convinced that only the freeing of trade between the colonies and the United States could keep them in the empire, Britain began to assist British North America to secure reciprocity with the United States. Even so, it took a war scare over American demands for access to the Canadian fisheries to make Congress look with any interest at freeing trade as a saw-off for giving the fishermen their due. The Reciprocity Treaty of 1854, with a term of ten years and the parties having the right of cancellation thereafter on one year's notice, provided for free admission into each country of the major natural products of the other, permitted joint access to all fisheries north of the 36th parallel, and gave Canadians access to Lake Michigan and Americans access to the St Lawrence canals. The treaty increased trade quite dramatically, and the reciprocity years were remembered as good times in the British part of North America.

After a decade, however, the United States repudiated the treaty. The bitterness that had built up in the North against Britain—and Canada—during the Civil War was one reason, but so, too, was the realization that in some years the United States was buying more from Canada than it was selling. There was also the charge that Canadian merchants and legislators played fast and loose with the Reciprocity Treaty's provisions by levying tariffs on items not covered under the 1854 agreement. The new American commercial hostility, and the genuine fear that the United States might consider invading British North America, helped push Nova Scotia, New Brunswick, and the Canadas into Confederation. Only the creation of the Dominion of Canada could give the British colonies a chance of survival, both economic and military, in the face of an angry United States.

Paradoxically, the memory of the good reciprocity times led dominion governments, Conservative and Liberal alike, to seek the restoration of free trade with Washington. Delegations regularly went south, beat their heads against congressional hostility and administration indifference, and returned home. Finally, in 1878, Sir John A. Macdonald, seeking to return to the office he had lost five years earlier, proposed a National Policy of high tariffs to protect infant Canadian industries—and, ironically, to encourage American firms to establish branch plants in Canada. His aim was to create employment and check emigration south of the line, as much as to give Canadian firms a boost. The National Policy soon forged links between business and the Tories, and the maintenance of high tariffs became an article of faith.

To bolster the policy psychologically, Canadians talked long and loud of the iniquities of the American nation and its government. "The United States began with an act of lawlessness," editorialized the *University Magazine*, "and their conduct ever since has been marked by that spirit." "I have always preached it to our people," George Taylor Denison, the fiercest nationalist and imperialist in the country, wrote candidly in 1888, "that the Yankees are our greatest if not only enemies and that we should never trust them."[2] The Great Republic was a land of corruption and scandal, of labour unrest and race hatred, of massive immigration that was bringing the dregs of Europe to North America and destroying the British heritage that Americans had once possessed. Industrialization, collapsing moral standards, urbanization, crime and the proliferation of guns—this was a society in which the only thing that mattered was money. Americans were materialists, the argument went, while Canadians were poor but proud. Here, rank and order still carried weight, men could rise on merit, and the social structure in which each knew his place was topped by the proud figure of the sovereign. "We have the freest institutions and most direct self-government in the world," bragged the *Canadian Methodist Magazine* in 1880. "We are free from many of the social cancers which are empoisoning the national life of our neighbours. We have no polygamous Mormondom; no Ku-Klux terrorism; no Oneida Communism; no Illinois divorce system; no cruel Indian massacres." Also, alas, no money. Still, America was different, not better, Canadians said, as they vainly tried to stem the flood of their most ambitious citizens south of the border and to deal with a stagnating economy in their frozen domain.*

---

* Stephen Leacock's fictional comment on emigration remains unsurpassed. The Liberal candidate in the 1911 election, Bagshaw, told a meeting in his mythical town of Mariposa that "I am an old man now, gentlemen, and the time must come when I must not only leave politics but must take my way towards that goal from which no traveller returns." There was a deep hush, Leacock noted: "It was understood to imply that he thought of going to the United States." *Sunshine Sketches of a Little Town* (Toronto 1931), 138.

In the circumstances, it was an astonishing testimony to the country's weak economy and to the power of reciprocity that Canadians still yearned for free trade with the Yankees. The country's growth in numbers of people and in wealth was slow—very slow indeed when compared with the booming United States. The hard years Canada suffered after 1867 could be traced in part to the end of reciprocity in 1866. While the United States was increasing rapidly in power, wealth, and population, Canada was doing little more than holding its own. It was "a time of gloom and doubt," the powerful journalist and publisher Sir John Willison later recalled.[3] Nothing else had worked to attract immigrants, to spur industrialization, or to develop the resources of the country; surely freer trade could get Canada moving again.

Two ideas took shape in Canada in the depressed 1880s—Commercial Union and Unrestricted Reciprocity. The first meant a complete customs union and a common Canada–US tariff against the rest of the world. It was popular with many in the United States, who saw it serving American interests. The Liberals could see this too: "Brother Jonathon wants all or nothing," one MP said, using the popular term for Americans. Commercial Union worried many, for inevitably the larger partner would set the rates and all key decisions would slide southward, culminating perhaps in Political Union or Annexation (the capital letters seem always to have been employed). As the firebreathing Colonel Denison put it, "the Commercial Union movement was a treasonable conspiracy on the part of a few men in Canada in connection with a number of leading politicians in the United States to entrap the Canadian people into annexation."[4]*

The second idea, Unrestricted Reciprocity, called for free trade between Canada and the United States, but allowed each government to set its own tariffs against other nations. A measure of independence could thus be preserved. This was the course favoured by the Liberal Party, led after 1887 by Wilfrid Laurier, although Laurier had not the slightest assurance that the Americans were interested in discussing, let alone concluding, an agreement with Canada.

---

* Denison was eminently easy to poke fun at. Phillips Thompson wrote in *Grip* in 1888 of "Swashbuckler Denison," who "curled his mustache and pawed the air,/ As he execrated the Yankees there./ Had the U.S. Army been anywhere near,/ The bravest had trembled in abject fear." In Ramsay Cook, "Neglected Pine Blasters," *Canadian Literature* (Summer 1979): 99.

Both Commercial Union and Unrestricted Reciprocity promised to shift much of Canada's trade out of its present east-west orientation and into a north-south direction. While this shift would be good for agricultural producers who could sell their products in the much larger US market, it posed problems for other sectors. The just-completed Canadian Pacific Railway was the iron road that tied Canada together, and its lines ran east and west; if trade shifted to the south, US railroads could be expected to extend spurs into Canada to capture the trade that the Canadian Pacific now carried. Moreover, the new-born industries that the National Policy had helped create could be swamped by cheaper American goods. That could cause ruin to businessmen and job loss to workers. Goods might be cheaper, but what if no one had work? Laurier had a major selling job to do.

National Archives of Canada C-6539

The first French Canadian to lead a national party, Laurier was fluently bilingual and charismatic. He had been born in 1841, took his law degree in English at McGill University, and understood English Canada better than most of his compatriots. Nonetheless, like many Quebec *rouges*, he had been cool to Confederation and, in 1885, had worried over Ottawa's use of force to put down the Riel Rebellion in the Northwest. "Had I been born on the banks of the Saskatchewan," he said, "I would myself have shouldered a musket" with Riel. Still, he believed that Canada's greatness lay in the partnership between French and English Canadians, and he did not chafe at Canada's position within the British Empire. As a francophone and a Roman Catholic, however, he was viewed with suspicion by many who remembered his 1885 remarks and feared that, if he were prime minister, the papacy would control Canada. His goal of discriminating against British exports and in favour of American did little to reinforce the impression that he was loyal to England and the Crown. Indeed, Laurier had flirted with anti-British and republican ideals in his youth and, although he did not want Canada to emulate such excesses of the American system as one man, one vote, he admired much about the United States and saw little reason to bow down before London. As one of his anglophone MPs said in Parliament, all that Canada owed England was Christian forgiveness for the way the Mother Country had handled Canadian–American relations.

Above all, Laurier was pan-Canadian in his views, properly viewing the unity of French and English Canadians and their well-being as more important than anything else. And what could glue Canada together more effectively than the prosperity increased trade could bring? Domestic peace would come to Canada if he could secure free entry for Canadian goods into the high-tariff markets of the United States. Workers would be happier, too, if they were able to buy cheaper manufactured goods from American sources. Otherwise, the continuing loss of the thousands emigrating to the south would go on, more than justifying the wry comment offered by Goldwin Smith that if the United States was not annexing Canada, it was assuredly annexing Canadians.

Prime Minister Sir John A. Macdonald would not have disagreed with Laurier in principle. In 1891 his party had been in office for thirteen consecutive years, and the Tory ranks were wracked by scandal and dissension. The National Policy was still good policy, Macdonald believed, but he knew it had not lived up to his party's expectations. He had genuine concerns about the intentions of the United States, and he believed in his heart, as he wrote in 1890, that "every American statesman . . . covets Canada. The greed for its acquisition is still on the increase, and God knows when it will end."[5]* To John A., Manifest Destiny remained American policy. But Macdonald knew that just as Americans might covet Canada, so Canadians wanted the prosperity of their rich neighbours—especially when the new American tariffs all but blocked access for farmers trying to sell their butter, eggs, barley, hay, and cattle into the vast market to the south.

* This was not a wholly unfair characterization. After 1888 the US Senate Foreign Relations Committee heard testimony that, while Canada was "a riddle to the American mind," nothing was "to stand in the way . . . of the 'Americanization' of the whole continent." Two years later, the Senate's Select Committee on Canada listened to a comprehensive account of how the dominion was gradually sliding under American control. It "has been coming to us and is coming to us steadily, more rapidly than ever before." Quoted in Gordon Stewart, "'A Special Contiguous Country Economic Regime': An Overview of America's Canadian Policy," *Diplomatic History* 6 (Fall 1982): 342, 345.

Perhaps Canada could have both the National Policy and Unrestricted Reciprocity. Late in 1890 the Old Man's government responded to feelers put out in Washington, but the results were predictably disappointing. Secretary of State James G. Blaine, a former Senator from Maine who looked on Canadians as competitors for markets, denied even that there had been discussions, denounced Canada's desire to have its cake and eat it too, and swore that he was "teetotally opposed to giving the Canadians the sentimental satisfaction of waving the British Flag . . . and enjoying the actual cash remuneration of American markets . . . So far as I can help it, I do not mean that they shall be Canadians and Americans at the same time."[6] Just like Haliburton's *Sam Slick* a half-century before, Blaine had summed up the Canadian dilemma with precision. Canadians wanted the British connection *and* free trade; they wanted their Loyalist anti-Americanism *and* the prosperity that economic integration with the United States could bring. There was more than a small element of hypocrisy in this approach, and Blaine, a man who knew Canadians well, was shrewd enough to spot it.

Rebuffed in Washington, Macdonald wrote that "we have burned our boats and must now fight for our lives."[7] As always, that most practical of politicians did what necessity demanded; the Conservative Party's strategy was to brand the Liberals as traitors who hoped to detach Canada from the British Empire. The government's election manifesto in 1891 set out the Tory view of the campaign bluntly: "The question which you will shortly be called upon to determine resolves itself into this: shall we endanger our possession of the great heritage bequeathed to us by our fathers, and submit ourselves to direct taxation for the privilege of having our tariff fixed at Washington, with a prospect of ultimately becoming a portion of the American union?"[8]

In his speeches, Macdonald played the same theme repeatedly. He was helped mightily by the cash contributions of the protected industries and railways his National Policy had helped, and all the stops were pulled in a brilliant, unscrupulous campaign. For the élites, the issues were thrashed through in detailed pamphlets and newspaper articles setting out the gains or losses that reciprocity might produce for Canada. For the ordinary voter, simpler, more emotive methods were used. Cartoons distributed by the Industrial League, the Tory-supporting manufacturers, made an open appeal to anti-Americanism. One, captioned "Keep Out the Wolves," showed a stalwart Canadian barring the door to the wolves of "American

Competition" and "Un-restricted Reciprocity." Another pictured the "Senator from the State of Ontario . . . Laying out the Grit Campaign" (see page 45). Others portrayed Uncle Sam setting his hired Liberal thugs on Miss Canada, who took refuge behind the well-armed Sir John A. and the British lion.[9] The party press picked up the themes set out by Macdonald and the manufacturers, denouncing the Grits as "the band of traitors who, with the aid of foreign gold, are seeking to debauch the electors and sell their country to the American rings and combines." In Quebec, the *bleu* clergy warned against annexationism, while *La Presse* accused Laurier of having no faith in Canada and of wanting to let the Yankees reign on the banks of the St Lawrence. "Is Canada to be wiped out?" asked the *Regina Standard*. "Shall the Union Jack droop and the British lion cower while the eagle screams and the stars and stripes wave triumphantly from Alaska to the Gulf of Mexico?" "Unrestricted Reciprocity," the headline of the *Saskatchewan Herald* went, "Means Annexation," and in Halifax the *Morning Chronicle* painted the election as "a contest between the Canadian people, on the one side, and a faction of one of the great parties and their Yankee allies, on the other." Anti-Americanism walked hand in hand with loyalty to Canada and the empire.

Relying on rational arguments as they did, Laurier and the Liberals were simply out-gunned. Their Unrestricted Reciprocity proposals had very strong appeal to the farm vote, to be sure. But though they protested their loyalty to the empire, they were confounded by the simple fact that, while not every supporter of Unrestricted Reciprocity was for annexation, without doubt every supporter of annexation was for Unrestricted Reciprocity. One New Brunswick MP wrote Laurier after the election that "the main thing was the loyalty cry. The changes were rung upon it in every way. . . . It really surprised me in the end we had any votes left." Another echoed the analysis: the Maritimes, he said, had been carried for Macdonald by "sentiment—the sentiment of loyalty fanned into a flame by the clergy and others and the fear of annexation."[10]

Goldwin Smith, the one-time Oxford Regius Professor of History who had moved to Toronto and become the country's one certified "intellectual," had been calling for both annexation and reciprocity for years. His tart pen lent respectability to the continentalist cause and did Laurier untold harm. Written before and during the 1891 election, Smith's *Canada and the Canadian Question* argued powerfully for reciprocity and annexation and poked fun at the overt loyalism of some Canadians:

"If a man makes a violent and offensive demonstration of it against those whom he accuses of American sympathies, you are apt presently to find him in the employment of some American company, peddling for an American house, or accepting a call to the other side of the Line." It sounded all too much like Sir John A., rebuffed by Washington, and only then turning to the defence of his National Policy.

But it was Macdonald who was put back into power with 121 seats against 94 for the Liberals, on March 5, 1891, by a country that desperately wanted to remain British and that continued to fear the designs of

PUBLISHED BY THE INDUSTRIAL LEAGUE FOR FREE DISTRIBUTION. F. NICHOLLS, SEC. TORONTO.

National Archives of Canada C-17233

the United States. "Thousands of simple Canadians," Laurier's biographer wrote, "had imagined that the country's national existence and national honour were at stake, and had voted to avert the dangers of too intimate trade connections with the United States."[11] That was likely true, for even on the grain-growing prairies the Conservatives captured all but one of the nine seats. The total popular vote, however, at 51.1 percent for the Conservatives and 47.1 percent for the Grits, was fairly evenly split. The rhetoric of the campaign, overblown even for an age that had raised bombast to high art, had nonetheless captured many of the worries that beset Canadians. The Tories had been financed by corporations that stood to lose if the tariff wall came down, and the issue at root was about money and who would keep it. That did not alter the fact that the Tories had found and struck the responsive chord: anti-Americanism still played well in Canada in the early 1890s. More precisely, anti-Americanism could be made a very effective weapon if the right images were created and pressed upon the people.

Sir John himself, prostrate from his electioneering efforts, died just three months after his victory. The great defender of the British tie, the man who had created Confederation and put in place the lineaments of the nation, was the country's greatest leader of the nineteenth century. In a final irony, he was laid to rest in a casket of rosewood-coloured rolled steel imported from West Meriden, Connecticut, which was proudly declared to be an exact facsimile of the coffin in which the assassinated President James Garfield had been buried a decade earlier.

*　　*　　*

Laurier learned from his defeat and from Macdonald's skilful playing of the loyalty card. The Liberals began to move away from their explicit policy of Unrestricted Reciprocity and towards support for the National Policy. By 1896, when Macdonald's lacklustre successors had demonstrated beyond doubt that they had none of the master's talents, Laurier took power with a platform of undeveloped promises and implicit understandings that the National Policy would not be altered in any fundamental way. There was still a yearning after the American market, however. The Conservatives had shamelessly sounded out Washington after the 1891 election and were again rebuffed, Secretary of State Blaine telling them that if they wanted tariff concessions they would have to abandon

Britain and expect to become an agricultural state of the Union. The Liberals also tried their luck in 1897 and offered reciprocity to the world, suggesting that Britain was especially qualified. Free trade with the United States was the goal, the Finance Minister said, but the Americans were simply not prepared to negotiate and, in the circumstances, all Canada could do was adjust the tariff to make it flexible. And so it did, giving preferences to Britain in 1897 and offering concessions to every country that treated Canada reciprocally. In 1898–99, there was another flurry of interest between Canada and the United States; again it came to naught.

No one seemed surprised, therefore, that the free trade issue gradually disappeared from view. In 1899 George R. Parkin, a prominent leader of imperial sentiment in Canada, wrote that Canadians no longer worried that "exclusion from the markets of the United States" would "threaten a comparative paralysis of Canadian farming." Most now believed "that the country will get along very well and perhaps will be better off in the long run without a Reciprocity Treaty. . . . The confidence of the people in the future of Canada was never so high as at present."[12] A similar reaction was offered a few years later by novelist Sir Gilbert Parker. "The country, its people," he wrote in 1905, "know where they are going; there is no longer national uncertainty; the Canadian stands no longer at the cross-roads—he is on the straight path of his destiny."[13]

There was good reason for the confidence. At long last, the economy had begun to boom, immigrants were beginning to enter the country in a flood, the West was being populated with productive farmers, and growth continued to gather steam—manufacturing increased by 6 percent a year in the first ten years of the new century. The country prospered. By the time the Liberals had been in power for a decade, Canada was the United States' third-best customer, with some 60 percent of the dominion's imports coming from the United States. Laurier told a British official he had no reason to believe the United States would offer the tariff concessions to Canada that were necessary for an agreement, but he did not seem noticeably upset at this prospect.

Otherwise, relations between the two countries continued to have their ups and downs. By the 1890s the United States seemed to be readying itself for a period of bumptious expansionism. The Venezuela Boundary Dispute of 1895 between Washington and London produced much presidential and congressional blather and briefly led in Canada to fears of an American invasion, fears that the United States would once again try to resolve its quarrel with Britain by attacking the closest imperial possession. After that chimera disappeared, the United States gorged itself on the Spanish colonies, including the Philippines, Puerto Rico, and Guam, that it had acquired after its war with Spain in 1898. But in 1903 the critical Alaska Boundary Dispute arose. President Theodore Roosevelt skilfully applied the "big stick" to frighten Canadians and to cow London into fearing the loss of potential American goodwill more than the "rights" of its Canadian colony. The resolution of the dispute in 1903 pleased no Canadian as a British judge cast the deciding vote in favour of the American position. Canada learned a sharp lesson in the disadvantages small nations faced in a world run by great power politics. Though their case was questionable in part, Canadians rightly believed that their interests had been sacrificed on the altar of Anglo–American amity. No one had been surprised that the greedy Americans had grabbed whatever they could, but few Canadians had been ready for what was popularly viewed as British perfidy. The US secretary of state could understand why the Canadians were furious, but, as he wrote to his wife, "serves 'em right if they can't take a joke."[14]

Canadians did not see the humour. The *Toronto Star* suggested stupidly that force was the only way for Canada to secure its rights against the United States. For his part, Sir Wilfrid said that he personally liked and admired Americans, but had been forced to the belief that they had a "grasping spirit" and were self-seeking, "caring only for Canada in so far as it may serve their purposes to be friendly." Why he should have expected anything else from any foreign nation was never stated.

Anglo–American relations grew warmer after the turn of the century, the resolution of the Alaska Boundary Dispute having contributed its mite to making Washington smile more favourably on Britain. Relations between Ottawa and Washington also improved. The British had learned that Canadian issues could become "an albatross round the imperial neck," and backed off from all but the most formal involvement in Canadian–American issues, leaving Ottawa generally freer to make its own deals with the United States. Peaceful resolution of boundary, sealing, and fishing questions that had long troubled the two countries became almost a routine matter, and free intercourse, if not free trade, across the international boundary increasingly became the norm.

Canada was evolving more like the United States every day, so much so that Samuel Moffett, an American progressive and journalist, published his doctoral dissertation at Columbia University in 1907 under the title *The Americanization of Canada*. He argued that Canadian society was being shaped by the industrialization of the United States, that Canadians were rapidly being assimilated into the American way of life, and that Canada was fulfilling itself as a liberal, progressive society. Certainly, the cities of English Canada had begun to look much like those of the United States. The *nationaliste* Quebecker Henri Bourassa told a Toronto audience in 1906: "You have little difference in language, in creed, in habits of living, in social intercourse. Toronto is more American than Quebec or Montreal."[15] (Quebec, in other words, was not a city like the others.) By 1910, speeches about the "undefended border" had become one of the staples of after-dinner oratory, and preparations had begun to celebrate the "century of peace" in 1914, marking the last time the two North American nations had come to blows. The pious platitudes had not made all Canadians love their neighbours, however. By 1910, when the United States at last was eager to talk seriously about trade with Canada, the rhetoric would be put to the test.

*   *   *

Many in Canada detested the National Policy. The tariff raised the prices of imported manufactured goods, and it encouraged Canadian factories to allow their prices to edge up towards those of the imports. This protection infuriated western farmers, in particular, who saw their neighbours to the south able to buy cheap tractors and ploughs from the great American firms while they had to bring in higher cost machines from Ontario's smaller and less efficient factories. As a large proportion of the prairie population had come from the United States in search of free land, the cost differential seemed especially unfair. In 1910, when Prime Minister Laurier undertook a tour of the West, he met repeated demands for lower tariffs and freer trade. In December a large delegation of farmers besieged the Parliament in Ottawa to demand relief from the high cost of protectionism.

By December 1910, in fact, negotiations between Ottawa and Washington for a reciprocity agreement were well advanced. With President William Howard Taft in office, the US administration seemed unusually friendy to Canada. Packing more than 350 pounds on his grossly obese frame, Taft was affable and hearty; he had summered at Murray Bay,

Quebec, every year from 1892 until he took office in March 1909, and he liked Canada and Canadians. His government, like him, seemed slow and ponderous, and the President feared that a rising tide of protectionism in Congress would give him serious difficulty in the elections of 1912. Perhaps an agreement with Canada could create the impression of movement; perhaps it could secure cheaper newsprint for newspaper publishers, something that might help the Republican Party's chances; and perhaps the word should go out to Ottawa that the Americans were ready to bargain. So they were, and a deal was soon in place.

Laurier's Finance Minister, Sir William Fielding, presented the Reciprocity Agreement to an astonished House of Commons on January 26, 1911. The two countries, Fielding said,

> have arranged that there shall be a large free list. We have agreed upon a schedule containing a large number of articles which are to be reciprocally free. These are chiefly what are called natural products. . . .
>
> In another schedule we have provided a rather numerous list of items on which there shall be a common rate of duty in both countries . . . we have had to make only moderate reductions while they, in many cases, have had to make quite large reductions.

It seemed almost too good to be true. The Laurier government had achieved what every Canadian government had wanted since the end of the Reciprocity Treaty of 1854—free entry to the United States for the agricultural products of Canada and, aside from the lower tariffs on agricultural implements and a few other items, continued protection for the manufacturers of Canada. In 1891 Macdonald had sought reciprocity and the National Policy; in 1911 Laurier had seemingly attained it. When the Conservative MPs in Robert Borden's opposition heard the details, with the cheers of the government benches ringing in their ears, they were dumbstruck. How could such a package be opposed?

When the Tory Members of Parliament went home to their constituencies, however, especially those from industrial parts of Ontario and Quebec, they were delighted to discover that reciprocity was not universally popular and that many wanted only to "bust the damn thing." Free trade with the United States reinforced all the concerns that had built up over Laurier's fifteen years in power. The critics had the inevitable grievances that arise against every long-lived government—spurned patronage expectations, real or imagined favouritism to another region or province, and the interminable grievances over language, religion, and ethnicity that have always disfigured Canadian politics. In English Canada, moreover, the old charges that Laurier, as a French-speaking Roman Catholic, was not enthusiastic enough about the empire and was too sympathetic to continentalism and republicanism were roused anew by the trade agreement. Laurier had been resisting British efforts to have Canada make a contribution of two dreadnaughts to the Royal Navy, opting instead to create a Canadian navy, so there was recent evidence to bolster this argument. In English Canada, many viewed Laurier as a leader ready to sell out the country to the Americans. In Quebec, the business elements, French and English, reacted to reciprocity much as had their anglophone counterparts elsewhere in the country, although some, not least *nationaliste* leader Henri Bourassa, worried about annexationist sentiment among Québécois. The French-Canadian *nationalistes*, long suspicious of Laurier as a leader who was too compliant to English-Canadian demands, chose to play up the government's creation of a Canadian navy as yet another demonstration of Liberal subservience to Imperial England. To many Quebeckers, in other words, Laurier was also a *vendu*, a sell-out. After governing for fifteen years, after balancing so brilliantly between the demands of the majority of the English-speaking and the appeals of the minority of the French-speaking, Laurier had made too many enemies on too many issues. The old magician had pulled the rabbit of free trade out of his top hat, but suddenly the audience was no longer cheering.

To industrial concerns like Massey-Harris, great commercial firms like Eaton's, the Canadian Pacific and Canadian Northern Railways, and the Bank of Montreal and the Dominion Bank, reciprocity in natural products was merely the thin edge of the wedge. Eventually, inevitably, once trade relations grew closer with the United States, the demand for free trade in manufactured goods would become irresistible, and the protectionist cause in Canada would be the loser.

Consider this theoretical example: Canadian widget makers, producing their widgets and selling them to Canadians at higher prices than Americans paid because of the protection offered by a high tariff wall, did not want to face the direct competition of The Great American Widget Co., its plants in Pittsburgh and Cleveland serving a much larger domestic market and producing widgets at a lower unit cost, thanks to the benefits of mass production. The entire Canadian widget demand could be met by stepping up the pace on one or two production lines in Pittsburgh and what would be the result? The widget makers in Valleyfield, Vancouver, and Brantford would be ruined, their workers laid off and driven to emigrate to the States, their families left behind dependent on welfare from the churches. And all so Canadian widget consumers could satisfy their needs at a saving of a penny or two. How, the Canadian producers asked, could this benefit the dominion? That some of the Canadian widget makers might be branch plants of US firms, lured north by the necessity of setting up factories as the only way of getting over the tariff wall, did not greatly lessen the force of the argument. If the tariffs dropped, the branch plant might shut down, with the Canadian market henceforth served by the parent company in Pennsylvania.*

So mesmerized had he been by the prospect of free trade in natural products, Laurier had unaccountably failed to realize that Canada's small but growing manufacturing industries had prospered and developed into comfortable, established patterns thanks to the National Policy's protection that his government had maintained. The aging Prime Minister—he was seventy in 1911—had lost his uncanny ability to cater to what his contemporaries called "vested interests" and to read the popular mood. Much like other leaders who grow too used to power, he had come to believe in his invariable rightness. But he was wrong. Understandably enough, the manufacturers of thousands of products in hundreds of towns did not want to face the direct American competition that would oblige them, at a minimum, to improve their efficiency and lower their prices and, at worst, to drive them into bankruptcy or into a forced sale of their plants to American interests. They were certain that Laurier's Reciprocity Agreement of 1911, while it did not yet open the border to manufactured goods, would be expanded to do so. Bust the damn thing!

The country's commercial interests did not wait long to organize. Less than a month after Fielding had presented the package to Parliament, the Toronto Eighteen, a group that included solicitor Zebulon Lash of the Canadian Northern Railway, Thomas White of the National Trust Co., Sir Edmund Walker of the Canadian Bank of

---

* Precisely the same arguments were made during the 1988 election about the effects of the Free Trade Agreement. After the election, moreover, a number of companies were quick to relocate to the United States and, in some cases, to Mexico.

Commerce, John Craig Eaton of the T. Eaton Co., and R.J. Christie of Christie, Brown, the biscuit makers, argued in their manifesto that the National Policy had created Canadian prosperity and had to be maintained.*

Economics and British nationality came together and, to the Toronto corporate élite and to those who agreed with them, Canada was threatened. What the Toronto Eighteen did not say was that they were placing their own financial interests before those of the country. This collection of railway lawyers, bankers, manufacturers, and department store owners had studied the trade agreement and decided it might threaten their profits. For the voters, the argument had to be phrased differently. The *Montreal Star* put it neatly: "Nothing but a high national spirit and a tariff which makes

National Archives of Canada C-133738

WHEN OUR INTERESTS CLASH WHOSE OX IS LIKELY TO GET GORED?

* The Toronto Eighteen, in effect a lobby group, represented the big businesses of their day—the railways, banks, insurance companies, major national retailers, and manufacturers. They were solidly against free trade. By contrast in 1988, the Business Council on National Issues, the lobby group for Canadian business and finance, was solidly behind the Mulroney government in its push for free trade, its members supplying advertising assistance and substantial corporate donations to the Progressive Conservative campaign.

the American frontier a reality can keep trade flowing across the empty country from Manitoba to Ontario and from Ontario to Manitoba."

Heartened by the campaign growing against reciprocity, on March 1 Borden struck a secret and all-embracing deal with the Eighteen's emissaries and Sir Clifford Sifton, the newspaper publisher and former Laurier minister who still remained a powerful figure in his party. Borden promised to resist "American encroachments and blandishments" in return for business support in contributions and assistance in propagandizing against the Reciprocity Agreement. To sweeten the pot for his new business friends, the Conservative leader also agreed to "recognize the necessity of introducing into his Cabinet from outside Parliament a number of men of outstanding national reputation and influence in order to give confidence to the progressive elements of the country, and strength and stability to the Government." Borden agreed to consult with Sifton and representatives of the Toronto Eighteen in forming his Cabinet "in order to ensure that his Ministry should be so constituted as to guarantee the effective adoption and application" of the anti-reciprocity policy. Crassly put, the Toronto Eighteen insisted on having representatives in the government as their price for supporting Borden, a stolid Nova Scotian who inspired confidence in almost no one. For his part, Borden saw the chance to deprive the Liberals of a massive portion of their financial and media support, to weld business to his party once more, and, possibly, to ride this alliance to victory. His promises were a cheap price to pay. After the election, Borden carried out his agreement with the Toronto Eighteen to the letter, exactly as the businessmen had delivered on their promises of material support. The alliance between the manufacturers and the financiers of Ontario and the Conservative Party, first created by Macdonald's National Policy, had been restored.

Laurier did not have to call an election in 1911. Forgetting that his party organization was creaking with age (and that the Conservatives were in very good shape indeed, especially in Ontario) and over-confident that his trade deal opened markets while protecting the tariffs, he rose to the bait thrown out by his obstructionist Tory critics in the House of Commons and called an election for September 21. With money no object, the manufacturers entered the fray, creating a firestorm of anti-American sentiment sufficient to topple the government. Using front organizations like the Canadian National League and the Canadian Home Market Association, they poured out propaganda both door-to-door and in the columns of the newspapers and magazines. By mid-August 1911 almost ten million pamphlets had been dispatched, with more going out every day. Laurier was in a war of words and sentiment, and the odds against him were lengthening.

The thrust of the anti-reciprocity campaign was not markedly different from that in 1891. Again, there were detailed analyses of the agreement and of its probable effect on trade figures and Canadian agriculture.* As before, the mix was one part analysis to two or three parts of nationalism, imperialism, and anti-Americanism, with a heavy topping of emotionalism. The Conservatives had found an issue they could effectively exploit, and they did so to the hilt.

An Appeal to the British-Born, a famous pamphlet written by journalist Arthur Hawkes, called on the recent quarter-million immigrants to Canada—and all those of British heritage—to save Canada once more for the empire. Canada had stayed within the empire in 1849 when annexation was rejected. "It was saved not because of Britain's love for Upper Canada and Lower Canada, but because of the love of the men in the Canadas for Britain." That was a grotesque misreading of events sixty years earlier, but Hawkes continued undeterred: "They knew deep down in their souls, that Canada possessed Britain in a far more magnificent sense than Britain possessed Canada, and that out of their tribulation rich fruits would spring. That is even more splendidly true today." The American way, Hawkes continued, "is not our way—it is neither Canadian nor British. . . . We are free from the woes that spring from the United States

---

* The definitive analysis of the 1911 election remains Stephen Leacock's in his *Sunshine Sketches of a Little Town* (124ff), where Liberal Bagshaw and Tory Smith battle for the soul of Mariposa with freely invented trade statistics pitched to the "high plane of national welfare," most notably "the price of marsh hay in Missinaba County," and the traditional election goings-on that characterized Canadian politics of the era. "For a month, at least, people talked of nothing else," Leacock wrote. "A man would stop another in the street and tell him that he had read last night that the average price of an egg in New York was decimal ought one more than the price of an egg in Mariposa. . . . People lived on figures of this sort, and the man who could remember most of them stood out as a born leader." As a McGill University economist, Leacock's own views of the Reciprocity Agreement were less humorous—he accepted money from the defenders of the National Policy to write election propaganda against Laurier and reciprocity. His biographer noted that one of his McGill colleagues told his class that "all economists are free-traders." But, one student protested, "Dr. Leacock is a protectionist." "I repeat," the professor said acidly, "all economists are free-traders." David Legate, *Stephen Leacock* (Toronto 1970), 59–60.

sowing its wild oats."[16] Another pamphlet, *Under Which Flag?* compared the slow evolution of British institutions with the revolutionary United States. Reciprocity would steal Canada's identity and, in an appeal to the most ambitious of Canadians and their sense of eventual power, "the chance that we will become the chief state in the British Empire and the most powerful and prosperous nation in the world." Yet a third widely distributed pamphlet saw reciprocity as weakening east-west links and harming trade between Britain and Canada. "Why take the risk?"

These emotional arguments made headway against the Liberals' rationalistic approach to the agreement, the detailed presentation of data and dollops of reassurance. And the anti-reciprocity campaigners received a flood of unexpected help from Americans both in Congress and out who trumpeted that reciprocity meant annexation. President Taft said stupidly that "Canada is at the parting of the ways." The Democratic Speaker-designate of the House of Representatives, Champ Clark, was just as foolish: "We are preparing to annex Canada. . . . I am for [reciprocity] because I hope to see the day when the American flag will float over every square foot of British North American possessions clear to the North Pole."* Senator McCumber avowed that "Canadian annexation is the logical conclusion of reciprocity with Canada." An Illinois congressman, George Prince, added: "I say to my neighbors in the north: Be not deceived. When we go into a country and get control of it, we take it. It is our history and it

---

* "That speech of Clark's," President Taft said privately, "has unquestionably sounded the death knell of the reciprocity pact and it was the plan nearest my heart." Possibly, but Taft's repeated comments about Canada being at the parting of the ways did him no good. Not even his later public remark that "the talk of annexation is bosh" could undo the harm. Cited in Lawrence Martin, *The Presidents and the Prime Ministers* (Toronto 1982), 74. Recent American analysts have suggested, however, that if annexation was not an immediate goal, "the real objectives of American policymakers were hardly more narrow. By 1910 they had come to the conclusion that an integrated North American economic order, organized around the needs of the American industrial system, would be little short of critical to the future prosperity of American business. They wished to block Canada's development . . . and to secure for American firms the Canadian market." Robert E. Hannigan, "Reciprocity 1911: Continentalism and American Weltpolitik," *Diplomatic History*, 4 (Winter 1980): 2–3; K.A. Clements. "Manifest Destiny and Canadian Reciprocity in 1911," *Pacific Historical Review*, 42 (1973): 32ff; Gordon Stewart, "'A Special Contiguous Country Economic Regime': An Overview of America's Canadian Policy," *Diplomatic History* 6 (Fall 1982): 339ff.

is right we should take it if we want it and you might as well understand it."[17] William Randolph Hearst's newspapers were just as open. His New York *American* stated, "Eventually Canada will come in. That will be when we want her."

All these remarks, sometimes uttered in ignorance and often for transparent domestic political purposes, fell like manna from heaven for the Tories, and the anti-reciprocity propagandists had an identifiable target. The newspapers opposed to the trade deal featured the comments of the most obscure congressmen as if they were pronouncements by President Taft. As one pamphlet, *Results of Reciprocity . . . By Canadians, For Canadians, About Canada*, put it, after quoting a long list of American statements of this sort: "It is our belief that they mean Annexation—that they want Annexation—that they regard this Reciprocity Bill as a first step toward Annexation." The Loyalists, this pamphlet argued, trotting out the still-popular myths, had come to the "Northern Wilderness of Canada that they might preserve the political affiliations in which they believed." These heroes stood by Canada, their wives and children beside them. They "did not keep a ledger account to decide whether it would not have been better for them to have foresworn their flag, refused the perilous pilgrimage into the Wilderness and fattened on the flesh pots of Egypt." So much for Liberal arguments that reciprocity meant prosperity.

Again cartoonists had a field day. The cover of *Results of Reciprocity*

THERE WAS A YOUNG LADY FROM NIGER
WHO WENT FOR A RIDE ON A TIGER
THEY CAME BACK FROM THE RIDE WITH THE LADY INSIDE
AND NEW STRIPES ON THE HIDE OF THE TIGER

showed Laurier and Fielding racing in a sleigh pulled by a horse called reciprocity along the "road to continentalism"—a road that took Canada over the precipice. Other favoured themes showed Champ Clark letting the cat of annexation out of the bag; Uncle Sam peering over the fence at "Prosperity Vineyard"; the dam that protected Canada from the United States with a huge leak labelled reciprocity; Laurier handing a box labelled "Canada's Destiny" to Uncle Sam over the caption, "Let Laurier finish his work"; or "a young lady from Niger/ who went for a ride on a tiger," labelled reciprocity, who "came back from the ride with the lady inside/ and new stripes on the hide of the tiger." Newton McConnell, the cartoonist of favour for the anti-reciprocity side, also drew Laurier cutting off the Canadian branch on the tree of the British Empire with a saw labelled reciprocity. "Bear down, you fellows," Laurier was saying to his ministers, "and she'll fall like ripe fruit from the parent tree." The Prime Minister was suspect in his loyalty exactly as he had been in 1891.

Borden and the Conservatives believed in the British connection and in Canadian greatness, and they genuinely feared the United States. Reciprocity would turn Canadians into hewers of wood and drawers of water, and oblige them to sell their birthright for the proverbial mess of pottage. Sir George Foster, a prominent Toronto MP, was certain that the Americans wanted Canada for its resources, and Canada, he proclaimed, had the right to "defend its resources from commercial rapine and plunder." The premier of Ontario, Sir James Pliny Whitney, who knew that his province was the most susceptible to the loyalty cry, referred to "Laurier, Taft & Company," and in his major address in the legislature spoke of how reciprocity would "reverse the policy which has brought Canada to her present enviable position" and "lead to Political Union with the United States." Conservative leader Robert Borden, for his part, concluded his campaign by harking back to President Taft's fatal words: "I believe that we are, in truth, standing today at the parting of the ways. . . . We must decide whether the spirit of Canadianism or Continentalism shall prevail on the northern half of this continent."

Laurier had gone into the election with a majority of fifty seats, but the people decided for Borden. The Conservatives won a substantial majority of 134 seats to 87 for the Grits, though the popular vote was closer: 50.9 percent to 47.7. Ontario gave Borden 73 of 86 seats, the decisive factor in the result. Apparently some Ontario farmers, much like the province's financiers and factory operators, were more concerned with American competition in their markets than with selling their production into the United States. Alberta and Saskatchewan, the agricultural provinces that stood to benefit most from reciprocity and where most of the half-million American immigrants to enter Canada since 1900 had settled, gave 15 of 17 seats to the Liberals. That was small comfort. In Quebec, where Laurier's navy and the charge that the Liberal leader was too susceptible to imperialist blandishments played better than anti-reciprocity, the Liberals took only 38 of 65 seats, with Conservatives and Conservative-supporting *nationaliste* candidates taking the rest.* The overall electoral calculus suggested very clearly that Laurier had grossly misjudged the potential support for freer trade and that his opponents had run a brilliant and unscrupulous campaign.** "Perhaps," Laurier said sadly on election night, "we have governed too long."

Reciprocity had been defeated in 1911 as in 1891 by a people who apparently wanted to keep their connection to the British Empire and who believed that to do so they had to remain separate and distinct from their neighbours. Imperialism and nationalism, in other words. Anti-Americanism had been a wondrously effective propaganda tool for the anti-reciprocity forces, one they had exploited to the full in playing on this two-in-one sentiment. As so often happened, once the bloody shirt of loyalism had done its work, Canadians were quick to take it off and ready to reassure Americans that they hadn't really meant it. Andrew Macphail wrote in 1911 that there was "something noble" in the upsurge in Canadianism during the election, "and something praiseworthy in this spectacle of a whole people swept by a wave of emotion and sentiment.

* Henri Bourassa's *Le Devoir* had initially been moderately sympathetic to reciprocity. Anxious above all to destroy Laurier, as the election drew nearer, *Le Devoir* began to find more to quarrel with in the trade agreement, to hint at annexation as an almost inevitable result of reciprocity, and to wonder if French Canadians could enjoy the same linguistic and religious guarantees if Quebec became a state of the American union. A good question, not without its present-day relevance.

** President Taft's reaction at the Canadian result was exact. "We were hit squarely between the eyes and must now sit tight. Of course I am very disappointed because I should like to have had this scalp dangling at my official belt." Think how that remark would have been interpreted in Canada! Cited in Martin, *The Presidents and the Prime Ministers*, 80.

In all sincerity many good and loyal souls were seized by a genuine alarm that their nationality was in danger. They were terrified."

Or, perhaps, the 50 percent of voters who cast their ballot for the Tories had been terrified by the scare campaign that Borden and his business allies had launched and that reinforced the fears that years of watching the United States had created. The American Consul in Ottawa, John S. Foster, was no unbiased observer, but his dispatches suggest the near hysteria that sprang into life in Canada once reciprocity again became the issue. "It is difficult to indicate . . . how bitter and excited the public opposition is becoming in Canada," he reported to Washington on March 15, 1911, months before the election campaign began. "Many of the people one meets in society are almost beside themselves." He added, "I have rarely known such manifestations of extreme feeling. They claim that reciprocity would destroy the home because divorces would immediately become prevalent, that the present judicial system would be replaced by an elected judiciary, and that every conceivable kind of ill would be let loose."* To Foster, the campaign was a scandal in which untruth, fuelled by irrational Canadian nationalism, had prevailed.[18] The governor general, Lord Grey, who recognized that the trade pact was very favourable to Canada, said much the same thing in March, demonstrating that he was no less prone to bias than Foster: "The feeling in Montreal and Toronto against the Agreement could hardly be stronger if the United States troops had already invaded our territory."[19] Britain's Ambassador in Washington, Lord Bryce, took a longer view: "What has happened here and in Canada illustrates the truth that nations may live close to one another and utterly misunderstand one another.

* Divorce statistics were frequently cited to suggest the differences between Canada and the United States. The dean of the Law Faculty at McGill University claimed, for example, that divorce was 320 times more frequent in proportionate terms in the United States. In the period 1867–1906, his statistics showed, there were 1.27 million divorces in the United States and only 431 in Canada (where divorce petitions had to be introduced one by one in the Senate and passed by Parliament). Colonel Denison, a police magistrate in Toronto, also noted that murder was much more frequent south of the border and that lynchings sometimes outnumbered judicial hangings. "We have no 'nigger question,'" one commentator wrote in 1900, offering an explanation for the disparity. Moreover, Canadians had seen three US presidents assassinated between 1865 and 1901. All these figures merely confirmed the Canadian judgement that their society was better, safer, saner. Carl Berger, *The Sense of Power* (Toronto 1970), 160–2.

Few persons in the United States had realised how deeply the arrogant superciliousness and almost brutal rudeness of American statesmen 30 or 40 years ago had sunk into the Canadian mind and made it supremely averse to all proposals from that quarter."[20] Canadians envied the United States its prosperity, but they had a smug and an almost unshakeable belief in the superiority of their system and their way of life. When they were whipped up into a high state of emotion, they emphatically chose the status quo. The barometer that gauged the weather of Canadian–American relations had plunged to its lowest level in decades.

Significantly, retention of the economic and political status quo was decided by the enthusiastic support of business and finance, the open manipulators of Canadian opinion and the chief beneficiaries of the Borden electoral triumph. Virtually as one, businessmen decided that their best interests were served by turning their back to the mammon of America. The issue of free trade would not again be posed so starkly until 1988, but then the response of Canadian business would be different.

3

ON THE AMERICAN ROAD:
THE CRITICAL YEARS, 1914-49

Roosevelt and King, as viewed by the Depression-wracked world.

Dale/Winnipeg Free Press

"English-speaking Canadians from all areas and all economic classes went off to war . . . honestly believing that they were . . . guaranteeing freedom and justice in the world," philosopher George Grant wrote in 1967 of the enthusiasm that gripped Canada in August 1914. Loyalty to Britain and loyalty to liberal capitalist democracy was identified with loyalty to freedom and justice. The slaughter of decent men that resulted, however, spelled out the implicit violence of the West and, Grant said, "it also spelled out Canadian fate":

It killed many of the best English-speaking Canadians and left the survivors cynical and tired. I once asked a man of that generation why it was that between the wars of 1914 and 1939 Canada was allowed to slip into the slough of despond in which its national hope was frittered away to the U.S. by Mackenzie King and the Liberal party. He answered graphically: "We had our guts shot away in France." The energy of that generation was drained away in that conflict so that those who returned did not have the vitality for public care, but retreated into the private world of money making. Canada's survival has always required the victory of political courage over immediate and individual economic advantage.

The Great War had calamitous effects, Grant argued. It divided French and English Canadians so sharply over the way to fight the war that Quebec saw itself "threatened more by English-speaking Canadians than by the deeper threat to the south." Moreover, the British ruling classes "acted as if their only hope of continuing power was to put their fate into the hands of the American empire," to accept American domination in return for Wall Street's support for the pound sterling. Whether this was the best result Britain could achieve was not the question for Grant. What was important to him was the effect England's turning towards the United States had on Canada's sense of nationhood.[1]

Grant's argument is unfortunately incorrect in its details, but there was no doubt he was on to something. Canada's enormous war effort in the Great War had simultaneously spurred nationalism and sapped the national will. It had bitterly split French and English Canadians on the issues of support for the war and conscription for the front. And it had left Britain much weaker and created a financial superpower in the United States, a power to which Canada was pulled like a moth to the flame. The terrible irony, however, something that Grant did not remotely grasp, was that Canada's war effort literally forced the country to turn to the United States for economic, financial, and even military assistance. Canada's imperialist nationalism, in other words, pressed it into the American embrace, and the process that culminated in 1917–18 was destined to be repeated twice more. During the Second World War and again in the early years of the Cold War, British economic and military weakness would again make Canada look to the United States for assistance. The result was decisive—Canada passed from being a British colony to an

American one. Britain's weakness, combined with the gallant imperial patriotism of Canadians, created the world in which Canadians live today.

* * *

Sir Robert Borden, leader of the anti-reciprocity forces in 1911, the man who had cried "No Truck Nor Trade with the Yankees," was compelled by the events of the Great War to seek American economic support for the dominion. In August 1914 this supplication was inconceivable, for Britain was the world's strongest financial power, and Canadians expected that Britain would be able to finance Canada's war effort, just as its investors had financed Canada's peacetime economic expansion. In 1914 Britons controlled 72 percent of foreign investment in Canada, while Americans, despite the profusion of branch plants that had come north to avoid the high tariffs with which Canada protected its domestic market, had only 23 percent, most in the form of direct investment.

But the staggering costs of total war soon revealed that Britain was no longer the world's financial superpower. Within two years, the United Kingdom was running out of the American dollars it needed to purchase critical supplies from the United States, selling investments there to cover its burgeoning trade deficit, and begging and borrowing to get more war material. The implications were serious for Canada. At the war's outset, Britain had agreed to finance Canada's war costs, but by the summer of 1915, as the pound sterling sank on exchange markets, the Treasury in London was urging Ottawa to find other sources of money. Float a loan in Canada, it said, a hitherto unheard of suggestion. The Minister of Finance did as he was told, and Canadians greatly oversubscribed the first war loan. Money was still scarce, however, and in July 1915 the federal government was obliged for the first time ever to go to New York for a loan—$40 million in one- and two-year loans at 5 and 5.25 percent. Canada had come to the parting of the financial ways, to use the terminology of the 1911 election, and, significantly, the move was made by Borden's Conservative government. There can be little doubt that Ottawa had no choice. The British government was so hard pressed, the City of London's financial markets so overstretched, that Canada had to relieve Britain of as many of its responsibilities in Canada as it could.

The same process happened in financing munitions production and sales abroad. At the beginning of the war, Canadian industry was weak and relatively backward, but war orders, for the most part paid for in London, created new factories and tens of thousands of jobs across the country. The British initially had paid in pounds sterling for their orders in Canada, but as the war went on and their difficulties mounted, they pressed Canada to cover more of the costs itself. By the time the United States entered the war in April 1917, Britain's debts in the United States amounted to more than $3 billion, a massive sum at the time, and London found itself reduced to pleading with Washington for assistance. That meant that London could no longer pay for the goods it bought in Canada. If Canada wanted to continue shipping food and munitions to the British market and to keep up employment in Canada's factories and farms, the Canadian government itself had to pay the costs. Facing an election in late 1917 in a country bitterly divided over conscription, Sir Robert Borden had no option, as the British knew.

Borden had additional problems. Every time a Canadian factory made an artillery shell or a truck for Britain, it had to import specialty steels and components from the United States. As shipments to the United Kingdom mounted, so too did Canada's trade deficit with the United States. The more Canada tried to help Britain, the deeper into the hole it went with the Americans. Sir Thomas White, the Finance Minister, tried to escape from his difficulties in the only way possible—by striking a deal with Washington that would let his government and Canadian firms float loans in the United States, despite an American government ban on foreign borrowing that came into effect when America entered the war. As he wrote to the Secretary of the Treasury in a letter that ought to have caused the Canadian to blush:

> We have in your time and mine always been good neighbors. Occasionally a verbal brickbat has been thrown across the fence but we have always sympathized with each other when brickbats have come from any foreign source. In our attitude towards constitutional liberty and all social problems our people are very much alike and understand each other better I think than any other two peoples in the world today. The struggle in a common cause will I am sure greatly cement our friendship and respect for each other.[2]

No anti-Americanism there, no reminder that White had been one of the Toronto Eighteen in 1911 and a bitter opponent of reciprocity. Now, tariffs had become unimportant. Instead, the war had turned Sir Thomas into a continentalist, one who did not hesitate in appealing to North American fellow-feeling if it could help Canada out of its difficulties.

It worked, too. When Britain borrowed from the United States government a few months later, the British insisted and the Americans agreed that Canada be allocated $15 million a month under the loan to cover the costs of raw materials and components that were to be included in Canadian goods destined for the British forces overseas. But Canada itself did not borrow from the US government, and Ottawa confined its money-raising efforts to the New York market. "We shall have to pay a fairly stiff rate of interest," White said, but "I would rather we should 'hoe our own road.'"[3] The same sensible approach would be followed a quarter-century later.

By late 1917 British orders in Canada began to tail off, and Canadian negotiators struck a deal with the US War Department for American orders so that Canadian employment could be kept up. At the same time, as the rapidly mobilizing American economy began to face shortages, Canada found itself forced to act like any American regional economy, bargaining in Washington for its allotments of coal and steel. As the *Financial Post* put it on December 15, 1917, "Canada's Prosperity to Depend on Close Cooperation in Aims and Objects with the United States." The rhetoric of 1911 be damned! Three years of war had changed everything.

The United States government, for its part, chose to forget the anti-American rhetoric that had been shouted across the line in 1911, and willingly helped its neighbour. It was a bonus that the influx of American capital and the allocations of scarce resources helped to achieve long-term American interests by cementing United States economic control and by weakening the United Kingdom's presence in Canada.

The outward sign of the shift caused by the war could be seen in the foreign investment and trade figures. In 1919 British investment still amounted to 57 percent of Canada's total and American investment to 39 percent, already a marked change from five years earlier; but by 1922, as Britain struggled to recover from the war's human and financial costs,

American investment reached 50 percent,* and, by 1939, it was 60 percent. Exports from Canada to the United States kept pace with the change in foreign investment. In 1901, exports to the United States were less than half those to the United Kingdom, but by 1918 they were four-fifths of a vastly greater total going to Britain. Imports changed even more dramatically: in 1901 imports from the United States were 250 percent of those from the United Kingdom; by 1918 they were 1000 percent greater.

At the same time, there were initial signs of military closeness between the two neighbours. Early in the war Canadians had feared that German or Irish Americans might launch attacks across the border, the former to help the Kaiser, the latter, much like the Fenians a half-century earlier, to assist Ireland's claims for independence. Ottawa had posted upwards of ten thousand soldiers to guard vital points. The US government closely monitored potential activities, nipping any schemes in the bud. Once the Americans entered the war, and once Britain diverted its hard-pressed anti-submarine vessels out of Canadian waters, Canada had to seek American assistance in convoy escort. The Americans not only willingly, if a little grudgingly, provided this help but they eventually offered air support, air training, and additional naval protection when needed. As a result, Washington won the gratitude of the Ottawa authorities, military and civil.

How times had changed. Despite the southward shift in economic, financial, and trade linkages caused by the war, there were no anti-American Tories to accuse Sir Robert Borden of continentalism or disloyalty during the Great War. He had done what he had to do. Wartime necessity showed irrefutably that the Conservative Party's anti-Americanism was simply words. It would linger on, but the force was gone.

---

* In 1923 American investors controlled 41 percent of the Canadian steel industry, 45 percent of the electrical industry, 52 percent of copper smelting, 52 percent of drugs and chemicals, and 70 percent of the auto industry. Such data, documenting the sale of Canadian resources by Canadian businessmen, led historian Frank Underhill to write that "our big businessmen are our chief American influences, and the tendency of their activities is not one whit altered by the vigour with which some of them wave the old flag. If they prevail indefinitely," he warned, "Canada will become only a geographical expression." FHU, "O Canada," *Canadian Forum* 9 (July 1929): 341.

*   *   *

Words still had some weight, of course. While the political order was changing, the vast majority of Canadians paid almost no attention, fixated as they were on events in France and Flanders. The four-year-long struggle in the trenches was so fierce, the Canadian and British casualties so high, and the outcome so unpredictable that the neutrality of the United States, with its industries and bankers profiting hugely from the war, offended them grievously. Governments may have been cooperating, but anti-Americanism flourished on a popular level. President Woodrow Wilson's refusal to join in the war against the Kaiser until April 1917 enraged poets and novelists alike. Captain H.B. McConnell, a self-styled soldier-poet, wrote in his 1916 book *Where Duty Leads* that "you have brought upon your name/ The shame of faltering, when you should have stood/ Take to yourself the curse of thousands slain." The usually benign creator of *Anne of Green Gables*, Lucy Maud Montgomery, resorted to bitter irony in her references to Wilson and the pious messages he sent the belligerents. "Ink," she wrote in *Rilla of Ingleside*, "is twice as high as it was last year. Perhaps it is because Woodrow Wilson has been writing so many notes." The American President was no one's favourite in Canada, even after he took the United States into the conflict. One Leamington, Ontario, writer complained that "Mr Wilson got into the war very much like a cat gets into a fight when someone catches her by the tail and throws her into the pit where forty cats are making the fur fly."[4] This attitude persisted in novels into the 1990s. In Robert MacNeil's *Burden of Desire*, a work set in Great War Halifax, his characters rant about the "Bloody Americans" and "how long it had taken the Americans to see their own vital interests while they watched the British Empire bleed itself to death." And when the Yanks finally saw their duty, "Now, like everything else they do, they have to make a big noise about it."

The sense seemed clear in later Canadian writing that Canada had achieved what writer Beckles Willson called "a position of admitted moral superiority" over the United States by her participation in the war from the outset; that it had, as Professor John Macnaughton put it, "morally annexed" the United States and eventually brought it into the war.[5] This was wishful thinking, of course, for Canadian opinion was scarcely noticed in the perpetually self-absorbed democracy to the south. Even when the Americans finally came into the fight, the tone of resentful criticism in

Canada changed only slightly. The newspaper editorialists expressed relief that America was in the war, but, as the Toronto *Globe* put it on April 6, 1917, "while Canadians believe that the United States would have fared better at the bar of history if she had drawn the sword sooner against the common foe of humanity and democracy, they must pay tribute to the vigor of the war measures taken or advised by the President." The Montreal *Gazette* took a similar tone the next day, urging its readers to remember that "while we welcome the cooperation of the United States . . . the first blow for democracy and the rights of small nations was struck by Britain and France and that the glory of victory will above all others be theirs."

At the front, there was said to be relief at the American entry. Large numbers of Americans had crossed into Canada to enlist in the Canadian forces while their country was neutral, but some in Canada, at least, had doubts about the fighting qualities of the Yanks. The Governor General, the Duke of Connaught, a bone-stupid soldier who had persuaded himself that he was Canada's commander-in-chief, worried that "experience has so far shown that American citizens do not always make the best of soldiers."[6] That was simpleminded bigotry and foolishness, but as 1917 turned into 1918 and the American armies only slowly made their way overseas, there was increasing bitterness, especially at the front. Soldier Will Bird wrote in October 1918 that at last "the Yanks were really fighting. They had long been a joke that left bad taste and were now seldom mentioned. For two-and-a-half years they had watched old England and France fighting the greatest war machine ever organized, and then had stepped in to lend a hand. A year later," he went on, "they had not done anything to help, and we forgot them; when remembered they were derided."[7]

The Americans, naturally enough, took a very different view—they believed that they had arrived in France just in the nick of time to save the Allies. The future scholar Harold Innis, invalided out of the army after service in France, wrote to his family from Chicago just after the July 4 celebrations in 1918: "The Americans however never get tired of talking about the things they do or the things they are going to do . . . I never heard such a line of bragging and boasting in all my life. It was really disgusting at least to Canadians. Personally I should have liked to have had the opportunity to tell them how long it took them to get into the war and if they were doing so much why there were so many young men on the streets. Some of them think they have won the war."[8] The Americans thought precisely that—and they were likely correct to do so—and their magazines, books, and politicians made no bones about it. In a parody of the initials of the American Expeditionary Force, they boasted they had won After England Failed. The *Canadian Annual Review 1919*, dealing at length with the question of just who had won the war, conceded that the Americans had much to bolster their claims, but noted "there was a side to it, however, of which the average American had never heard." A long account followed of British and Canadian financial costs, manpower contributions, and casualties compared with those borne by the United States.

The calm refutation of American boasts made no impression in the United States which remained utterly oblivious to Canada and Canadian sensitivities. Ten years later, the first scholarly assessment of the entire history of Canadian–American relations denounced the provocative American claims. Author Hugh Keenleyside observed that the major and most unrestrained American celebrations at war's end seemed to take place close to the border: "Thus in a few short weeks was undone much of the good that had been accomplished by the months of co-operation and mutual sacrifice during the war."[9] This theme was to be played out again and again during the interwar years, and Major George Drew, then assistant master of the Supreme Court of Ontario, first made a name for himself in 1928 with a *Maclean's* article on "The Truth About the War." The piece, a statistical comparison that lumped Canadian and other Dominion efforts into the British totals, attracted public attention, and *Maclean's* distributed more than 100,000 copies in pamphlet form. The response revealed the antagonism to American war bragging to which Canadians had been exposed for years in American magazines such as the *Saturday Evening Post*. The impact of all this discussion on anti-Americanism in Canada is unmeasurable, but it was likely substantial.

The Canadian entry to the war in 1914, in contradistinction to the American delay until April 1917, demonstrated just how different the two countries still acted. Canada had spent decades desperately trying to resist the Americanization of European culture practised so assiduously and so successfully in the United States. Its citizens, as Ramsay Cook observed, "believed that an Americanized culture, one cut loose from its European roots, would destroy the distinction between Canada and the United States." Canada was *British* North America.

But was it any longer? If they were unhappy with American braggadocio, Canadians could have stopped reading American magazines and books. They didn't, and they couldn't, but even that extreme response might not have saved them. Writing early in the century in his book *The Americanization of Canada*, the American social scientist and journalist Samuel Moffett noted that Canada's newspapers and magazines, though Canadian in sentiment, were "American in their whole tone, their makeup, their typography, their estimate of the value of news and their manner of presenting it." Moreover, much of the material they published came from American sources and "in consequence is furnished by American writers from an American viewpoint." The *Mail and Empire* in 1905 agreed: "Of Americanizing literature this country is getting altogether too much." The Toronto newspaper added that "the ports of entry between Canada and the United States are so many sluices through which Americanizing reading matter is pouring every day. The minds of our people are being saturated with social and political teaching that is bad for the country." The Toronto *Globe* was blunter still two decades later: American pulp fiction magazines presented Canadians with the "off-scourings of the moral sewers of human life," a veritable flood of "undisguised filth." What made this worse was that the Canada of the early twentieth century offered little to its own artists and writers and, in consequence, had only the most rudimentary culture. The *Mail and Empire*'s answer to the problem was to bring in "British books of the same literary class," as if that would create a Canadian culture. A foreign critic could dispose of Canada's literary history in five pages, said another.*

Where is Canadian literature? the founder of the Canadian Authors' Association asked, then answered his own question with the comment that

---

* One reason for the dearth of Canadian literature may have been the intense reluctance to venture into the modern. Lewis Wharton in *Canadian Bookman* bemoaned American periodicals, some "so studiedly pornographic as to constitute a standing source of corruption." Andrew MacLean, editor of the *Canadian Magazine*, sounded the same note: "The magazine press of the United States is the filthiest the world has ever seen." But Canada was different. Lorne Pierce, one of the leading editors of his day, boasted in 1924 of Canadian literature's wholesome purity: "No sex obsession, no morbidity, no psychoanalysis but rather the purifying and purging effect of our land." He might have added: "no readers." Quoted in Mary Vipond, "National Consciousness in English-Speaking Canada in the 1920's: Seven Studies" (PhD dissertation, University of Toronto 1974), 346; John Weaver, "Imperilled Dreams: Canadian Opposition to the American Empire, 1918-1930" (PhD dissertation, Duke University 1973), 337.

it was "on the road to New York." Virtually every successful writer either moved to the United States or sought an American publisher as soon as he or she was able. The problem had been apparent for generations. The editor, publisher, and journalist Mercer Adam, just prior to departing from Canada for the United States in 1889, had written that "we talk with horror of political annexation, yet we pay no heed to the annexation of another kind, which is drafting off across the line not only the brains and pens of the country, but the hopes and hearts of those who move and inspire them."[10]

It wasn't only literature that was a problem. "Our Art is not Canadian," one critic noted of Canadian painting before the Group of Seven emerged to make it so. Another complained that Canada's theatres, their offerings controlled by booking offices in New York, existed solely for the benefit of foreign playwrights and actors. Arts patron and sometime politician Vincent Massey added that theatre in Canada was "under alien influences," and the editor B.K. Sandwell said bitterly that "Canada is the only nation in the world whose stage is entirely controlled by aliens [of course, Sandwell meant Americans, not the British whose actors and plays toured Canada extensively] . . . the only nation whose sons and daughters are compelled to go to a foreign capital for permission to act in their own language on the boards of their own theatres."

As Archibald MacMechan put it in the *Canadian Historical Review* in 1920, the situation was such that Canada faced "the very real danger of bondage" to the United States. The danger came not from actual invasion but from "gradual assimilation, peaceful penetration, in a spiritual bondage—the subjection of the Canadian nation's mind and soul to the mind and soul of the United States." The American view of the world, of social life, of republican thought, of European conditions, of the British government at home and in India and Ireland was not good for Canadians, the *Canadian Annual Review* observed in 1922.[11] For MacMechan, the *Review*, and many others, however, subjection to the mind and soul of the United Kingdom remained virtually the essence of Canadianism in the 1920s. Some questioned this alignment. F.H. Underhill wrote in the *Canadian Forum* in 1929 that "those colonially-minded persons who think to save us from the flood of Americanism by appealing to English traditions might as well start a campaign to bring back the horse and buggy."

At the root of complaints against American influence was money. The American publications had too much of it, the Canadian too little. "Publishing," an industry representative argued in 1926 when some three hundred US magazines sold fifty millon copies a year in Canada, "is like any other manufacturing problem and we, the Canadian publishers, are just as entitled to protection as the manufacturer of lamps or lingerie."[12]*

Should Canadians have feared the continuing influx of American money? The *Canadian Forum* in 1926 published an article on "The Penetration of American Capital in Canada," one of the earliest studies to view the situation with alarm. Even so, there was no fear that the Stars and Stripes would follow investment northward. "In the first place, the dominion is not a backward country, peopled by a race indifferent to the development of their country." Then, Canada, though not a great power, was part of the British Empire. "This nullifies any idea of annexation of Canada by force." The Americans could secretly buy up the press, endow the churches and universities, and gradually persuade Canadians that annexation was the best course to follow. However, the *Forum* concluded that the British connection would always be an effective counterweight to any such propaganda "unless the country was in the midst of severe economic distress."[13]

In Quebec, it was a different kind of protection that was wanted. In the 1920s American investment had stirred mixed emotions, though, as in the rest of the country, it was generally welcomed as a positive force: it industrialized the province, provided jobs for the people, and stopped emigration to the greener pastures of New England. But American money brought Americanization, so much so that by the early 1940s, writers noted that "le franco–canadien vit de plus en plus comme l'américain."[14] And the Comité permanente de la survivance française en amérique told the Massey Royal Commission in 1950 that "le peril le plus grave qui menace l'avenir de cette culture [canadienne–française] est ce que l'on appelle 'l'américanisme.'"

Many Quebeckers were greatly disturbed by this threat. In 1936 the clerical journal *Revue Dominicaine* devoted an entire issue (later published in book form) to a sustained diatribe against all things American. The United States was damned for its effect on the cinema and on sport, on religion and philosophy, on financial life and the media. Georges Pelletier, editor of the influential *Le Devoir*, wrote about the impact of American newspapers on Quebec in terms that anglophones will have no trouble

---

* Nothing much has changed in the intervening seventy years. Publishers still argue for cultural protection on the basis of unfair competition. See chapter 9.

understanding: "Les défauts, les vices américains les plus affichés, dans ce type de presse importée, ce sont: le matérialisme intense qui ramène tout à la possession de l'argent; le gout des futilités les plus stupides, élevé presque aux proportions d'un culte pour des idoles sportives, cinématographiques, etc. . . . enfin en matière de religion, une ignorance totale qui conduit a l'agnosticisme absolu."[15] Vice, materialism, money, a cult of sports and movie idols, religious ignorance and agnosticism—Pelletier sounded much like the Loyalists or the late nineteenth-century critics of the United States in English Canada, albeit with a more modern tone.

André Laurendeau, one of the best and most subtle minds in the province, did not disagree. In 1937 he decried the insidious dangers of American materialism, and even a quarter-century later he still worried that an independent Quebec would be weaker than a Quebec that was part of Canada: "The non-US mass would fall to six million from the

High US tariffs in the late 1920s roused Canadian ire—and pride.

Hunter/*Toronto Daily Star*/Reprinted with permission—Royal Ontario Museum 929.39.26

eighteen million it was before. Our economy would become still more fragile, still more vulnerable, still more subject to the economy of the United States; we would be a 'banana republic.'"[16]

For all the complaints, for all the lingering anti-Americanism, relations between Canada and the United States in the interwar years had become close and generally comfortable. The irritants caused by Canadian pride versus American boasting, US prohibitionist attempts to sink Canadian boats ferrying whiskey to grateful Americans, and the Smoot-Hawley tariff that raised American duties against Canadian goods to record highs were blips on a straight line of rising good will. The church in Quebec might complain about the Americanization of the people, but Québécois, like their English-speaking compatriots, avidly sought to become as much like the Americans as they could. The élites still aped the British in dress, manner, and culture, but ordinary Canadians, while sentimentally attached to Britain and occasionally subject to fits of anti-Americanism, were North Americans.

Early in the 1930s, the peaceful character of Canadian–American relations seemed impressive enough to be a model for the world. Under the guiding hand of James T. Shotwell, a Canadian-born historian at Columbia University, the Carnegie Endowment for International Peace commissioned a series of scholarly volumes on the North American relationship to show that neighbouring states could live in peace if they traded with each other, moved freely across their borders, and followed rational, non-ideological policies.

Such ideas were widespread. Even an unabashed imperialist like W.L. Grant, the headmaster of Upper Canada College, could write in the 1920s that, while he worried that "in this country with 3000 miles of American frontier, American influence seeps in like drainage . . . hostility toward the United States is absurd. There is at times a certain bad manners toward them on the part of some old Tories which I abominate."[17] Chief Justice Charles E. Hughes of the US Supreme Court said much the same in a different way: "While we will have much to discuss, we will have nothing to fight about." A Canadian writing in *Foreign Affairs* in April 1932 picked up this point, saying there was nothing to fight about because the habit of peaceful settlement had overtaken the desire to resort to arms. So it seemed to the good burghers reading the daily newspapers with their heavy diet of American news, while listening to "Amos and Andy" or the Metropolitan Opera direct from New York.

*   *   *

Was there any basis to this optimism? Could the United States yet be a threat to Canada? Some in the Canadian military believed so. The Canadian forces, reduced to a few thousand as soon as government could demobilize the Great War's mighty Canadian Corps, still had planners who drew up their schemes, much as their counterparts in Washington prepared their own detailed plans for every eventuality. Colonel James Sutherland "Buster" Brown, the Army's Director of Military Operations and Intelligence, had the task of preparing a defence plan for Canada if the Americans attacked, and his chosen strategy was to launch offensive operations against selected points in the United States. Doing reconnaissance himself, collecting road maps and postcards of strategic points, Brown reckoned that Canadian attacks aimed at occupying Spokane, Seattle, Portland, Fargo, Detroit, Albany, and other key points might shock the Americans, disrupt their own offensive plans, and allow time for the forces of the British Empire to be rushed to the dominion's aid. (The real folly in Brown's planning was in assuming that the British, who knew who buttered their bread, would send an expeditionary force across the Atlantic to rescue Canada.) That Canada had no trained forces capable of accomplishing these offensive aims did not seem to trouble him. Brown did not anticipate a war between Canada and the United States as sole belligerents, but he argued, as did many others in the 1920s, that there were credible scenarios in which Britain and the United States might be drawn into war. If that occurred, it was entirely reasonable to expect that the United States might again launch its forces at the closest British possession. Indeed, American war planners were proceeding on precisely those assumptions.

Buster Brown was without question a rabid and confirmed anti-American, one whose Loyalist ancestry, reading, and observations of individual Americans confirmed him in his unshakeable view of the superiority of Britain and the British dominions and the rapaciousness of the Great Republic. But Brown was not, as some historians who came across his plans in the archives have assumed, acting on his own in preparing Defence Scheme No. 1. He was carrying out the directives of the army's Chief of the General Staff and the responsible ministers of the Crown. Moreover, Brown's plans survived virtually intact until 1931, when they were finally scrapped as anachronistic. Even then, the planners at National Defence Headquarters had to consider other possibilities, such as the need to protect Canadian territory in the event of a Japanese-American war in which Canada was neutral and the combatants might try to seize Canadian territory for its own offensive or defensive purposes.

The American planners, at the same time, continued their planning and, as some writers have noted, even accelerated it. Their work, it appears, was not intended simply for exercise and training purposes. In May 1930 the Secretaries of War and the Navy approved "War Plan Red," which had as its aim "ultimately, to gain complete control of Crimson," the code name for Canada. The "Red" plan was amended in 1934 to authorize immediate first use of poison gas against Canadian targets and to allow strategic bombing of Halifax if the port could not be captured. The next year, Congress allocated money to build air bases near the Canadian border to permit pre-emptive strikes against Canadian airfields (there were almost none and no first-line aircraft). Much of this planning was a desperate attempt by US Army generals to find some way to extract funds from Congress during the Depression, but not all of it. Buster Brown was not insane in assuming that the United States—or at least some of its military planners—had designs on the dominion.

* * *

If there was an American military threat to Canada, global events soon eliminated it. The rise of fascism in Germany, Italy, and Japan threatened the democracies as never before, and the Americans' conquest of Canada proceeded by peaceful means. The Second World War effectively completed the process of continental integration accelerated by the Great War; indeed, it carried integration directly into military areas that had largely been untouched by the 1917–18 period.

Mackenzie King, the Liberal Party politician who was widely viewed in imperialist circles in Canada and the United Kingdom as "the American," was prime minister. King had done graduate work at Chicago and Harvard, and had laboured as a social worker at Jane Addams's Hull House in Chicago. He had also spent much of the Great War in the United States working for the Rockefellers in developing company unions to bring "labour peace" to the Colorado mines. His critics unfairly charged then and later that King, a pudgy, neurotic man already in his forties, ought to have been in the trenches. In 1917, moreover, and much to the anger of Canadian imperialists, King had stayed loyal to Sir Wilfrid Laurier and opposed conscription. As Prime Minister in the 1920s, he had pressed for Canadian autonomy in imperial conferences, and he had destroyed the already wobbly diplomatic unity of the empire by sending a Canadian Minister to the United States in 1927, giving Canada for the first time its own diplomatic representative in the American capital.

Worse yet to those suspicious of the Americans and "the American," in 1935 King returned to power after five years in the political wilderness, and he instantly called on the American Minister in Ottawa to discuss trade. It was King's policy "to seize every occasion possible to show Canada's solidarity with the United States on matters affecting their mutual interest and well-being," and if the United States was reasonable on tariffs, Canada under his leadership would prefer to travel "the American road." By that, the Prime Minister meant putting an end to destructive tariff wars and the "beggar-thy-neighbour" policies that in his mind had been typical of the Conservative government led by Richard Bedford Bennett from 1930 to 1935. He also meant, though he did not say so, America's high-tariff policies that had shut out Canadian goods. The Americans were pleased with the overture, and the negotiations begun under Bennett for a trade deal between the two North American states were pushed ahead at full speed to a conclusion. King and President Franklin Delano Roosevelt crafted a deal that substantially lowered tariffs. This first Canadian–American trade agreement to reach fruition since 1854 upset some manufacturers and many Tories, especially those who believed in the Ottawa Agreements of 1932 that had tried to carve an empire trading bloc out of the Depression-wracked dominions and colonies.The Depression had so sapped the country's economy, however, that protests were limited by the hope that the new pact might get some trade flowing again.

King then compounded matters by negotiating another trade agreement in 1938 that further lowered trade barriers. It was not as big as reciprocity in 1911, but it was a step towards freeing trade in North America. Bennett denounced the deals as a complete sell-out to the Americans, and the Canadian Manufacturers Association bitterly complained, but the press response on the whole was positive. Whether the 1938 trade agreement might have increased exports and imports was never determined. The coming of war the next year eliminated normal trading relations.

When Canada went to war at Britain's side in September 1939 and the United States remained neutral, the same testy attitudes that had marked the 1914–17 period began to re-emerge. The Premier of Ontario, Mitch Hepburn, for example, was no friend of either the Liberal government in

Callan/Reprinted with permission—The Toronto Star Syndicate/National Archives of Canada C-143284

Ottawa or the neutral United States. After Britain and France fell victim to the Nazi blitzkrieg, after Dunkirk and Italy's entry into the war at Hitler's side, the Premier, on June 11, 1940, warned Canadians that there was a Nazi Fifth Column in the United States "only waiting for orders from across the Atlantic." Ontario, he cautioned, lay alongside "the most thickly populated sections of the United States, where undoubtedly there are hundreds of thousands of Nazi and Fascist sympathizers." Hepburn implicitly accused the United States authorities of condoning this largely imaginary threat, which was simply untrue. At about the same time, Hepburn tried to ban a film on the Canadian war effort, jointly produced by the National

Film Board and "The March of Time," a popular American series, from Ontario theatres on the grounds that it was federal Liberal propaganda. To those who urged that propaganda in an American series was good for the country and might even help thaw American neutrality, Hepburn turned a deaf ear.[18] Others, upset by the favourable press that the isolationist Colonel Charles Lindbergh, the first man to fly solo across the Atlantic, was getting in the *Saturday Evening Post* in July 1940, wanted to ban that US magazine from circulating in Canada. Still another indication of wartime anti-Americanism occurred when the University of Toronto moved to fire historian Frank Underhill for remarks he had made at a conference at Lake Couchiching, Ontario, in August 1940. The historian, always a provocateur, had said that Canada "can no longer depend on the power of Britain and France standing between us and whatever may develop on the continent of Europe. And so we can no longer put all our eggs in the British basket. . . . we have now two loyalties to be followed in practice when we plan our defence policies," loyalties to Britain *and* the United States. Those ought to have been truisms, but they upset the powerful in Toronto, and Underhill's job was saved only by dint of a long struggle.[19]

Such attitudes in Ontario verged on the idiotic at a time when Canada's dependence on the United States was never more apparent. The Allied defeat on the Continent and the very real prospect of a Nazi invasion and conquest of Britain meant that for the first time the dominion potentially lay open to a serious attack from across the Atlantic. If the Royal Navy fell into Hitler's hands, there would be a real threat to North America. The American Minister in Ottawa, Pierrepont Moffat, reported that Canadians seemed aware of the shift in global power: "Even elements which in the past have been least well disposed to us such as the Toronto public and the English-speaking sections of Montreal are now outspoken" in favour of a defence arrangement with the United States. Even "the old die-hards," the unthinking Tory imperialists who mistrusted everything American, welcomed a defence agreement, Moffat said, certainly exaggerating matters.[20]

In the circumstances, and much like Borden a quarter-century before, King did what he had to do. Britain's military weakness (along with Canada's) forced the dominion to seek the help of the United States, and Roosevelt provided the opportunity when he called King and asked to meet with him at Ogdensburg, New York, a small town on the St Lawrence just 80 kilometres from Ottawa, on August 17, 1940. The President had long been concerned by the relative defencelessness of the Canadian Atlantic and Pacific seaboards, and he had been speaking since 1935 of the good neighbourly relations that existed between the two countries. In 1938 he had authorized secret defence discussions between the Chiefs of Staff of Canada and the United States, and the coming of war and its disastrous course in the spring and summer of 1940 increased his sense of urgency. Hence the invitation to Mackenzie King to join him at Ogdensburg.

The Permanent Joint Board on Defence that was the product of their meeting altered Canada's strategic future. From being a British military dependency, Canada was now America's and, to judge by the title of the PJBD, permanently so. That the board, by guaranteeing Canada's military security, also allowed the country to do its utmost for Britain by continuing to send every trained man, every piece of equipment, and vast quantities of food overseas for the prosecution of the war, and that it formally associated the neutral United States for the first time with a belligerent member of the Commonwealth, seemed to escape the critics.

And there were critics. The leader of the Conservative Party in Parliament, R.B. Hanson, attacked the agreement as "political window dressing" designed to help Roosevelt's prospects of re-election, and he hinted darkly at Prime Minister King's longstanding leanings towards the United States. The Conservative leader in the Senate, former prime minister Arthur Meighen, privately wrote with scorn about "this world-shaking achievement that King and Roosevelt have staged in Ogdensburg. . . . Really I lost my breakfast when I read the account this morning . . . and gazed on the disgusting picture of these potentates posing like monkeys in the very middle of the blackest crisis of this Empire." King had never wanted Canada to sit on the Committee of Imperial Defence in London because it might entangle Canada in war, Meighen added, his bilious anti-Americanism spilling onto the page. "He has no objection, though, to such an arrangement with the United States. Neither have I for that matter. There is no danger of it entangling us in war because there is no Spain left that the United States could lick."[21] The apoplectic Meighen, convinced that the Ogdensburg Agreement was very much "in line with Mr King's life long inclinations," soon repeated his criticisms of Ogdensburg in the Senate. What was interesting, however, was that almost no one joined in. The English-language Tory press did not pick up Hanson's or Meighen's line; indeed, Hanson had to spend much time explaining that he had not really meant what he said. In August 1940, with Hitler triumphant in Europe, the Ogdensburg Agreement made eminent good sense, and imperial relics like Meighen and Hanson stood out only because their attitudes were so out of tune with reality. Anti-Americanism, in other words, hurt the war effort and was unpatriotic.

The military links forged at Ogdensburg bound Canada and the United States closer together than ever before. So, too, did the Hyde Park Declaration of April 1941. Exactly as in the Great War, Canada found itself in difficulties because of Britain's economic weakness and inability to pay for the goods it needed in Canada; exactly as in the earlier conflict, Canada, running short of American dollars, had to seek assistance in the United States. This time, however, the scale of the Canadian war effort was vastly greater, and the difficulties, again caused by the need to import American raw materials and components for munitions destined for Britain, greater still. The problem was compounded by the Roosevelt administration's proposed Lend-Lease Bill, which, by offering Britain American war supplies "free," threatened to eliminate London's orders—and the jobs they created—in Canada. The way out was provided by the 1941 Hyde Park Declaration, signed on "a grand Sunday in April" by King and Roosevelt. The Americans agreed to buy more raw materials in Canada, thus increasing Canadian holdings of scarce American dollars; they also consented to charge the cost of imported components and raw materials to the British Lend-Lease account, thus saving Canada's economy by preventing a dollar shortage that could have all but shut down the country. Significantly, the Canadian government refused to accept Lend-Lease itself, Mackenzie King observing shrewdly that, however good relations were with Washington, it would not do to be indebted to the United States. After the war, the Americans might use such an advantage to drive a hard bargain on tariffs.

The agreement made at Hyde Park was a lifesaver for Canada, one that allowed the Canadian economy, finally hitting high gear, to do its utmost for victory. But the short-term gains had to be set against the long-term results. Britain's economic weakness had again pushed Canada southward, and the declaration increased US demand for Canadian resources. The bilateral economic links had tightened, and the figures made this very clear. American foreign investment, 60 percent of the Canadian total in 1939, reached 70 percent by 1945; exports to the United States also tripled during the war, while imports rose by an astounding 250 percent. Ogdensburg had made Canada an American military dependency; Hyde Park and the forces unleashed by the war simultaneously made her more prosperous and an economic dependency.

While these changes took place, the public mood was relatively benign towards the United States, and so it should have been. In 1917 the Allies had greatly benefited from American money, resources, and soldiers, but it stretched the truth to argue that the doughboys had singlehandedly won the war. After 1941, however, once Roosevelt galvanized the enormous productive capacity of America and ten million men and women enlisted, there were fewer doubters that the US entry was the decisive factor in the war. The Soviet Union chewed up the Nazi legions, to be sure, but the trucks, aircraft, and food the Red Army used came in large measure through Lend-Lease. The equipment and the food Britain used also came from America, including Canada.

The newly powerful United States worried government officials in Ottawa. At the PJBD, American officers in the autumn of 1940 had pressed Canada hard to concede tactical and strategic control of Canadian forces to the United States military in the event of a British defeat; in a situation in which North America would be gravely imperilled, this arguably made sense, and Canada agreed. But in 1941, with Britain still fighting and its powers of resistance increasing daily, the Americans sought the same control and the effective integration of Canadian defences into their own if and when they joined in the war; this time Ottawa resisted fiercely and won its point.* Although he understood Canada's dependence on its neighbour, Mackenzie King had a backbone and was prepared to fight for his nation's military autonomy.

Still, some American intentions could not be resisted. Before the United States entered the war, it won the right from Britain to send troops to Newfoundland, the island dominion-turned-Depression-era-Crown Colony that Canada had long coveted. After Pearl Harbor in December 1941, the United States demanded that Canada permit the construction of the Alaska Highway, a land route through the dominion to Alaska, now threatened by Japanese attack. Canada agreed, and more

---

* Perhaps this persistence in defending the Canadian position was the kind of attitude that led Fiorello LaGuardia, the New York City mayor named by Roosevelt to head the US Section of the Permanent Joint Board on Defence, to refer to "the usual difficulties" he was encountering in Canada, something he attributed to "pride and the little brother attitude with which you are familiar." F.D. Roosevelt Library, Hyde Park, NY, Roosevelt Papers, OF4090, LaGuardia to Roosevelt, May 28, 1942.

than 15,000 American troops poured into the northwest, spending money with apparent abandon. The US Army headquarters in Edmonton, Canadians and Americans both joked, answered the telephone, "Army of Occupation." Vincent Massey, from his post as Canadian High Commissioner in London, sourly noted that the Yanks "have apparently walked in and taken possession as if Canada were unclaimed territory inhabited by a docile race of aborigines."[22] The federal government, absorbed by events overseas, initially paid little attention until the British High Commissioner, returning from a trip to the North in 1943, pointed out to the government that the Canadian official presence was all but non-existent and that there might be some difficulty in persuading the Americans to leave at the end of the war. Ottawa promptly appointed an army general as special commissioner and told him to show the Red Ensign. When the war ended, the Canadian government paid the United States in full for every installation it had built in Canada, thanked the Americans profusely, and bade them adieu.

That attitude was apparent elsewhere, though tempered by the new sense of reality produced by wartime experience. Postwar planners, warily considering the prospect of Soviet-American antagonism and weighing Canada's geographic position between the two new superpowers in their calculations, now understood that the United States had a legitimate interest in Canada's defences. Their studies made clear that Canada had to accept full responsibility for all future defence measures on Canadian territory. If Canada did not, the United States would insist on doing the job on its own, whatever Canada and Canadians might say.

Friendly with Roosevelt, fully aware of the critical importance of the United States to Canada and to victory, Mackenzie King nonetheless worried about the new US influence on Canada. In 1942 he had written in his diary that "America has had as her policy, a western hemisphere control which would give hemispheric immunity . . . from future wars but increasing political control by US." A few days later, he remarked on "the fingers of the hand which America is placing more or less over the whole of the Western hemisphere." Canadian national interests during the Second World War, exactly as in the Great War, had obliged Canada to cooperate closely and to mesh its economic life with the United States. But caution remained the watchword.

* * *

The two wars had sped up the process of making the North American continent a single economic unit. The cold peace that followed after 1945 would largely complete the task.

In 1945 Europe was in ruins and, in a world struggling to repair itself, two countries, Canada and the United States, had emerged from the conflict strengthened. North American goods and foodstuffs were essential to rebuild Europe, but the all-but-bankrupt British, French, Dutch, Belgians, and Scandinavians had no dollars. The British, for their part, set out to negotiate loans in Canada and the United States in 1945–46 and, after hard bargaining, secured $3.75 billion from Washington. The Canadian discussions were almost equally difficult, and in the end Canada, a nation with one-twelfth of the US population and one-seventeenth of its productive capacity, offered to lend $1.25 billion, or something above 10 percent of the Gross National Product, and, moreover, wrote off a substantial sum in British war debts. The reasons were clear: first, Canadians felt enormous sympathy with the Mother Country's effort to rebuild; second, if Britain could not purchase goods in Canada, postwar reconstruction could be disrupted by the collapse of overseas sales; and third, and most important, the Canadian government desperately wanted to avoid a situation in which Canada's only source of imports and destination for exports was the United States. For the same reasons, credits were advanced to other European states. In all, Canada put up an astonishing $2 billion in loans and credits to keep its overseas markets, a sum vastly greater in proportionate terms than that offered by the United States. Mackenzie King, a sentimental imperialist at heart, had been the key player in pushing the government towards generosity. "It certainly will be difficult for my political opponents through generations to come to say that I have been anti-British with what has been done for Britain under my administrations in the war and post-war years," King wrote in his diary. He could not have been more wrong about his opponents.

The loans and credits disappeared quickly, swallowed up by the scale of reconstruction needed to get Europe functioning again. By 1947–48, with the Soviet Union no longer even pretending to be friendly towards the West, with Eastern Europe groaning under the tight Soviet yoke, and with Communist parties apparently poised to take power in elections in France and Italy, there was a desperate need to galvanize European democracy. The American response was the Marshall Plan, a huge and generous scheme to let the Europeans have access to American goods without cost. The United States had its own interests in mind, too, but the Marshall Plan was the peacetime equivalent of Lend-Lease.

Much like Lend-Lease, the Marshall Plan threatened Canada's markets in Europe. Why pay for goods, why devote what was left of Canadian loans to supplies when everything could be secured free from the United States? The British pound sterling still could not be converted into dollars and, just as in 1941, Canada's surplus in the United Kingdom could not be used to cover the trade deficit with the United States. Even worse, Canada's own postwar reconstruction, although hugely successful, had seen Canadians with money anxious to buy American goods or take American holidays after fifteen years of depression and war. The country's holdings of American dollars, the world's essential hard currency, had begun to shrink rapidly. Just as in World Wars I and II, moreover, every time the British or Europeans received a Canadian manufactured product, it contained American components or raw materials. It seemed that every effort to help Europe, every attempt to keep up employment in Canada, put Canada further into difficulty with the United States.

The answer—the only answer—was a special arrangement with Washington. Canada was granted a line of credit in American dollars, and Marshall Plan recipients were advised they could make "offshore purchases," or purchases outside the United States.* In practice, that meant Canada. By 1949, as sales of Canadian products boomed, the economy had recovered, and the dollar crisis passed into history, thanks to a billion dollars of US–financed European purchases from Canada. The difficulty was that Canada had become even further integrated into the American economy, and a huge proportion of its export trade was either with the United States or financed by it under the Marshall Plan.

That set officials to thinking. The Canadian High Commissioner in London, trade expert Norman Robertson, wrote to Ottawa to ask

---

* Why was the United States so helpful? Robert Bothwell and John Kirton surmise correctly that Canada was "one of the few countries not obviously dependent on American handouts for its internal stability and national survival; if anything, many senior American officials overestimated Canada's capacity to contribute" to Europe's economic recovery. "'A Sweet Little Country': American Attitudes Toward Canada, 1925 to 1963," *Queen's Quarterly* 90 (Winter 1983): 1085.

"whether we should not . . . be thinking of a real reciprocity arrangement with the United States, which would strengthen our dollar position in the short turn, and in the long run, ensure us against too great a dependence, relative to the United States, on the European market."[23] Canada's dollar shortage, brought on in substantial part by the effort to assist Britain, had forced Canada to consider a free trade agreement with the United States.

To some officials in Ottawa, this was not a threat but an opportunity. Instead of railing at the fate that had constrained the possibility of independent action, Canada should run with Robertson's idea by moving to free trade with the United States. Knock down the tariff barriers, integrate the economies, and ensure prosperity, they said. Canadian negotiator John Deutsch admitted privately to his friend Grant Dexter at the *Winnipeg Free Press* that there was a price to free trade: "The loss of political independence in the sense that we would no longer be in effective control of our national policies. Things have changed since the reciprocity campaign of 1911. Then reciprocity simply broadened the area of trade . . . [but now] . . . we would inherit a vast structure of American government policy." Prime Minister King, elderly and just months away from retirement after more than twenty years in office, initially had agreed that secret talks could be held on a free trade agreement. Surprisingly, however, when Deutsch and the other negotiators returned in March 1948 with a draft agreement for a special form of customs union, King began to baulk.

As Mackenzie King wrote in his diary, "What has been suggested to me today is almost the largest proposal short of war any leader of a government has been looked to to undertake. Its possibilities are so far-reaching for good on one hand, but possible disaster if project were defeated that I find it necessary to reflect a good deal before attempting a final decision." And when the Prime Minister who had been through it all before began to reflect, the worries poured out. What would the opposition say? They would accuse him of selling Canada to the United States and it would be 1911 all over again, with anti-Americanism sweeping everything before it on the hustings. King had lost his parliamentary seat in that election, and he remembered it well. Another reciprocity election would be even worse, and it would destroy him just as it had destroyed Laurier. Worse, free trade would destroy the moral unity of the British Empire—a curious concern about an empire that scarcely existed any longer from a leader who was widely reputed to have devoted his life to constraining its power. The Prime Minister refused to go along, rebuffing the repeated pleas of his officials and ministers and scuppering free trade. "I would no more think of at my time of life and at this stage of my career attempting any movement of the kind," King noted on March 24, 1948, "than I would of flying to the South pole." Whether King was correct in his assessment of the force of anti-Americanism in 1948 is unknowable; it scarcely mattered, however, for free trade had been eliminated as a possibility for forty years more.

The best the officials could secure from the obdurate Prime Minister was a promise that once the North Atlantic Treaty was put into place—secret negotiations had begun initially between Britain, the United States, and Canada, but soon expanded to include the Western European states—perhaps an economic clause could be included that might lead to North Atlantic free trade. A political leader who always recognized pie in the sky when he saw it, King conceded this as a possibility.

Although the North Atlantic Treaty did contain Article 2, "the Canadian clause" that looked to economic and social cooperation among the signatories, NATO was and remained a military alliance. Britain and Western Europe quickly used up the Canadian loans, took all the Marshall Plan–supported goods they could, and began to move to create a European trading unit. Their shortages of hard currency made this necessary, but it left Canada by the wayside. Canadian exports to Britain, for example, were 15 percent of Canada's total export trade by 1950; in 1937, they had been 40 percent. The result was clear. The only sure market for Canadian goods was in the United States, and Canadian consumers preferred American products over the sometimes shoddy British goods (Hillman automobiles, in particular, as I know from bitter experience) that broke down because they weren't built for Canadian expectations or conditions. American investment also poured north in a torrent that accelerated year by year. With Western Europe and Great Britain effectively excluded as paying destinations for Canadian exports, only the United States remained as a market willing and able to purchase large quantities of Canadian goods. Ottawa tried repeatedly to diversify its trade, but success was limited. Henceforth, the United States was the only sun in the Canadian economic constellation.

King, key figures in his Cabinet such as C.D. Howe, and his successor as prime minister, Louis St Laurent, have been demonized as those who sold out Canada, not least by some of the country's best-known historians. Donald Creighton, the leading Canadian historian of this century and a strong Conservative sympathizer, was always scathing in his treatment of

King Liberalism. To him, after the Great War, the essential elements of Canada's national existence were allowed, indeed encouraged, to decay:

> The main direction of Canadian economic activity shifted from east to south. The American market became increasingly important in Canadian trade and American capital increasingly dominant in Canadian development. Along with the gradual dwindling of the old economic ties with the United Kingdom there went a corresponding decline in the historic Anglo–Canadian alliance and the virtual dissolution of the British Commonwealth. Mackenzie King, the archetypal Canadian continentalist, broke up the Britannic union without even attempting to devise policies for a separate and independent Canada. Since 1940, Canada has stood alone, its independence exposed to the penetrative power of American economic and military imperialism, its identity subjected to the continual hammering of American mass media.[24]

Creighton wrote frequently about Canada's decline from an honoured place in the "Anglo–Canadian alliance" to branch-plant dependency as "a military satellite of the American Republic." The moral and cultural personality of Canada had come under attack from the south, and the key decisions on defence, foreign policy, economics, and cultural development now were destined to be made by Americans. Canada, in other words, had been "offered up to meet the voracious demands of the American military machine and [the] unappeasable appetites of a lavish American society." The American Empire, he lamented, was "taking over the birthright of Canadians; and its imperial religion is taking over their minds."[25]

As Charles Taylor wrote of Creighton, "his big subject—almost his only subject" in his last years was "his beloved Canada" and how it had been destroyed by "Liberals and Americans, collaborators in our downfall." The Liberals—King and Lester Pearson especially—were virtually traitors. The Americans? "I have an incredible dislike and hatred of the United States," Creighton said flatly. "I've always had it. I never met one I liked."[26] Creighton actually told a junior American colleague in the University of Toronto history department that it "would take a car load of flea powder to make one of you fit to enter a dog kennel." (In the circumstances, it was only justice that his daughter married an American—and a draft evader to boot!)

Another well-known and equally distinguished conservative historian was every bit as outspoken, if somewhat more polite, in his condemnation of the United States and its baleful influence over Canada. W.L. Morton of the University of Manitoba and Trent University wrote in his once widely used text, *The Kingdom of Canada*, that Canada was in danger from "the strident tones, the careful conformity, the insidious and calculated mediocrity of the mass American culture." America, he said in *The Canadian Identity*, was a "messianic country periodically inspired to carry the republic into other lands for the liberation of the Gentiles, the lesser breeds without the covenant." Was the distinctiveness of Canadian culture, the French, British, Ukrainian, Icelandic, Polish, and Dutch influences that made Canada what it was, to be "processed and homogenized to soft music and dreamy lighting and sold in the accents of Madison Avenue to increase the earnings of American stockholders? The Americanization of American life," Morton added, did seem a fate "as ignoble as . . . possible." But those harsh words paled beside Morton's denunciation—without presenting a shred of evidence—of Canada's condition in 1964, a country "so irradiated by the American presence that it sickens and threatens to dissolve in a cancerous slime."[27]

Other academics jumped on the anti-American wagon, particularly economists who were studying the increasing control exercised by American corporations over the economy or political scientists who were researching the defence linkages between the two countries. Philosopher George Grant was equally critical in his *Lament for a Nation*, pronouncing it "extraordinary that King and his associates in External Affairs did not seem to recognize the perilous situation that the new circumstances entailed. In all eras," he said, "wise politicians have to play a balancing game. How little the American alliance was balanced by any defence of national independence!"* Writers like Kari Levitt, Mel Watkins, and James Laxer have sung repeatedly from the same page in the hymnbook. Even playwrights attacked King. Michael Hollingsworth, the author of an eight-part account of *The History of the Village of the Small Huts*, a theatrical history of Canada and a *tour de force*, portrays Mackenzie King as a political weasel actively selling out his country. In his newer series, *The Global Village*, the first episode on "The Cold War" has the ghost of Franklin Roosevelt appearing to King to advise: "You have nothing to fear but fear

---

* For more on Grant, see chapter 9.

4

WITCH-HUNTS AND FELLOW-TRAVELLERS: COLD WAR ANTI-AMERICANISM

EGERTON HERBERT NORMAN (1909-1957)

Reidford/*Globe and Mail*

The mood in the House of Commons was boiling with anger as Lester Pearson, the Secretary of State for External Affairs, rose to his feet. "I must deal with these very serious points that have been raised," Pearson began that April 12, 1957:

> we bear a share, and I bear the major part of that share as Minister
> of the Department, for Mr. Norman's death. That is a statement I
> hate to see on the record of this House. I do not have to defend

my part in Mr. Norman's case, because I was convinced of his loyalty and decency as a Canadian from the first day he entered the
Department of External Affairs until the day of his tragic death. I
have defended him whenever defence was necessary to the best of
my ability, and I have done my utmost to keep the innuendoes,
suspicions and implications as a result of the witch-hunting tactics
of another country from being made public. Am I now to be held
responsible for his death because I have tried to stand up for him?

Deeply shaken, Pearson went on: "Am I to be attacked now because I did
not make public all the evidence taken at this enquiry of the security agency
of the United States, the effect of which might have been disastrous to
people's good names, merely on suspicion?" A CCF member interjected,
"We are in Ottawa, not in Washington." "We are in Ottawa, that is true,
and we do not do that kind of thing in this country," Pearson said, uttering
one of the truisms that Canadians held dear. Turning to the impact that the
provision of security information from Canada to the United States had
had on the Norman case, the foreign minister added: "We cannot run the
risk, after what has happened, of giving them security information about a
Canadian citizen without some assurance—if we can get that assurance—
that it will not be passed on to witch-hunting agencies."

On April 4, a week before that debate in Parliament, Herbert Norman,
the Canadian Ambassador to Egypt, had jumped to his death from the
roof of a Cairo apartment building. In hearings of the United States
Senate's Subcommittee on Internal Security in mid-March, his name and
his alleged Communist political affiliations had been bandied about,
exactly as they had been a half-dozen years before. The Canadian government had investigated, cleared Norman of any wrong-doing in
1951–52, and promoted him, but the revival of the McCarthyite allegations in the congressional committee had pushed him over the brink and
to his death. The resulting furore in Canada produced an extraordinary
outpouring of anti-American sentiment, and it led Pearson to threaten to
cut off key components of Canadian security relations with Washington.

The grinding Korean War, the fearful development of Soviet hydrogen
bombs, the fracturing of the North Atlantic alliance during the Suez
Crisis, and Moscow's brutal suppression of the Hungarian revolution all
kept tension high throughout most of the 1950s. In the United States,
and to a much lesser extent in Canada, domestic Communists were

hounded and reviled, investigated, and jailed or removed from their posts. For their part, Canadian leftists, both Communists and sympathizers, lashed out at the behemoth to the south and at what they saw as its compliant partner in Ottawa. It was a troubled decade, and Herbert Norman's suicide was one of the events that helped sow mistrust between Canada and the United States. Mackenzie King, Franklin Roosevelt, and the events of the war years had forced Canada and the United States together, but in the postwar years the partnership was destined to be a stormy one.

*   *   *

Canadian Communists were an endangered species in the years after the Second World War. The party had been outlawed in Canada in 1940, thanks to its anti-war crusading, and many of its members were interned. Not even the Nazi attack on the Soviet Union in June 1941, which at last made Communists into fervent supporters of the war effort, led to the release of those who had been locked up, a decision that was delayed until 1943. But the Labour Progressive Party, the old Communist Party under a new name, was allowed to operate, and the LPP proselytized, cooperated with the Liberals against the social-democratic Cooperative Commonwealth Federation in the 1945 election, and devoted itself to infiltrating trade unions and the public service. The defection of Igor Gouzenko from the USSR Embassy in September 1945 revealed widespread Russian spying in Canada and directly implicated LPP members in this effort, not least the party's sole Member of Parliament, Montrealer Fred Rose. The LPP never could recover from that blow, however much members and sympathizers argued—wrongly—that the Gouzenko case was a frame-up. By the beginning of the 1950s, estimates of the party's membership put it around ten thousand. The Canadian Communists, sustained by quarterly subsidies from Moscow, remained loyal through every twist and turn of Soviet policy.

This won them few friends, because of the protracted and sharp antipathy in Canada to Soviet policy. The Gouzenko case turned wartime admiration for Russian resistance into fear of Soviet aims, and Soviet intransigence and brutal aggressiveness continued and repeatedly confirmed it. Meanwhile, as the LPP faithfully followed the Moscow line, Canadian government policy gradually moved towards support for the idea of a Western defensive alliance to galvanize the European democracies and to resist Soviet and domestic Communism. By April 1949, with all Eastern Europe and China under Communist control, the North American and Western European countries at last joined together in the North Atlantic Treaty Organization. The North Korean invasion of South Korea in June 1950 led an American-dominated United Nations to fight a "police action" to restore South Korea's independence. Canada provided an infantry brigade group to the Korean effort, as well as Royal Canadian Navy destroyers and RCAF transport aircraft. Just as important, the Korean crisis, which appeared to demonstrate that the USSR was prepared to countenance military force to expand its empire, obliged NATO to turn itself into a strong military organization in Europe. In 1951, as part of this process, Canada sent yet another brigade of infantry and an air division of fighter aircraft to France and Germany, the first peacetime overseas military deployment to Europe in Canadian history. At home, meanwhile, the development of radar nets to detect attacking Soviet bombers began apace, an effort that culminated in the American construction of the Distant Early Warning Line in the middle 1950s and the formation of the North American Air Defence Command, a joint Canada–U.S. air defence organization to protect the continent, in 1957–58. The Americans were generally grateful. "The Canadians," one official in the Department of State noted with just a hint of irritation in 1952, "are almost always with us on the major issues."[1]

Although there was strong support in Canada for NATO, the Korean War effort, and the increasingly close defence relationship with the Pentagon, there was no unanimity. The LPP, naturally enough, railed against Ottawa's policy and tried to mobilize Canadians against the United States, the leader of the Western alliance. A variety of "peace" offensives took place under party control, their supporters, not all of them Communists, arguing strenuously against the American monopoly of the atomic bomb—at least until Moscow exploded its first nuclear device in 1949. Those who took this line suffered attacks, sometimes vicious in their intensity. "In this era," Reg Whitaker and Gary Marcuse wrote with substantial naivety, "it was the fate of those who espoused peace to be vilified as the enemies of freedom."[2]

Not that Stalin was the friend of either freedom or peace, but it served Soviet interests to mobilize the well-meaning do-gooders of the West against the United States. One such organization, the Canadian Peace Congress, took shape in 1948, clearly under party direction, but led by sympathetic fellow-travellers. The most interesting figure in this movement was James G. Endicott, a longtime United Church missionary in

China who returned to Canada in 1947 and, in the following years, played a leading and controversial role.

Born in China to prominent Methodist missionary parents in 1898, Endicott spent his first dozen years there, then attended school in Toronto. He served overseas in the Great War, and returned to the University of Toronto, where he earned his MA in 1925. He married Mary Austin the same year, an attractive young woman to whom a history professor, Lester Pearson, was also drawn, and he returned to China with his bride to carry on the missionary work into which he had been born. Completely fluent in Chinese (and "probably the only Westerner alive who, speaking in Chinese, can move a Chinese audience to laughter and tears," Blair Fraser wrote in *Maclean's* in July 1952), Endicott came to know and love the Chinese people and to oppose those enemies, domestic and foreign, who oppressed them. He also worked with many of the Chinese leaders, including Chiang Kai-shek and his extraordinary wife, with whom he helped to create the New Life Movement that Mme Chiang used to build support for her husband. Endicott soon convinced himself that the Chiangs were corrupt, however, and he found his new soulmates in Mao Tse-tung's Communists, who opposed the Nationalists and who were, in his eyes, much more honest, idealistic, and, in their own atheistic way, Christian. By the time he returned to Canada for good in 1947, Endicott was a crusader for Chairman Mao's revolution, exulting in its success in 1949. Such views marked him as a "pinko" in the early Cold War years, but there were very few Canadians, in or out of government, prepared to defend Chiang's appalling corruption and incompetence.

What first gave Endicott public notoriety was his leadership of the Canadian Peace Congress, where he was a full-time employee at a salary of $2000 a year. The Congress, though nominally independent, was a Communist front organization, part of the worldwide network of similar organizations created by Moscow to brand the United States and its allies as nuclear warmongers. Probably 80 percent of its active workers were party members. But who, after all, could be against peace? Many thousands of Canadians, always suspicious of the imperialistic capitalism and global manifest destiny espoused by government and business figures in the United States, signed petitions and called for the Americans' atomic bombs to be banned. Endicott and his wife stayed out of the Labour Progressive Party—"It seems more like joining a sect than a political party," Mary observed—but, as his son wrote in a biography of his father,

"Fortunately, Endicott soon developed a personal relationship with the leaders of the Canadian party" which "permitted him to be in touch with their thinking and them with his."[3] Fortunately.

As such, Endicott's Peace Congress—at least until the Hungarian revolution of 1956—unfailingly argued the party line. Everything socialist Moscow and Beijing did was right; everything the capitalist United States and its allies did was monstrously wrong. In Endicott's view, Christ would certainly have been on the side of the Marxists, and, as a Christian soldier, so was he. The North Atlantic Treaty, for example, was "a War Pact directed at the Soviet Union." "The framers of the Atlantic Pact have set up a company union, it came from the home of company unions, the United States, and you know that company unions never bring peace."[4] The ideological blinkers were as firmly in place as if Reverend Endicott was in the pockets of Josef Stalin and LPP leader Tim Buck—as, in fact, he was. The LPP line was also regularly presented in Endicott's *Canadian Far Eastern Newsletter*, which he began shortly after his return to Canada as his "personal interpretation" of the revolutionary changes taking place in Asia.

At conferences around the globe sponsored by the World Congress of Peace, Moscow's umbrella organization, Endicott could be counted to denounce American policy with vigour. A superb, passionate speaker, a man who could use the Bible, humour, and ridicule to great effect, the youthful-looking, stocky, and vigorous Endicott was a powerful spokesman for "peace." At a meeting of the Congress in Moscow in early 1950, for example, Endicott denounced the FBI for spying on Canadians and the United States for closing its borders to left-wing Canadians.* In North America, he argued, "a police state is in the process of forming and the battle for peace has become a battle for civil rights." His views were cheered by the delegates and, presumably, by the members of the Supreme Soviet, who were also addressed by Endicott. They were less well received in Canada by government and media figures, who denounced Endicott as a Soviet dupe, the very personification of what Lenin had called the "useful idiots" who could serve the Soviet state's interests at almost no cost.

---

* This was Endicott's first visit to the USSR, and he wrote his wife: "I have seen Socialist Russia—it is a success." A little later he compared Warsaw—"the miracle of the postwar world"—with Paris, which seemed to him like 1946 Shanghai, "degenerating into poverty, police and oppression." Quoted in Reg Whitaker and Gary Marcuse, *Cold War Canada* (Toronto 1995), 380.

The charges were hurled with even greater frequency after North Korea invaded South Korea on June 25, 1950. Although President Syngman Rhee's government was a brutal dictatorship, most historians would quarrel with Endicott's argument that the United States had "stamped out the Korean people's movement for independence and restored a government of pro-Japanese Korean quislings." North Korea's Communist regime was in every way much more repressive, and the opening of the Soviet and some Chinese archives has revealed that Josef Stalin and Mao Tse-tung connived at and supported North Korea's invasion of South Korea as an expected easy gain for Communism.[5] Few in Canada doubted this objective in June 1950 except the Labour Progressive Party, the Canadian Peace Congress, and the Endicotts. In his *Newsletter* of July 1950, Endicott offered his "personal opinion" on the beginnings of the war:

> John Foster Dulles [then negotiating the peace treaty that finally drew war with Japan to an official close and two-and-a-half-years later the U.S. Secretary of State] gave them the nod to go ahead and attack. Dr. Rhee had just previously been to see General [Douglas] MacArthur [in Tokyo] and also got a nod. The South Korean forces attacked on June 25 and advanced six miles. But a mass rising of guerillas in their rear spread panic and when they were hit by the northern forces they collapsed. The Americans found themselves holding the bag with a small force of Japanese-trained professional soldiers and an aroused people buzzing around their ears.

In an address to the Manitoba Peace Council delivered immediately after the reports of fighting reached Canada, Endicott declared categorically that "there is no shred of evidence for terming the Korean outbreaks as manifestations of 'Russian Communist imperialism.'" Instead, it was American imperialism that was directing matters. As Endicott's filial biographer noted, "Within a few hours the sweeping nature of American plans was revealed," as President Harry Truman ordered troops into Korea and directed the United States Navy to protect Taiwan. The American conspiracy to swallow all of Korea had been exposed for those with the eyes to see. Endicott told the World Peace Congress meeting in East Germany in early 1951, "The peoples of Europe and of the rest of the world must know that the rulers of North America have decided on war, are furiously preparing for war, and are scheming to deny and suppress every measure toward peace." That there was genuine uneasiness about the foreign policy of the United States in Europe and Asia was true. That many feared that the United States might, if pushed into a corner in Korea, use its nuclear arsenal was also true. Canadians shared these concerns. It was, however, an uphill struggle to persuade the Canadian public that the democracies were aggressors and the Communists benign, and the public evinced little interest in Endicott's organization or its leader's views. An opinion poll in August 1951 asked Canadians if they had heard or read anything about the Canadian Peace Congress led by Dr James Endicott. More than two-thirds said they had not, and only 31 percent knew what the CPC was or who led it. Of those who had heard of it, 4 percent approved of the CPC, 14 percent disapproved, and 13 percent had no opinion. Those who disapproved either disliked Endicott or considered the CPC "run by the Reds."

Endicott's warnings about Western preparations for war, therefore, tended to be discounted, when they were heard at all. Nonetheless, part of those preparations was the development of techniques of germ warfare, something that many countries, East and West and including Canada, had been researching for years. Endicott escalated his anti-American campaign in the spring of 1952 with a flat-out charge that the United States had secretly begun to use germ warfare against China and Korea.

In April 1952 Endicott had visited China "as part of a tour . . . arranged by the Chinese Committee for World Peace." To go to China when Canadian troops, as part of the United Nations forces in Korea, were fighting Chinese "volunteers" was in itself surprising. In the northeast of Mao's China, he discovered that "the chief topic of conversation everywhere was the large-scale American bacteriological war being carried out against the Chinese people." Admittedly no scientist, Endicott nonetheless had spoken to Chinese researchers who told him of the atrocities, and he had ventured "out into the fields to talk with farmers and interview those who had actually seen and collected various insects, feathers and some of the receptacles in which they had been dropped. To me," he wrote on his return to Canada as the first and for some time the only Westerner who claimed to have been an eyewitness to American germ warfare, "the evidence is unquestionable and overwhelming."[6] Endicott also was reported to have told a press conference in Mukden that infected insects were being bred for the American military by Canadian scientists working at the government's Suffield, Alberta, Experimental Station. This statement he subsequently retracted, if in fact it had been made, but

Endicott did wire Pearson from China about "incontrovertible evidence" of germ warfare, and he released his claims to the media.

The younger Endicott noted that his father found it hard to credit that the United States, "which had sent so many missionaries to China, could do so great an evil." Yet he believed that no nation was more open to the charge of "waging wars of mass extermination by means of brutal, scientific weapons," including the use of atomic weapons against Japan and napalm in Korea. Those who would use such weapons, Endicott believed, would not hesitate to use germ warfare. He "could not escape the evidence that had been presented to him," but he did not wish to be a martyr, and he did not go to North Korea for fear of being charged with treason. Why China, equally a belligerent, could be visited was unclear.

To no one's surprise, the Beijing government refused to allow impartial bodies such as the International Red Cross or the World Health Organization to examine their purported evidence. The International Red Cross, China said, was a "tool of American aggression," and the Soviet Union vetoed a UN Security Council proposal to investigate the Chinese claims on the ground. Thus the details of the "crimes" presented by Endicott and by others, including the "International Association of Democratic Lawyers" and Chinese and tame foreign bacteriologists, were and are essentially unproven and unprovable. Claims that typhoid, rickets, and cholera-carrying insects, paper bags full of anthrax-laden feathers, and botulism toxins blended with dust and gelatin had been dropped on Chinese territory were presented by Endicott and others and promptly ridiculed by Western scientists. The Vice-Principal of McGill University's Macdonald College, for example, complained about the "biological illiteracy" in the charges that had insect species spreading diseases they did not carry. "A great deal of secret work is said to have been done on germ warfare," Professor W.H. Brittain said correctly, but these charges sound like the "futile attempts of someone lacking the most elementary knowledge of insect transmission of disease."[7] Moreover, had germ warfare been used, high casualty rates might have been expected in a country plagued with relatively primitive sanitation standards and health care. Endicott attributed the lack of damning statistics to the Chinese imposition of military secrecy so as to prevent the aggressors from learning of their successes or failures. Most inspiring to the credulous Canadian peace activist, however, was what he described as the spirit of the Chinese people, their "excellent health service," and their demonstration how even germ warfare could "be checked and defeated by an aroused and liberated people."[8] There were apparently genuine epidemics in North Korea and, although there were charges that germ warfare had been employed there, Endicott did not attempt to exploit them. In any case, disease in North Korea was not unusual.

Endicott's charges—which, Blair Fraser wrote in *Maclean's*, made him "for the moment, at least . . . one of communism's major assets in the whole world"—resulted in a storm of protest in Canada. There was and continued to be substantial unease in government and the media over the way the United States was prosecuting the United Nations' war in Korea, and over the near hysteria that sometimes seemed to motivate congressional committees hunting down Communists and fellow-travellers. But the differences between Ottawa and Washington, especially on the tactics and strategy of the war, were ones of degree, and no one in government believed Endicott's claims of bacteriological warfare. The media called him a traitor who aimed to demoralize the Canadian public and weaken its support for the war. Conservative MPs John Diefenbaker and Gordon Graydon denounced him vigorously, questioned why he had been allowed to go abroad, and, greatly overreacting, called for his citizenship to be revoked to prevent his return to Canada. Stuart Garson, Justice Minister in the Liberal government of Louis St Laurent, began an inquiry to see if Endicott could be prosecuted.

While the government investigated, Endicott fearlessly, even brazenly, continued his efforts. He addressed a meeting of ten thousand supporters at Toronto's Maple Leaf Gardens soon after his return. His son observed that Endicott "stirred deep emotions in the collective consciousness of Canadians, Christian and Jew, believer and non-believer, alike," with his denunciation of those who had impugned his loyalty to Canada and his assaults on "McCarthyism" and "MacArthurism" and "the lawless American militarists in the Far East":

> *My stand on germ warfare was forced upon me by the actions of law-less American militarists* [Endicott's italics]. I saw with my own eyes, I heard witnesses with my own ears, I was profoundly disturbed and my conscience would not let me keep silent. . . . I declare that germ war has been tried out on a large scale. . . . I declare that the die-hard colonial exploiters, the white-skinned plunderers of the long-suffering millions of Asia and Africa, are becoming homicidal maniacs. . . . There is one government in the world today

which is financing and supporting most of this wickedness and that is the government of the United States. . . .

The [Americans'] air of injured innocence [about the germ war charges] would sit more convincingly on the shoulders of the American militarists if they did not have such bad records. Let me ask them 'Would you use an atom bomb?' 'Yes, of course, and we are going to use thousands if we can.' 'Would you use jellied gasoline?' 'Yes, of course. . . .' 'Well then, would you use a germicidal [sic] bug?' 'Oh, no, never!' 'What, never?' 'No, never!' 'What, never?' 'Well, hardly ever!'

Endicott also told the roaring Gardens' crowd that American prisoners of war confirmed they had been trained for germ warfare in Japan.[9] The "confessions" carried substantial weight at the time, but only because the Chinese techniques of brainwashing POWs had not yet become known in the West.

What was most significant in this whole episode was that, in the middle of a war in which Canadians were fighting and dying, ten thousand people turned out to cheer a man who was spreading stories that only the most credulous could have believed. The power of Communism and the desire of fellow-travellers to believe the worst of the United States was such that, in 1952, Endicott could draw substantial crowds to cheer his anti-American tirades. It was almost enough to make one believe that Canadians on the left had imbibed anti-Americanism with their *Das Kapital*—as in fact they had.

The Canadian government in the end did nothing more than label Endicott a tool of Moscow and Beijing and present to Parliament scientific testimony that destroyed the "evidence" he and others had disseminated. Pearson told Parliament in May 1952 that Endicott's charge "is so false and so fantastic that it would normally be unwise to dignify it by official denials. Nevertheless, it has become such a central feature of Soviet propaganda, and has been repeated so violently and so often for the transparent purpose of deceiving persons who may not be aware of the Soviet purpose behind the charge, that I think some statement should be made. . . ." Pearson went on to denounce Communists and fellow-travellers in Canada who followed every "twist and turn of Soviet policy." The claims of germ warfare raised by Endicott were denied absolutely.

In the more than four decades since his charges of American bacteriological warfare were laid, no hard evidence has been produced to substantiate Endicott's claims definitively, an unlikely outcome if there were substance to them, given the thousands who would have had to be involved in such warfare, the openness of American society, the post–Vietnam War desire to wash the United States' dirty linen in public, and the end of the Cold War. Until his dying day, however, James Endicott continued to believe that he had been right, and the award to him of the Stalin Peace Prize in December 1952 merely confirmed him in the rightness of his judgment.

What did this extraordinary episode involving Endicott and his germ warfare charges signify? Until the beginning of the Cold War, anti-Americanism in Canada was largely an idea propagated by the United Empire Loyalist element and used by politicians and business for their own ends. Now the United States had become a superpower, the leader of the capitalist world in a battle against Communism; as a result, anti-Americanism now became firmly entrenched in the left-wing Canadian psyche. Moreover, the germ warfare campaign showed that Canadians could be as credulous as any other people and that committed Christians could be gulled into believing that the benevolence of Soviet and Chinese Communism could outweigh the evils inherent in capitalist American and Canadian society.* Marxist ideology, even if it was never sealed by formal membership in the Labour Progressive Party, could turn an otherwise intelligent man into an anti-American of such venom that he believed absolutely that the United States was guilty of monstrous crimes, aided and abetted by his own government and its men who were fighting under the United Nations flag. Christian do-goodism, anti-colonialism, and a gullible mind could combine to create a virulent, ideologically motivated anti-American. Even more extraordinary, such was the suspicion of the United States, its leaders, and its atomic weapons that some thousands of ordinary Canadians, desperately hoping for a peaceful world, were prepared to follow the Moscow-directed cause of the Canadian Peace Congress and to put credence in Endicott's foolish, unsubstantiated charges of American germ warfare. Some, regrettably, still do.

Endicott's campaign of anti-Americanism was so extreme that, while it initially fed the anti-Americanism of the Canadian left, in the longer run it

---

* An opinion poll released on September 20, 1952, found that 3 percent of Canadians believed the germ-war charges to be "definitely true," 10 percent believed they might be true, and 71 percent thought them probably or absolutely false. The most likely person to believe the charges was a man or woman under forty years of age, who lived in British Columbia, and who was inclined to vote CCF. Press Release, Gallup Poll of Canada, September 20, 1952.

began the process of discrediting anti-Americanism as a popular force in Canada. The old Tories and the younger Conservatives in academe and business who were instinctively disposed to think ill of Washington's works could scarcely align themselves with Endicott, especially when the United States was carrying the burden of defending the capitalist and free-enterprise West against the collectivism of Soviet and Chinese Communism. The social-democratic left, which harboured its own dark suspicions of American globalism and drew on the British Labour Party's deep distrust of the United States, nonetheless supported the creation of NATO and the Canadian part in the Korean War. Not wanting to be tarred by the Muscovite brush, the CCF scrambled to put as much distance as it could between itself and the Communists. And the Canadian public? Trying hard to cash in on the boom generated and sustained by Cold War rearmament, average Canadians were more interested in automobiles, suburban bungalows, and the effort to emulate Americans' life styles than in denouncing Washington. Extremism in the defence of Moscow and Beijing was no virtue in Canada, and Endicott's germ-warfare campaign and slavish following of the party line ultimately did his cause great disservice.

*　　*　　*

Scorned as he was by most Canadians, James Endicott did strike a responsive chord in his countrymen with his denunciations of American McCarthyism. The Republican Senator from Wisconsin, Joseph McCarthy, had made his reputation by purporting to have lists of card-carrying Communists in official positions in the United States government and military, and he and his imitators in the Senate and the House of Representatives and their supporters in the media whipped up domestic anti-Communism and increased Cold War tensions through well-publicized hearings during the early 1950s. Canadians watched the violations of civil liberties and the witch-hunting with substantial unease, though their leaders tended to be more concerned than the public at large.* Lester Pearson

* In 1950 opinion polls showed that 70 percent of Canadians, compared with 77 percent of Americans, thought that Communists should be made to register their names with the Department of Justice. Three years later, 62 percent of Canadians said that freedom of speech should not permit Communists to make speeches in public whenever they wished. Press Releases, Gallup Poll of Canada, March 11, 1950, May 16, 1953.

"Mind keeping that shadow on your side of the line?"

called the American hysteria "mass frenzy," and he wept over "the dreadful trail of McCarthy . . . one of the most horrible creatures of the twentieth century. I loathed and detested him."[10] Pearson and many others in government, the universities, and the public at large also shared widespread concern over the rigid policies of President Eisenhower's Secretary of State, John Foster Dulles, an anti-Communist zealot (in Canadian eyes) who threatened massive retaliation at Moscow at every opportunity. Eisenhower himself, though venerated for his wartime role, was popularly seen as old and ill, ineffective, and uninformed.

The discomfort in Canada, while temporary, was such that political scientist James Eayrs could write that the "traditional friendship" Canadians felt for Americans had been "strained by tensions and stresses unrelated to any of the usual sources of difficulty between the two nations." Anti-Americanism among students, in the media, in the CCF and the Progressive Conservative Party, and among Canadians generally was so sharp for a period that "the chief parlour game seemed to be panning Americans," one student said, while a professor described his colleagues' discussions of the United States as "violently, irrationally anti-American." The mood, Eayrs noted, had been created largely by the reaction against McCarthyism, "a fear that the United States' great capacities for leadership were being stunted and withered by a frightening species of national paranoia."[11]

Paranoia was not a uniquely American phenomenon, of course, and Ottawa's hands were not wholly clean when it came to prying into past and present political beliefs. The Canadian government, spurred by the revelations of Soviet spying provided by defector Igor Gouzenko in September 1945, toughened security checks and probed for ideological (and, later, sexual) deviations. A relatively small, but significant, number of civil servants were fired or shifted within the bureaucracy to non-sensitive areas, and preparations were put in place for the confinement of potential saboteurs and Communist troublemakers in the event of war with the Soviet Union. Yet the differences between Canadian and US approaches to the problem were substantial enough for Canadian officials and the media to point to yet another area of life in which their quiet methods were superior to those of the Americans.

The Royal Canadian Mounted Police and the Federal Bureau of Investigation cooperated extensively in sharing information on domestic leftists and their sympathizers. If the Canadian public generally had its anti-Americanism reinforced by McCarthyite excesses, the RCMP sometimes appeared to wish that Canada had a Joe McCarthy of its own. The Canadian government was too cautious for the Mounties, and some officers believed that secret Communists in high places were protecting their comrades against removal.

Herbert Norman was a case in point. Like Endicott, Norman was a "mish kid," born in Japan to Methodist missionary parents. His early youth there gave him a love and understanding of Japanese culture and life, and his education in Canada, Britain, and the United States made him one of the leading Japanologists of the pre-Second World War years. His education in the dreadful decade of the 1930s, when Hitler and Mussolini seemed to have cowed the democracies into spinelessness and only the Soviet Union among the larger nations evinced any desire to resist the triumph of fascism, also helped to make him an active Communist. During his time at Cambridge University in the mid-1930s he was, as his friend Harry Ferns wrote, a Marxist and a Communist. "Both of us did the same party work as students. Norman was in charge of . . . the recruitment to the Communist party and political education of students mainly from . . . India and Ceylon."[12] There was nothing illegal in this, since the British Communist Party was a legitimate political organization, even if Norman's colonial recruiting was conducted in secrecy. Nor was there anything illegitimate about the Communist connections Norman had in the late 1930s at Columbia and Harvard universities and in Toronto, where he taught briefly at Upper Canada College.

Norman's problems began when he joined the Department of External Affairs in 1939. He underwent no serious security check (External Affairs amazingly did not begin vigorous screening of employees until 1946) and said nothing of his Communist past. Subsequently, he occupied posts in the Canadian Legation in Tokyo and in wartime intelligence work in Ottawa that brought him into contact with highly secret materials. With the Soviet Union an ally in the struggle against Hitler, wartime unity ordinarily prevented hard questions from being asked. Thus no problems arose until well after V-J Day when Norman, back in Tokyo and assigned as a research and analysis specialist on the staff of the Supreme Commander, Allied Powers, Pacific, General Douglas MacArthur, aroused the suspicion of one of the General's key military aides, Major-General Charles Willoughby. Some of the Canadian's memoranda and actions seemed soft on Japanese Communists, Willoughby believed, and he passed his suspicions on to Washington. Then Norman's name turned up in belated investigations being run by the FBI on Gouzenko-related material. In October 1950, by now Canada's Minister to Japan, Norman was called back to Ottawa, and for fear of what "the Americans" and "particularly [FBI director J. Edgar] Hoover" might make of the issue, subjected to a serious security check by External Affairs and the RCMP for the first time in his career. Norman was cleared, in part at least because he lied about ever having been a party member, which at this time would have appeared far more sinister than it did in the 1930s. The RCMP, clearly convinced Norman was a Red, was not pleased with the result of the inquiry, but its doubts were overridden by External Affairs. Soon after, Norman's name turned up in congressional testimony. Shocked, External Affairs not only cleared Norman of wrongdoing, but in January 1951 the department placed him in charge of the American and Far Eastern Division, a particularly sensitive post at the time of the Korean War, the military build-up of NATO, and increased Canadian–American concern about the possibility of a Soviet attack over the North Pole.

In August 1951 the US Senate's Internal Security Subcommittee, investigating the Communist links of members of the Institute of Pacific Relations, an academic-business grouping that did research, held conferences, and published on the Far East, came across Norman's name. Certainly the regular links between the RCMP and the FBI ("the logical result of Ottawa's continentalist policies," journalist Charles Taylor criticized) had transmitted data on Norman to Washington, and someone had tipped off the subcommittee staff. During his time at Columbia University, the Senate subcommittee heard, the soon-to-be Canadian diplomat had apparently been a member of a Communist study group. Pearson defended Norman, weakly some thought, and the Canadian media denounced the congressional inquisitors.*

When new information about Norman's past continued to surface in Britain and the United States, the Americans showed a "very apparent unwillingness to deal with Norman in his official capacity," Pearson's biographer observed, and there was a renewed Canadian investigation of the diplomat early in 1952. Again he was cleared, though by this time it was known that he had been a Communist Party member in Britain and that he had formed Communist connections, though possibly not Canadian party membership, in Toronto on his return. The RCMP's ever increasing fears that Norman might be a Canadian version of Guy Burgess or Donald Maclean, the Cambridge-educated Foreign Office officials whose defection to the USSR in the early 1950s had been both damaging and excruciatingly embarrassing to Britain, continued to fester. Norman's departmental masters, who tightly controlled the investigation, had no such worries. Convinced that even if he had once been a Communist, he had served Canada loyally since joining External Affairs, Pearson and his Undersecretary, Arnold Heeney, protected their man, though in July 1952 they shifted Norman to the department's less-sensitive Information Division and then to the beautiful diplomatic backwater of New Zealand as High Commissioner. In 1956 Pearson gave Norman a much more important post, Ambassador to Egypt and Lebanon, with his base in Cairo.

Norman distinguished himself during the Suez Crisis that began in late October 1956. His task was to interpret President Nasser to Ottawa and to persuade Nasser that Pearson's plan for a United Nations Emergency Force, with Canadian troops included, was a workable way out of the chaos caused by the Anglo–French–Israeli invasion. By every account, he did his job brilliantly, and he particularly won Pearson's gratitude for getting Canadian troops into the Emergency Force after Egypt initially had

---

* John Holmes, a senior officer of the Department of External Affairs, wrote a friend that opinion in the department was "incensed" at the "weak statements put out by the Department at first, and there would have been some angry rumblings if the Minister had not come through eventually with a firm protest" at the congressional witch-hunting of Norman. "Some of us were, I think, shaken for the first time by doubts as to whether the Department would be loyal to us if we needed support." Bishop's University, T.W.L. MacDermot Papers, file/54, Holmes to MacDermot, Labour Day 1951.

barred them because their uniforms, traditions, and weapons were indistinguishable from those of the British invaders.

The reaction of the Canadian public to Pearson's and the Liberal government's role during the crisis, however, was not wholly favourable. Opinion polls showed 43 percent of Canadians approving the Anglo–French invasion, 40 percent disapproving, and the remainder with no opinion. To many, not least the leaders of the Progressive Conservative Party, Canada had turned its back on its two mother countries and "meekly" followed the "unrealistic policies of the United States." There were cries of betrayal in press and Parliament, and a marked hostility to American policies and leadership in the months following the crisis. What could not readily be denied after Suez, however, was that Britain and France had demonstrated irrefutably that they were no longer great powers; Canadians had to face up to the fact that the United States was the sole and unchallenged leader of the Western alliance. Prime Minister St Laurent said as much to President Eisenhower during the crisis when he spoke of the criticism of American policy: "We have trouble up here, with people who look upon bigness as a sin." The truth rankled those who were nostalgic for the British connection, and who pointed the finger at Pearson's actions during the crisis.

In fact, with Hungary in revolt against the Soviet Union that October and November and with the United States in the midst of a presidential election, Pearson's main aim had been to rescue the British and French from the consequences of their political stupidity and military incompetence at Suez; to prevent the Western alliance and NATO from breaking up in acrimony; and to preserve the British Commonwealth, whose non-white members were on the verge of bolting because of Britain's invasion of Egypt. He largely succeeded in all those goals. Moreover, the UN force Pearson cobbled together won him the Nobel Peace Prize and made him the inevitable successor to St Laurent as Liberal leader. Pearson and Suez also established peacekeeping as Canada's métier, but almost certainly helped the Liberals lose the June 1957 election.*

---

* In a campaign that generally played on latent anti-Americanism, Progressive Conservative leader John Diefenbaker made much of Suez as demonstrating the Liberals' disregard for Britain. In one address on the Prairies, he charged that "the government had wasted no time in protesting to Britain over the Anglo–French invasion of Egypt. Why, then, hadn't it been just as punctual in protesting US [surplus disposal] policies which could reduce wheat to an almost valueless commodity?" Cited in John Meisel, *The Canadian General Election of 1957* (Toronto 1962), 58.

So too did the dénouement of the case of Herbert Norman. In March 1957 the Senate Internal Security Subcommittee was exploring the extent of Soviet activity in the United States, and again, just as in 1951 and possibly because of the same RCMP–FBI linkages, Norman's name and his activities, this time in Japan, the United States, and the Middle East, came out in testimony, which was made public. Norman's subsequent suicide created an extraordinary public response in Canada that severely roiled the waters of Canadian–American relations; for once, the expressions of anti-Americanism were entirely justified.

"Murder by Slander," the *Toronto Star*'s headline screamed on April 4. Norman's death, the *Canadian Forum* wrote, "was attributed solely to persecution by the committee and the word 'murder' was uttered by the intemperate." Not just the intemperate or the *Star*. Professor Eayrs observed that "if there were those who felt" the word murder "too extreme they kept their feelings to themselves," and his colleague Burton S. Kierstead was scathing in a letter to the *New York Times*. "What has really happened is that Canadian attitudes toward the United States have crystallized sharply. Let no politicians deceive with soft bromides. The present (temporary, I hope) feeling of the Canadian people toward the United States is not a negative disapproval. It is a positive dislike. . . . It is not just that a couple of Senators and their counsel have killed Mr. Norman. . . . The point is that your people do not seem to care sufficiently to put a stop to an inquisition which shames you, betrays the ideals you and we give homage to, and leaves us unsure whether in you we have a partner in righteousness, as we had supposed, or whether we have made a bargain with the forces of tyranny and evil."[13]

The Norman affair had begun on March 14, when the Internal Security Subcommittee published its testimony implicating Norman. In what the *Globe and Mail* two days later called "as scathing a denunciation of the activities of a foreign government as has ever been heard in the House of Commons," Pearson told Parliament that "these slanders and unsupported insinuations" should be treated with "the contempt they deserve." Though Canada protested strongly to Washington about the committee's "making and publishing allegations about a Canadian official" without consultation, the protests had absolutely no effect on the subcommittee, which released still more testimony on March 28. After Norman's suicide on April 4, rage in Canada reached its peak, as every grievance of the last decade was once again recycled in anger.

Diefenbaker said in a public statement that Norman's death was "attributable to the witch-hunting proclivities of certain Congressional inquisitors in Washington who, lacking local targets, felt impelled to malign and condemn Canadian public servants as well." The CCF stated that "he was killed as surely as if someone had put a knife in his back." Students at the University of Toronto burned effigies of Senator McCarthy and Internal Security Subcommittee counsel Robert Morris (who was photographed "smirking as he held up a newspaper with the headline: Envoy Accused As Red Kills Self"). Nor were matters eased when President Eisenhower seemed to dismiss Norman's suicide as a minor matter that should best be forgotten. Canadians understood "our . . . three-branch coordinated form of Government," Ike said, suggesting he could do nothing to control Congress, and therefore they "do not hold such things too much against the Government when they occur." Eisenhower was right, but he had refused to confront McCarthy and McCarthyism, even when his old friend and patron, General George C. Marshall, became a target. The President "meant well," Pearson wrote a friend, but his dismissal of the affair had "infuriated" Canadians. The *Globe and Mail* went further, characterizing the President's remarks as "impudent and patronizing."

In Washington, meanwhile, Canadian Ambassador Arnold Heeney told his diary that "the state of Can.–U.S. relations" had become "thoroughly bad." The subcommittee's charges and Norman's death "infuriated Canadians and produced a wave of anti-Americanism at home which Mike [Pearson] says exceeded anything in his experience."[14] Ottawa threatened to withhold security information from US agencies unless it could be guaranteed that such breaches would not again occur.

The response to Canadian protests in Washington was cool. In the United States, the separation of powers gave the administration little real control over such matters, no matter how helpful the State Department might wish to be (and there was some doubt about that). If Canada, a minor player in the provision of intelligence, cut off the United States, the Americans in retaliation would certainly stop providing Canada with their technically much more sophisticated and valuable product. The media recognized that Pearson was trying to exert pressure on Washington, but the *Globe and Mail* on April 11 wondered if it was worth it. Pearson's speech had emphasized that Canada's friendship with the United States must not be jeopardized by this unhappy affair. Nevertheless, "a growing number of Canadians are beginning to question that 'friendship.' It seems to take the form, over the years, of a long series of insults and injuries by those Americans, in Congress and elsewhere, who hold the actual power in the United States, followed by effusive editorials and speeches by other Americans, deploring what has happened and urging Canadians to forgive and forget. It must be the most one-sided love affair in international history." That the *Globe and Mail*, then and now the voice of the business and financial community, could argue in this way was an indicator of the broad-based Canadian disgust at American Cold War witch-hunts and Herbert Norman's suicide.

The Norman affair stayed in the public forum for several more weeks, but debate in the House of Commons ended on April 12 when Parliament was dissolved. The Conservatives had turned their attack onto Pearson, attempting to discover just when the government had learned that Norman had been a Communist in his youth.* Although these charges against Pearson muddied the waters, the suicide of the diplomat in the face of American witch-hunting did not become a major issue in the June 1957 election. Nor did later charges, emanating from congressional committees, that Robert Bryce, the Secretary to the Cabinet, had been a Communist at Harvard in the 1930s, stir much interest in Canada. Even less credible were charges levelled at Pearson himself, though some Canadian politicians—including Diefenbaker—quietly tried to make use of them.

Nonetheless, as US Ambassador Livingston Merchant wrote confidentially to the Department of State, the Norman suicide raised an "issue which holds highly charged appeal to latent anti–United States feeling."[15] The Ambassador was right. The Norman case undoubtedly

* Later historians tried to determine if Norman had in fact been a spy for the Soviet Union. Extraordinarily, two biographical accounts, both by Americans, appeared at the same time, one arguing that he was not, the other that he was. See Roger Bowen, *Innocence Is Not Enough: The Life and Death of Herbert Norman* (Vancouver 1986), and James Barros, *No Sense of Evil: Espionage: The Case of Herbert Norman* (Toronto 1986). The titles convey the bias of each. The issue became controversial enough in late 1989 for the Mulroney government to commission former diplomat and political scientist Peyton Lyon to write a report so as to resolve the issue once and for all. Lyon's hasty and badly argued paper, "The Loyalties of E. Herbert Norman," released on March 30, 1990, was so vicious in its personal attacks on Professor Barros that it lacked all credibility. The gradual opening of Soviet archives should be able to let some diligent researcher answer the questions raised about Norman by the United States, the RCMP, and Barros.

fuelled an atmosphere of anti-Americanism that contributed to the election of John Diefenbaker and the ouster from power of the Liberals, viewed by many voters as too continentalist, too soft on the Americans.

*   *   *

The 1950s saw a resurgence in Canadian anti-Americanism. There was a genuine uneasiness that the United States, rash, impulsive, generous, and powerful, was in command of the free world's destiny. There was a concern that Britain, stable, sober, and impoverished, was now so reduced in its strength that it scarcely mattered. With Washington pressing for Ottawa to play its part in defending the North American continent and to participate in a major way in NATO and in Korea, the lines that had separated the two nations were beginning to blur.

The Communists and their friends saw an opportunity, and they tried to exploit it. A militaristic, aggressive America was the only threat to global peace, they cried, a sentiment that many Canadians, their eye focused on the south rather than on Soviet control over its satellites or Chinese expansionism, might have been persuaded to listen to with a sympathetic ear. When the strategists of the left like James Endicott foolishly decided to raise the ante by tossing a germ-warfare allegation on the table, however, the opportunity to influence Canadian opinion disappeared like the chimera it was. Canadians were always prepared to accept that their neighbours were loud, pushy, and hyper-nationalistic. Many believed that United States policies were often misguided, but few accepted that they would use germ warfare in Korea. Left-wing ideological anti-Americanism never recovered from the damaging impact Endicott and his friends had upon it.

In large numbers, however, ordinary Canadians did believe that congressional witch-hunters had murdered Herbert Norman. The McCarthyite hounding of Americans who—in a different time and in different circumstances—had once accepted Communism as a sounder creed than democracy was appalling enough. But when the witch-hunters focused on Canadians like Herbert Norman, and when the effects were fatal, this was blatant US interference. The barometer that measured Canadian–American relations fell precipitately, and the storm of anti-Americanism combined with and fed the public's uneasiness about the increasing dominance a sometimes erratic United States had over Canada's political, economic, and military life. Even trade unions were under sway. The result saw John Diefenbaker raised from relative obscurity on the opposition benches to power. The new Prime Minister himself would not hesitate to play the anti-American card.

5

TOO CLOSE FOR COMFORT: JOHN DIEFENBAKER AND THE POLITICAL USES OF ANTI-AMERICANISM

Macpherson/Reprinted with permission—The Toronto Star Syndicate

In 1958 and 1959, movie theatres around the world still showed newsreels each week. In the months after the Soviet Union put up *Sputnik*, the first satellite launched into an earth orbit, the newsreels featured the United States' effort to develop the huge missiles necessary to duplicate the Russians' feat. The American missiles, however, blew up with amazing frequency, collapsing back to earth in showers of smoke, flames, and explosions. For a time, as Nikita Khrushchev gloated and postured, the Western alliance seemed to be in genuine danger from the Russians' intercontinental ballistic missiles.

The newsreels of these disasters played in Canadian movie houses to a startling response. When the huge missiles strained off their launch pads only to collapse in ruination, audiences all across Canada, and certainly in Toronto, as I cannot forget, clapped, laughed, and cheered, revelling in the Americans' humiliation and failure. Canadian anti-Americanism was alive and well at the end of the 1950s, even though the Soviets' missile successes posed a threat to Canada.

No one could suggest that John Diefenbaker singlehandedly created this mood in Canada. Anti-Americanism existed long before Diefenbaker, and it survived his departure from the prime ministership. But there can be no doubt that Diefenbaker's prickly nationalism had fed Canadian concerns about the Americans, and that those cheering audiences believed their government had major differences with the United States administration. They were right.

*　　*　　*

The Conservative Party had stagnated in opposition since 1935. Its leadership lacklustre, its policies musty, the party had slipped irretrievably into irrelevance. Tory policies still reeked of imperial sentimentality when the British Empire was on the cusp of history. The African and Asian colonies and territories were grasping for independence, the dominions were at last becoming truly independent nations, and Britain's economic and military power, wasted by war, had collapsed everywhere. The Progressive Conservative Party's rhetoric had a permanent tinge of anti-Americanism at a time when the United States was the leader of the Free World and the magnet that attracted the best and the brightest from all over the world, not least from Canada. Tory support, battered by successive defeats in the elections of 1935, 1940, 1945, 1949, and 1953, seemed on the verge of disappearing as Canada urbanized and modernized. The Liberals under Mackenzie King and Louis St Laurent had ridden the wave of the future.

Suddenly, almost inexplicably, everything changed. John Diefenbaker, chosen leader of the Progressive Conservative Party at a national convention in December 1956, won a stunning minority election victory in June of the next year over St Laurent and became Prime Minister. A spellbinding orator, an experienced parliamentarian, and a fervent believer in the British connection, Canadian nationalism, and the Western alliance against the Soviet Union, Diefenbaker personified those Canadians who clung to past imperial glories and looked with increasing desperation for the twentieth century to belong to Canada.

Diefenbaker was born in rural Ontario in 1895, but raised in the western province of Saskatchewan. His mother's maiden name was Campbell, Scottish to the core, but his father's Baden ancestors had come to Canada early in the nineteenth century. Germans laboured under no discrimination in Canada until the outbreak of the Great War in 1914, but then the lash of public opinion fell heavily on those whose language or names suddenly attracted attention. John Diefenbaker, in 1914 a university student, suffered along with his family. From that point on he opposed the hyphenated Canadianism that characterized everyone by their "old country" origins and supported "one Canada," his later descriptive phrase for pan-Canadian nationalism. The young Diefenbaker enlisted in the Canadian Expeditionary Force and served briefly as an officer in Canada and Britain. Either injured in a training accident or suffering from psychological problems, as his most recent biographer suggests, he was demobilized by the Canadian Expeditionary Force before he saw any action in the trenches.[1]

Countless Canadians like Diefenbaker had resented the way the republican United States, always loud in its protestations of virtue, remained neutral in the Great War until 1917. He was even more offended by the Americans' postwar bragging that they alone had won the war. On the Prairies, where large numbers of Americans had settled in the years around the turn of the century, these attitudes would be hardened by the United States' delay in entering the Second World War.

Thus, John Diefenbaker was a bundle of contradictions. His Scottish forebears gave him a burning interest in Britain and British forms of government and law. A fervent monarchist, he believed that the Crown had a mediatory effect on politics and that the British connection was good for Canada, not least because it provided a counterweight to the sometimes overpowering influence of the United States. At the same time, sensitized by his Germanic surname, he wanted to see a country where foreign elements subsumed their ethnicity in a common Canadian nationalism. As a pro-British pan-Canadian nationalist with anti-American attitudes, he typified many Canadians. At the same time, as a westerner, he resented the financial and political dominance exerted by central Canada over his region. The control exercised by Toronto and its paymasters on New York's Wall

Street, along with the weight the federal government gave to French Canada's attitudes and sensitivities, rankled in him and his region.

Diefenbaker took his hardening attitudes into politics. He failed to win election to Parliament in the 1920s, he lost out as a municipal candidate in his home town of Prince Albert in the 1930s, and he failed as a provincial Conservative in the last years of the Great Depression. But in the general election of 1940, an election in which Mackenzie King and his Liberal Party swept back into power with a huge majority, he finally won a place in the House of Commons as a Conservative. His party was in ruins, reduced to a mere forty seats, all but leaderless. Diefenbaker tried to become House leader in 1940 but failed, and two years later he sought the national leadership, running poorly at a convention. In 1944 he was one of only two Tory MPs to argue in favour of family allowances, an indication that he leant towards social welfare—and away from the free enterprise rhetoric still espoused by the Ontario group that controlled the Progressive Conservative Party. In 1948, by now reasonably well known across the country as a compelling speaker with firm views on domestic and foreign policy, he tried for the gold ring again, losing this time to Ontario's Premier George Drew, a man with strong backing from Toronto's financial circles. Not until 1956, his party still becalmed in the political doldrums it had occupied since 1935, did he finally struggle to the top of the greasy pole. The leadership of the Progressive Conservative Party did not seem much of a prize.

At the beginning of 1957, Diefenbaker's attitudes were much as they had been since his youth. The Suez humiliation of the previous year notwithstanding, he continued to believe in Britain's greatness and in the majesty of the Crown, and the highlight of his accession to the prime ministership was his almost immediate flight to Britain for a Commonwealth Prime Ministers' conference and a meeting with the Queen. Diefenbaker remained suspicious of the United States and its policies, deeply resentful of the way Washington had turned its back on Britain in the Suez Canal crisis and of the way the Liberal government had cooperated with the Americans in humiliating London and Paris by forcing them to withdraw their armies from Egypt. At the same time, as American investment increased to some 76 percent of all foreign investment in Canada in 1957 and dominated crucial areas of the national economy, he fumed at what he saw as a too-close link between the Liberals and American high finance. He worried about the inevitable loss of control over Canada's economic destiny. Moreover, his dislike for the central Canadian nexus within his

The 1956 Pipeline debate increased Canadian
concerns about US economic control.

Callan/Reprinted with permission—The Toronto Star
Syndicate/National Archives of Canada C-143285

own party had not been appeased by his convention victory. Suspicion was
John Diefenbaker's middle name.

In the general election campaign of 1957, Diefenbaker, his extraordinary eyes flashing, his arms waving, his voice full of seemingly genuine
passion, had appeared meteor-like on the political scene. His stock in
trade was Canadian nationalism, which equalled a large dose of under-
stated anti-Americanism. Canada ought to have stood by Britain at Suez,
not followed Washington's lead. American investment was too large and
threatened a loss of control to the south: "If the St Laurent government
is re-elected," Diefenbaker proclaimed, "Canada will become a virtual
49th state of the American union." Canada's great future was yet to
come, and it would be based on an unhyphenated nationalism that would
create a wholly independent nation on the northern half of the continent.
That attitude guaranteed that there would be flareups in relations with
the United States—and there were.

Yet when he became Prime Minister, Diefenbaker was quick to sign

Canada on to the North American Air Defence Agreement, an alliance that joined the Royal Canadian Air Force's home defence squadrons and radar lines and the United States Air Force under a single command headquartered in Colorado Springs. He was so quick in this decision that he failed to consult his Cabinet, his Cabinet Defence Committee (which had not yet even been formed), or the Department of External Affairs, which learned about the agreement's signature from the Americans. Diefenbaker had not acted wisely, though he was not playing at anti-Americanism. It was present, however. When NORAD finally came before the House of Commons, the CCF voted against the agreement, the first major break in the widespread support Cold War Canadian foreign and defence policy had commanded.

Diefenbaker soon demonstrated that he was an admirer of President Dwight D. Eisenhower, then in the early part of his second term in the White House. A centrist Republican with a Germanic name (exactly as Diefenbaker was a middle-of-the-road Conservative with a Germanic name), Ike was a war hero, the leader of the great military coalition that had won the Second World War. Now he was the leader of the free world in the conflict with Soviet Communism. Eisenhower was older, a genuinely pleasant and courteous man, and he had the innate good sense to treat Diefenbaker well, to call him "John" in their correspondence, and to flatter the Canadian leader politely. As Diefenbaker wrote in his memoirs: "Unlike his successor, [Eisenhower] did not regard the United States presidency as a glittering jewel; he saw it as a job to be done. I found Eisenhower a warm and engaging person, and we became the best of friends. He had an appreciation of Canada and Canadians. . . . Eisenhower was a man that one could talk to . . . he was prepared to listen to my point of view."

Eisenhower, in other words, played Diefenbaker shrewdly and well, offering him invitations to visit Washington and sending warm telegrams to mark significant events, political and personal. He appeared to understand Diefenbaker's concerns about US influence over Canada, and he went out of his way to relieve them, something he accomplished with remarkable success. The President was also well informed. As a briefing paper prepared in the Department of State for a ministerial meeting put it: "Canadian sensitivity to the actions and policies of the United States is a political reality in handling the problems inherent in the close relations between our two countries. . . . A complicating factor in dealing with the Canadian Government is that relations with the United States inevitably play an important role in Canadian domestic politics . . . the Government feeling itself impelled to outdo the Opposition in defense of Canadian interests."[2]

The public mood fed this attitude in Ottawa. There was still affection for Americans and a general, if very soft, confidence in the world leadership of the United States, though this trust co-existed uneasily with a widespread and hardening anti-Americanism on the part of all those who had been outraged by the hounding of Herbert Norman and who worried about the aggressive anti-Communism that characterized Washington's foreign policy. Diefenbaker himself professed to worry about this attitude. In an interview with Arnold Heeney, the Canadian Ambassador in Washington in 1960, the Prime Minister pronounced "anti-American sentiment . . . now worse than at any time in his lifetime." It was growing into an "avalanche." Heeney characterized the mood as "not ill will but combined asperity and cockiness," and he described the Americans of that era as "generous, charming and often frightening."[3] It was the "frightening" part that troubled Canadians, who were worried about nuclear war, American pressure on the dominion, and the cultural tide sweeping across the border.

Robert Thomas Allen, a popular journalist, wrote in *Maclean's* on September 24, 1960, that his countrymen had "gone slightly out of their minds on the subject of the United States. They've become the victims of a fixed idea—the idea that the first step toward being right is to establish that the United States is wrong. It's turning them," Allen argued, "into a spectator nation, a breed of carping Monday-morning quarterbacks. . . . They can't speak intelligently about Americans, or civilly about Americans, or calmly about Americans, or get their mind off Americans."

Matters were destined only to worsen. One of the bestsellers in Canadian publishing in 1960 was a slender book by James M. Minifie, the CBC correspondent in Washington. *Peacemaker or Powder-Monkey: Canada's Role in a Revolutionary World* called on Canada to cut itself loose from the Americans' chariot wheels and to proclaim its neutrality proudly. A Canadian-born, Oxford-educated, American citizen, Minifie seemed to believe that Canada and the United States existed in isolation, that there was no Soviet Union with missiles and bombers poised to strike over the North Pole, and scarcely any need for Canadian defence. His little book sold thousands of copies and stirred debate on the apparent loss of Canadian sovereignty set in train by the Cold War. He did not persuade John Diefenbaker, whose anti-Communism co-existed with his anti-Americanism.

The degree of understanding, the concern for Diefenbaker's sensitivities that the Eisenhower administration had shown, had welded the Prime Minister solidly into the Canadian–American alliance, however much he might bridle on occasion. When John F. Kennedy won election to the presidency in November 1960, however, the new administration proved much more impatient with Canada. In his early forties, good-looking, forceful in speech, Kennedy's attractiveness drew the world's interest, and Canadians were captivated by him every bit as much as Americans.*

Diefenbaker had preferred Richard Nixon, Eisenhower's Vice-President whom he had come to know, to Kennedy. He nonetheless paid an early visit to the new American leader on February 20, 1961, and seemed to believe that he had established a good working relationship with the much younger, charismatic Kennedy. The President, however, had been briefed in ways which painted Canada as a potential trouble spot and which suggested that the major problem might be the Prime Minister:

> Canadian support cannot be taken for granted and there will most probably be a variety of Canadian initiatives, some of which will be most annoying to the U.S. . . . [Diefenbaker] is not believed to have any basic prejudice against the United States. He has appeared, however, to seek on occasion to assert Canadian independence by seizing opportunities for Canada to adopt policies which deviate somewhat from those of the United States, but he has done so only when it has been possible without overwhelmingly serious consequences to U.S.–Canadian relations.[4]

When Kennedy repaid Diefenbaker's visit by coming north to receive a rapturous welcome in Ottawa in May 1961 (and to injure his back seriously in an unfortunate tree-planting ceremony at Government House), his briefing book again was tart—but completely correct in capturing Diefenbaker's typically Canadian attitudes. Indeed, the briefer's shrewd assessment of Canadian feelings towards the United States in 1961 could

---

* The Canadian Institute of Public Opinion reported on January 18, 1961, that Canadians, by a five-to-one majority, believed Kennedy would improve US–Canada relations. On December 26, 1962, Canadians ranked Kennedy as the person they admired most, 21 percent naming him first. Diefenbaker ranked fifth, the choice of only 3 percent.

likely have been mirrored at most points in the half-century after 1945: "The projection of the United States image in Canada during the Presidential visit should take into account the long-standing tendency of some Canadians to believe that we are dominated by a trigger-happy military, that we are not regardful of cultural values, that we are harsh and discriminatory in our attitudes toward minorities, that we are inept and lacking in perception in our handling of relations with under-developed countries in both diplomacy and aid, and that we tend to be absent-minded and neglectful of the interests of Canada."[5]

Difficulties quickly arose at this meeting in Ottawa. A memorandum prepared for the President was apparently left between the cushions of a sofa, and Diefenbaker, who found it and failed to return it as protocol demanded, apparently (and wrongly) interpreted some penned scratches written on the paper as referring to him as an "SOB." As important, there were sharp disputes about Canada's continuing trade with Fidel Castro's Cuba, while the United States, just a month after its humiliating failure in supporting a Cuban exiles' invasion at the Bay of Pigs, was becoming increasingly hard-line in its approach to Cuban Communism and all who lent it aid. There were also continuing differences over Canada's acquisition from the United States of nuclear warheads for the weapons systems Diefenbaker's government had purchased in the late 1950s for use in NORAD and in Europe with the forces of the North Atlantic Treaty Organization. There was no doubt that Canada in 1959 had agreed to go nuclear, but while construction of Bomarc missile sites in Canada went ahead, the negotiations to lay out the agreed terms under which warheads for the surface-to-air missiles would come to Canada made no progress whatsoever. Howard Green, Diefenbaker's Secretary of State for External Affairs, was pressing hard for nuclear disarmament at the United Nations and in Allied councils, and the delay, as Diefenbaker wavered uneasily and watched his pro-nuclear Defence Minister, Douglas Harkness, had begun to be very noticeable. It wasn't that Diefenbaker was not anti-Communist—not at all. The luxury his government had of sheltering under the Americans' nuclear umbrella made the Chief complacent. The government felt free to carp and complain at Washington, secure in the belief that the Yanks would protect them if the Cold War turned hotter.

Complacency could turn to spitefulness. At their May 1961 meeting in Ottawa, Diefenbaker persuaded himself that Kennedy was too cocky for such a young man and too inclined to use American muscle to push him and Canada around. The Prime Minister developed a sharp and growing dislike for the President, a nostalgic yearning for the camaraderie and respect that Eisenhower had shown him, and a stiff-necked attitude to burgeoning American power that did not bode well for the future of Canada's relations with the new American administration.

Relations grew worse. In early May 1962, with an election campaign in its early stages, the Prime Minister was furious after Kennedy gave a forty-five-minute private interview to Liberal leader Lester Pearson before a dinner to honour Nobel Prize winners. Diefenbaker ranted to US ambassador Livingston Merchant that the Americans were out to get him and that he might feel obliged to reveal the "SOB" memorandum to the voters. Basil Robinson of the Department of External Affairs, Diefenbaker's foreign policy aide in the Prime Minister's Office, later observed that the Ambassador "had clearly been staggered by the vehemence of the prime minister's tirade against President Kennedy."[6] But Diefenbaker, cautioned by Merchant in a subsequent meeting and obviously having second thoughts of his own, did not make the 1961 memorandum public.

While relations deteriorated during the campaign, Diefenbaker's Cabinet continued to avoid a decision on accepting the nuclear warheads, without which the Bomarcs were only useless, expensive metal. The government was in trouble, its popularity sagging under the strains of a major downturn in the economy, and facing a run on the Canadian dollar that required it to fix the dollar's value at 92.5 cents US. There were increasing doubts about the Prime Minister's leadership capacity and even his mental health. The election results on June 18 reduced the Tories to minority status, leaving Diefenbaker clinging to power. The United States, asked immediately after the election to help bolster Canadian dollar reserves, gave its assistance, but this renewed evidence of his country's dependency on American largesse did little to improve the Prime Minister's humour. Depressed by his political misfortunes and in pain from a broken ankle, Diefenbaker brooded over the summer. When American reconnaissance aircraft revealed that the Soviet Union was installing intermediate-range nuclear missiles in Cuba, a crisis that brought the world to the brink of war erupted with startling suddenness in October 1962. A political storm along the Canada–US border was almost inevitable.

Canadian intelligence officials had brought word of the Cuban crisis to Ottawa a day or two before Kennedy's envoy flew north to brief Diefenbaker. Although he listened to the briefing calmly, the Prime

Minister quickly came to believe that he and his country had been excluded, despite the NORAD treaty's provisions that should have guaranteed Canada a privileged place and early consultation. That fed his belief in Kennedy's impetuousness and, on the advice of and with the support of senior officials in the Department of External Affairs, the Prime Minister gave a speech in Parliament calling for neutral members of the United Nations Disarmament Committee to investigate the situation on the ground in Cuba. An infuriated Washington interpreted the Canadian suggestion as casting doubt on Kennedy's honesty, which, of course, it had. More important, Diefenbaker refused to permit Canadian interceptor squadrons in NORAD to move to a heightened state of alert, and preparatory measures for ground and naval forces also were officially placed on hold. The Americans were properly outraged. *Maclean's* reported from Washington in March 1963: "What Canadians don't always realize is that if there is anti-Americanism in Canada, there is anti-Canadianism in the US. The Americans, constantly bombarded by the propaganda of the military-industrial complex and the hysteria of John Birchers and other right-wing extremists, are highly emotional about Cuba. . . . many Americans regard us as traitors to the cause of freedom."

So too did many Canadians. "The Red Scare had reached its zenith," Pierre Berton wrote in his memoirs of the atmosphere in 1962. "Almost every organization slightly to the left of centre was smeared with the Red tag." Berton was well aware of the mood because he had asked Liberal leader Lester Pearson on television in June 1962 if he would rather be Red than dead, and Pearson's reply—that he would rather live under the Communists and work to throw them out of power—had led Conservatives to smear Pearson as soft on Communism. Now Diefenbaker would find the charges thrown at him. Canadians evidently believed it was important to back their ally.

The refusal to bring the Canadian components of NORAD to alert status apparently left the centre of the continent open to a Soviet air attack. In fact, the danger was never there. The Minister of National Defence, acting in defiance of the Prime Minister and on his own authority, placed the RCAF on "Defcon 3," a high-alert status, and turned a blind eye when the Royal Canadian Navy's commander on the East Coast put his ships to sea to track Soviet submarines.[7] The Kennedy administration said nothing officially about Ottawa's dilatoriness—its tolerance can only be described as remarkable—but its extreme displeasure was made clear to Canadian officials and, inevitably, quickly leaked into the press.

While some Canadians that October scrambled to dig fallout shelters in their backyards or basements and stockpiled water and canned goods to help them survive the coming nuclear war, their government did next to nothing. Diefenbaker and several of his key ministers were blinded by their anti-Americanism, their dislike for Kennedy, and their stiff-necked insistence on the right NORAD gave them to be consulted in the greatest crisis of the Cold War. Once the story became public, the impact on Diefenbaker's credibility was devastating. The Cuban crisis eased when the Soviets, eyeball to eyeball with Kennedy, blinked and agreed to pull their missiles out. In this first great Cold War confrontation in which television brought events into people's living rooms, Canadians all across the nation looked to President John F. Kennedy as their leader, not to the ineffectual, indecisive Diefenbaker. The Prime Minister's authority crumbled.

Canada's own crisis was about to begin, helped by the fact that a clear majority of Canadians in a poll on December 22 wanted the Canadian military to be armed with nuclear weapons. The US administration felt no need to hold back in its attack on the Canadian leader. When the retiring NATO Supreme Commander, US General Lauris Norstad, paid a farewell visit to Ottawa on January 3, 1963, he told a press conference that Canada had not lived up to its alliance commitments because of its failure to arm Canada's CF-104 fighter-bombers, stationed in Europe and intended for a strike role against eastern European targets, with nuclear weapons. Norstad's remarks still further undermined the Diefenbaker administration, already weakened by the critical public response to the Prime Minister's inaction during the Cuban crisis and by a Cabinet that was increasingly polarized over the nuclear question. Diefenbaker desperately tried to explain and justify his government's defence policy in a major speech in Parliament on January 25, 1963. His "on the one hand/on the other hand" tone momentarily satisfied some of his critical Cabinet colleagues, but his remarks about American–British nuclear negotiations twisted facts and broke Allied confidences. The State Department in Washington issued a blistering press release on January 30, declaring Diefenbaker a liar, a man whose government "has not as yet proposed any arrangement sufficiently practical to contribute effectively to North American defense." The damning press release did the trick: within days the Conservative Cabinet fell apart, the government suffered defeat in a confidence motion in the House of Commons, and an election was duly called for April 8. Historian Donald Creighton exaggerated dramatically, "About the only manifestation of American power which was spared Canada in the crisis was the sight of American tanks rumbling up Parliament Hill in Ottawa." The Americans, he went on, had indicated to Canadians where their best interests lay, and Pearson's Liberal Party readied itself to seize power from Diefenbaker's faltering grasp.

* * *

The Department of State press release had been suggested by the US Ambassador to Canada, Walton W. Butterworth, who had arrived to take up his post in December 1962. An experienced diplomat, a vigorous defender of his nation's positions, Butterworth could be very rough in his advocacy. His acquaintances in Canada included Pearson, whom he had known since their prewar service in London and with whom he was on first-name terms, but Butterworth was not especially admired by his Canadian counterparts. Diefenbaker, who quickly came to despise the Ambassador, called him "Butterballs" or "Butterfingers." Still, his job was to advance American interests, and Butterworth was unrepentant that his press release had caused a storm in Canada. Even opponents of the Diefenbaker government denounced the Kennedy administration for its interference in the country's domestic affairs, but Butterworth's view was that no apology was necessary: "He feels the statement was very useful," Vice-President Lyndon Johnson was told, "and will be highly beneficial in advancing US interests by introducing realism into a government which has made anti-Americanism and indecision practically its entire stock in trade." To the Ambassador, the Diefenbaker government had been characterized by nothing so much as "neurotic political leadership," an "essentially neurotic Canadian view of the world." It was prey to the "traditional psychopathic accusations of unwarranted US interference in domestic Canadian affairs."[8]

Diefenbaker's instant response to the American intervention was to believe he could secure a dissolution of Parliament on the issue. He was convinced, Justice Minister Donald Fleming wrote, that "we've got our issue now." His disillusioned Defence Minister, Douglas Harkness, later noted that the Chief believed "he could win an election on an anti-US appeal and this, to him, was all that mattered." Such a possible campaign

Macpherson/Reprinted with permission—The Toronto Star Syndicate

"Somebody up there doesn't like us."

approach appalled many Cabinet members, and Finance Minister George Nowlan bluntly told the Halifax *Chronicle-Herald* that he had served notice he would quit the Cabinet immediately if an anti-American program was presented by his party and his leader. Richard Bell, the Minister of Citizenship and Immigration, was another minister who told the Prime Minister he would not be party to an anti-American campaign. In response, Diefenbaker raged at Bell: "I will do whatever I bloody-well like and I don't care whether I have your resignation or not." For their part, the traditionally Tory-supporting *Globe and Mail* and the Montreal *Gazette* warned against "the extravagant use of anti-Americanism," which could "shatter our relations with the United States."

The complaints of the newspapers and his colleagues notwithstanding, Diefenbaker's election campaign in the winter of 1963 featured a strong anti-American thrust. Deserted in the large cities by influential supporters and the media, the Chief travelled by train to the small towns, drawing large and enthusiastic crowds. "It's me against the Americans," he told crowds sporting "Vote Canadian, Vote Conservative" buttons, "fighting for the little guy." "We are a power, not a puppet," he said on another occasion, and he frequently referred to the "great interests" against him, "national and international." "Canadians have the right to decide what is right for Canada," he said in Winnipeg. "We make our policy in Canada—not generated by special interests or even by visits across the border." His Agriculture Minister, Alvin Hamilton, told a Montreal audience that the Yanks "think we're a Guatemala or something. . . . In fact, this country is larger and has immensely more natural resources than the US, so don't push us around, chum!" (The Guatemalan Ambassador reportedly was not amused and protested to the Department of External Affairs.)

Diefenbaker's anti-Americanism was frequently overt. When he blasted the State Department press release as an attempt to treat Canada as if it were a satrapy, he was in full cry. More often, however, he resorted to innuendo: the Americans, preaching the needs of defence to Canadians, had been slow to enter the two world wars, unlike Canada. "When some nations start to point out to us what we should do, let me tell you this. Canada was in both wars a long time before some other nations were. . . . We don't need any lessons as to what Canada should do after that record of service in two world wars."* There were slurs at President Kennedy's youth and inexperience, assaults against American investment in Canada, and attacks on the American media, most notably on the February 18 issue of *Newsweek*, which had featured a cover photograph of Diefenbaker looking positively Satanic and a story that made his actions appear similarly motivated.

---

* When Cuban fighters shot down two small American aircraft in early 1996, the US Congress took tough action against President Castro's regime and countries like Canada that traded with it. North Carolina Senator Jesse Helms was especially scornful of Canada as an "appeaser," treating with Castro much like Neville Chamberlain had dealt with Hitler. The *Globe and Mail* was quick off the mark on March 7, 1996, in phrases that sounded much like Diefenbaker's: "If Mr Helms wants to talk about the Second World War, may we remind him that Canadians were fighting Hitler for a good two years before the Americans showed up? Three years, in the First World War. Next time the senator from North Carolina goes hunting for appeasers, he should take a look in his own backyard." Some attitudes evidently die hard.

When Congress released secret testimony by US Defense Secretary Robert MacNamara that the primary military worth of the Bomarc anti-aircraft missiles was their ability to draw Soviet ICBM salvoes away from the United States and towards Canada, Diefenbaker was quick to seize on the issue as a virtual American plot to have Canada destroyed in a nuclear war. "Are they going to make Canada into a burnt sacrifice?" he shouted to voters at Dorion, Quebec. The Liberals, who had come out in support of nuclear warheads for the Bomarcs and Canada's defence commitments only on January 12, 1963, when party leader Pearson reversed his long-standing position, clearly were in league with the United States. The proof, for Diefenbaker, was that Pearson had attended the dinner Kennedy had thrown in early May 1962 for Nobel Prize winners, a dinner at which, by clear implication, he had received his orders in a private conversation with the President to take on the nuclear weapons issue and destroy John Diefenbaker. The Prime Minister neglected to mention to voters that it was his government that had signed the NORAD agreement and had purchased the Bomarc missiles, but his brilliantly unscrupulous attacks kept the Liberals on the defensive. At one Vancouver Liberal Party campaign meeting, Pearson's address was disrupted by protesters calling him a "Yankee stooge" and burning American flags. In Hamilton, picketers carried signs labelling the Liberal leader a "Pentagon Pet" and "the All-American." The opinion polls, initially showing very positive trends for the Liberals, began to turn around under the lash of Diefenbaker's extraordinary campaign energy and anti-American rhetoric.

Late in the campaign, the Prime Minister's staff began to drop hints about the so-called SOB memo of May 1961 and about a mysterious letter that, they suggested, would prove that the Liberals were in league with the Kennedy administration. This letter, copies of which had arrived early in April at newspaper offices across Canada, purported to be a private communication dated January 14, 1963, from Ambassador Butterworth to Pearson congratulating him for reversing his party's policy on nuclear warheads two days before. "I was delighted with the timing," the letter said,

> which I considered perfect. It will be quite evident to the electorate that the policy of the Conservatives is narrow-minded and that they are unfit to continue governing the country.
>
> At the first opportune moment, I would like to discuss with you

> how we could be useful to you in the future. You can always count
> on our support.[9]

"How we could be useful to you in the future." It is only fair to note that
the Kennedy administration kept itself completely aware of the mood in
Canada, one of the few times in this century that the White House watched
Canadian anti-Americanism with concern. The President allowed the
Democratic Party's polling expert, Oliver Quayle, to work for the Liberals
(just as in 1962 he had agreed that Lou Harris, another Democratic poll-
ster, could assist the Pearson campaign), and he offered additional aid in a
telephone call from a White House intermediary to Pearson during the
election. The horrified Liberal leader was quick to turn down that offer,
which was not yet known to Diefenbaker. "This was a narrow escape,"
Pearson said later, "since I knew there were people abroad in the land who
would insist . . . that [the offer] was a deep dark American plot to take over
the country. . . . To my relief [the call] was never reported."

The Butterworth letter, however, was in the Prime Minister's pocket
late in March. While Diefenbaker campaigned across the country, Donald
Fleming, whose decision not to run again for personal and family reasons
had already been announced, was minding the store in Ottawa. On
March 26, Diefenbaker sent him the Butterworth letter and asked his
opinion. "I said I approached the matter with great caution," Fleming
wrote. "I did not believe that the ambassador could be so stupid as to
confide such thoughts to paper, that I did not think he could be so crude
and inept as even to express such thoughts in any form, that the whole
letter was so 'pat' as to suggest it was carefully planted, that the timing
alone raised the most serious suspicion, that I had concluded it was a
carefully baited trap laid for Dief and in my opinion it could have disastrous and very far-reaching effects for him to be enticed by the bait
without full proof of authorship."[10]

Fleming's sound prudence must have been discouraging to the over-
eager Diefenbaker. Nonetheless, there were veiled hints about the letter
in his speeches. On April 6, two days before the election, the letter was
printed in the Vancouver *Province*, which had not troubled to check with
the United States Embassy or Pearson before printing the text. The
Winnipeg Tribune, one of the four or five major urban newspapers supporting Diefenbaker which had been couriered the letter by the
Diefenbaker campaign, did check. Butterworth repeatedly and flatly

denied writing such a letter, while Pearson adamantly denied receiving it. As a result, the *Tribune* did not print it, nor did any other of the mainstream media that were openly opposing Diefenbaker's anti-Americanism and his nuclear weapons policy, along with his government's drifting economic stewardship. The result, as Butterworth said, was that the letter did not hit the presses "at a moment when denials could not catch up with or neutralize the allegation."[11]

The American Embassy had heard rumours of the letter several days before it appeared in the *Province* and had raised it with the Secretary to the Cabinet, R.B. Bryce. "Obviously taken aback" by the letter's contents and its sudden surfacing during the campaign, Bryce said that the letter "must have come from someone in PM's [campaign] party. He could imagine no other way."[12]

In fact, all or almost all the copies of the Butterworth letter distributed to the Canadian media, including a covering letter over an undecipherable signature, had been mailed from Great Britain on March 24 in air-mail envelopes. Unfortunately for those who hoped to benefit by the letter's release, insufficient postage had been applied, and (mail moving faster then than three decades later) the letters reached Canada by sea mail early in April. Diefenbaker's copy, without the covering letter, had been brought to him by Conservative Senator Gratton O'Leary, the former publisher of the *Ottawa Journal*, who had received a message from Britain indicating that "an important person"—journalist Knowlton Nash says it was George Drew, the Canadian High Commissioner in Britain—had a vital communication for Diefenbaker that he "must get to him urgently." O'Leary later told Butterworth that Diefenbaker checked other letters with the Ambassador's signature and decided, because they were the same, that the letter was genuine and that he would use it in a speech. Presumably unaware of Fleming's advice, O'Leary claimed that he persuaded the Prime Minister to hold off because this would worsen Canada–US relations. The Senator also said that Diefenbaker wanted to send for Butterworth and confront him with the letter, but O'Leary reasoned that the Ambassador was certain to ask where the letter had come from and would insist it was a forgery.[13] When Diefenbaker asked him if he should use the letter in a speech, O'Leary told the Prime Minister, "No, it looks too good to me."[14] Cautioned by Fleming and by an influential journalist for whom he had substantial regard—O'Leary was widely credited with stopping a mushrooming caucus revolt in February 1963 with an emotional speech—the

Prime Minister refrained from any direct references to the Butterworth letter, contenting himself only with innuendo.

Thus, because of an error in mailing and because one key newspaper was professional enough to check, the Butterworth letter did not become a major issue in the election. Diefenbaker lost, but the Liberals won enough seats to form only a minority government. The political survival of the Progressive Conservative Party and its leader was attributable, partly if not largely, to Diefenbaker's vigorous campaign and its skilful, if unscrupulous, use of anti-Americanism. He had appealed to the innate Canadian mistrust of the United States, and there was more than enough evidence, even without the Butterworth letter, to stoke the country's emotions.

The election had turned out just the way the Kennedy administration had hoped. Pearson quickly met with the President to restore amicable Canadian–American relations and to accept the nuclear warheads for the Bomarcs and the Canadian forces in NATO. The Department of State wanted to drop the matter of the forged letter, but a furious Butterworth argued that it would be a serious error for the United States to revert "to its old ways of treating Canada like a problem child for whom there was always at the ready a cheek for the turning." At the same time, the Ambassador took full credit for offering the advice that led to "the defeat and destruction of the Diefenbaker Government and the ensuing favorable change in the formation of a government headed by Pearson. In the process," he said in a cable to the State Department, "a somewhat more mature Canada has emerged from the electoral crucible and a measure of its neuroses has been exorcized."[15] There was some truth in Butterworth's claims to have played a decisive role. He had suggested the idea of a frontal attack on Diefenbaker to the Department of State and, as Canadians belatedly learned, Butterworth had also held secret briefings on the flaws in Canadian nuclear policy for journalists in the cellar of the embassy. Not until years later did journalist Charles Lynch reveal the American Ambassador's activities.

Butterworth had not written the letter, though the signature was genuine. Embassy staff concluded after close examination that the letter had not been typed on one of their typewriters but had been put together in three parts by photography: the embossed letterhead, the body of the letter, and the signature. Moreover, the type size did not correspond proportionately to the standard official paper on which the letter appeared. Later investigation found the paper to be of British origin. The letter was a forgery—a fact that ought to have been immediately apparent whatever the result of the technical assessment. No ambassador, and especially not one with Butterworth's long experience, would have made the mistake of writing such a letter when its contents could have been conveyed safely in conversation. Moreover, Butterworth's bread-and-butter correspondence with Pearson was on a first-name basis, and the forged letter reeked of formality.

The issue soon moved to the House of Commons where Diefenbaker, now Leader of the Opposition, continued his anti-American attacks. In an address on May 21, 1963, referring to Pearson's January reversal of

"You can't cook?"

Liberal Party nuclear policy, he said darkly: "Possibly it will not be very long before we know some of the things that took place, some of the words of deep approval that were given to the Prime Minister for giving this remarkable calisthenic performance." No one had very long to wait. Six days later, Gordon Churchill, latterly Diefenbaker's Minister of Trade and Commerce and then of National Defence, read the text of the forged letter into Hansard.

If the press had restrained itself and withheld publication during the election, now the lid was off. Every major newspaper featured the story, with Butterworth's brief statement that the letter was "a complete forgery." Editorials generally denounced the Conservatives for what was widely viewed as a malicious smear campaign, and the *Montreal Star* said, rather prematurely, that "strident anti-Americanism no longer has political currency in Canada." Other papers played variations on the same tune, burying the idea of anti-Americanism as a factor in Canadian public and intellectual life.

The criticism had no effect on Conservatives in and out of Parliament. Until his death, Churchill continued to believe the letter to be genuine, and he had his own technical analysis done of it in 1965, predictably confirming him in his opinion. No evidence, however, was presented for public scrutiny. Similarly, Diefenbaker proclaimed in his memoirs, published in 1977, that he had "confidential knowledge which will be revealed in due course that it was a true copy"; such evidence, two decades after Diefenbaker's death, has yet to be made public. The Chief added, in one of his very rare confessions of error, that he had made a major mistake in not using the Butterworth letter to the fullest in the 1963 campaign.

*   *   *

Was this extraordinary little episode nothing more than a reflection of John Diefenbaker's unreasoning dislike for John F. Kennedy? Or was it a symptom of a deeper-seated, irrational, and paranoiac anti-Americanism in the Canadian psyche? That Diefenbaker disliked Kennedy is beyond doubt, as even a casual reading of his memoirs makes clear. He resented Kennedy's youthful style and popularity, his good looks, and his attractive wife. Canadian women tried to dress as much like Jackie Kennedy as they could, adopting her hats and trying to emulate her style; none tried to pattern themselves after Olive Diefenbaker, a matronly, even dowdy, woman with a vicious disposition hidden behind a cold smile. Diefenbaker fumed at what he saw as the way the United States took Canada and its leader for granted. The assumption in Washington seemed to be that the Kennedy administration decided and Canada obeyed, and sometimes, it must be admitted, Diefenbaker was justified in this belief. His anger had existed when the Republicans were in office, but Eisenhower jollied Diefenbaker along and most overt manifestations of prime ministerial rage were suppressed; when Kennedy came to power and the efforts to appeal to Diefenbaker as a colleague and friend largely ceased, the rage became visible. By January 1963, beset by enemies foreign and domestic, Diefenbaker was ready to clutch at any straw, and the State Department's press release guaranteed that anti-Americanism played a major role in his election campaign. Significantly, key members of the Progressive Conservative Party were embarrassed, not to say humiliated, by their government's inaction first during the Cuban crisis and then on nuclear weapons. They refused to go along with their leader, and warned against an overt assault on the United States. For the first time in its history, the Conservative Party was not united in the anti-American cause; for the first time, the Ontario members turned away from the issue that had been their bread and butter since John A. Macdonald's time. The United States was the leader of the Western alliance, the economic mecca, the investor of choice, and Tory ministers and members, sensitive to the arguments of their friends in business and finance, had no stomach for a fight against the Yanks—especially when their government was so clearly in the wrong.

Diefenbaker's own decaying fortunes let the dissidents get away with their disobedience. The Prime Minister's almost uncanny hold over his party had weakened by the beginning of 1963 and Diefenbaker, realizing his predicament, understood that he had to keep as much of his party as possible on his side during the campaign. Despite his contemptuous rejection of his critics on an individual basis, therefore, he never let himself go against the Americans completely, and he hesitated to do anything more than make oblique references to the SOB memo and the Butterworth letter.

Only a psychiatrist can adequately explain Diefenbaker's mental state. To this historian, he appears to have been a paranoid personality whose world divided almost automatically into "us" versus "them." By the time of the election of 1963, the "us" side comprised only a few loyal party supporters of a pro-British bent and the "little guys" in small town and rural Canada. By contrast, the "them" side was massive—big business, the cities, the Canadian and American media, the Conservative defectors, the Kennedy administration, and the Pentagon. The campaign might have been expected to be a disaster, given the government's appalling record of indecision and confusion and the manner of its collapse, but the extraordinarily resilient Diefenbaker thrived in the face of the challenge and won 97 seats to Pearson's 131, making the election far closer than anyone would have believed when Diefenbaker's government collapsed in disarray early in February.* There can be no doubt that the anti-American tenor of his campaign contributed substantially to this result.

But in many ways, Diefenbaker was a typical Canadian. He reflected the usual Canadian dislike of Americans: the antipathy towards the more powerful neighbour; the dislike of America's crass style, popular culture, and greedy big business; and the fear of Washington's big stick, the stick that had been used against Cuba in October 1962 and against him and his country in the press release of January 30. But Diefenbaker's paranoia reinforced these dislikes, and his rampant anti-Americanism was much like Canada's at its worst and most juvenile. Historically, the nation's weak identity had demanded that anti-Americanism form a large component of Canadian nationalism. People such as Diefenbaker who had long relied on the link with Great Britain as a counterweight to the overwhelming presence of the United States found themselves with nothing to hold onto once Britain lost its power and began to move towards the European Community, as it was trying to do in the early 1960s. Diefenbaker-style imperial and monarchical loyalism was no longer sufficient or relevant in a world and a continent dominated by the brash and confident superpower to the south.

The 1963 election was the first in which a campaign motivated by anti-Americanism had not triumphed. The tide had turned in Canada, and political leaders such as John Diefenbaker had lost their trump card. Anti-Americanism was still strong, but it could not prevail over the forces of continentalism, especially when they were combined, as in 1963, with the attractive force of President Kennedy and the potent anti-Communism that made Canadians believe their country had to work in concert with the United States in defending North America.

* The opinion polls demonstrated that Diefenbaker's anti-American campaign hurt the Liberals and helped the third parties more than it improved his own position. In January 1963 the Canadian Institute of Public Opinion showed the Liberals with 47 percent and the Conservatives with 32 percent. Two months later the Liberals were down 6 percent, the Conservatives were holding, and the minor parties were gaining strength. The election on April 8 gave the Liberals 41.7 percent, the Conservatives 32.8, the NDP 13.1, and the Social Credit 11.9. In Quebec, the anti-nuclear Créditistes drew 27 percent of the vote and twenty seats; nationally the anti-nuclear NDP won seventeen seats. In essence, the Diefenbaker campaign held the Tory vote intact and drove voters away from the pro-nuclear and—in the public eye—pro-American Liberals.

The forged Butterworth letter was a minor issue in political terms, but it had substantial significance as an indicator of the paranoid style in Canadian and Progressive Conservative politics. In truth, the Prime Minister and his loyal Conservative ministers had to believe that the letter was genuine, for it offered a ready explanation for their political difficulties. So fierce were they in their resentment of the United States and so angry at the Kennedy administration's actions against them and their defence policy (or non-policy) that the letter gave them both solace and justification. After all, how could they have won the 1963 election once the Americans trained their big guns on them? The Americans, their patience tested to the limit, had finally lashed out against Diefenbaker, thereby confirming their demonic status.

The Butterworth letter, when added to the State Department press release and the other private American attempts to influence the 1963 election, all contributed to the assiduously cultivated legend that the Americans had done in the Chief. Novelist and journalist Heather Robertson encapsulated the continuing force of this myth when she wrote in 1989 of Diefenbaker's "political assassination." The Canadian leader "had not gone to Harvard. When President John F. Kennedy, who had gone to Harvard, suggested that the American missiles on Canadian territory (what the hell were they doing there anyway?) should be armed with nuclear warheads, John Diefenbaker raised his eyebrows and shook his jowls. No." Robertson's parenthetical question was the critical point, even if she, like other proponents of the myth, did not realize it. The American missiles had, of course, been bought and paid for by Diefenbaker's government, which understood and accepted that they required nuclear warheads. Thwarted, Robertson continued, Kennedy then turned nasty: "Who was this guy?" As the 1963 election neared, Kennedy issued an ultimatum: "If nuclear warheads were not accepted, the Americans would see to it that the Canadian government was defeated. And it was."[16] The legend, propped up as always by a few facts and much pop psychological mythologizing, lives on, and not only in bad novels. The true believers evidently cannot accept that Diefenbaker's dithering incompetence brought down the Tory government.

The key point was missed by the mythologizers. In 1891 the anti-American cry had helped to hold power for John A. Macdonald. In 1911 it had propelled Robert Borden into power, his party bound hand and foot to Canadian businessmen who resented reciprocity's challenge to their Canadian markets. But in 1963, even if Diefenbaker's attack on the

United States was not as full-throated or as uninhibited as Macdonald's or Borden's,* anti-Americanism could not have swept all before it. Indeed, so sharp was the opposition within his own party to Diefenbaker's planned use of anti-Americanism that the Chief had to hold back. As it was, there remained more than enough anti-Americanism in the Tory campaign to discredit it. For all practical purposes, Progressive Conservative anti-Americanism died with John Diefenbaker's leadership of the party.

Canada was evidently in the throes of change. The forces on the right of the political spectrum no longer feared the Americans the way they had a half-century before. Business interests were now much more responsive to the imperatives of Wall Street than they were during the free trade elections of 1891 and 1911. The military and its domestic clients looked to Uncle Sam as the great power which they, like every little brother, wanted to emulate. Sophisticated urbanites, watching American TV and reading American books and magazines, saw Diefenbaker as a Prairie rube whose anachronistic anti-Americanism was crudeness personified and whose government was inefficient and unsuccessful. The forces against the Chief could not be overcome, though his wresting a majority from the Liberals demonstrated that the remnants of the old Canada were stronger than the proponents of change had realized.

The United States, as novelist Graeme Gibson wrote in his *Gentleman Death* in 1993, "embodies the times we must live in. The times to come." Society is imploding and a terrible exhaustion has set in. "It must be true," Gibson says, "that what passes for anti-Americanism, apart from simple envy, is little more or less than a fear and loathing of the future, a despair at the loss of our collective pasts."[17] Diefenbaker was not a reflective man, but somehow he must have sensed that, with the help of the powerful in Canadian society, the American future was destined to wash away the collective past that Canadians had constructed with so much struggle and difficulty. His visceral anti-Americanism reeked of his despair at "the times to come."

---

* In his *Right Honourable Men: The Descent of Canadian Politics from Macdonald to Mulroney* (Toronto 1994), 211, historian Michael Bliss argues that Diefenbaker wallowed "in a crude anti-Americanism that would have seemed demagogic even in the days of Macdonald and Borden." But there was nothing like the vehemence of 1891 and 1911 in Diefenbaker, who generally pulled his punches in the face of a less receptive public.

6

CLASS TRAITOR:
WALTER GORDON AND AMERICAN INVESTMENT

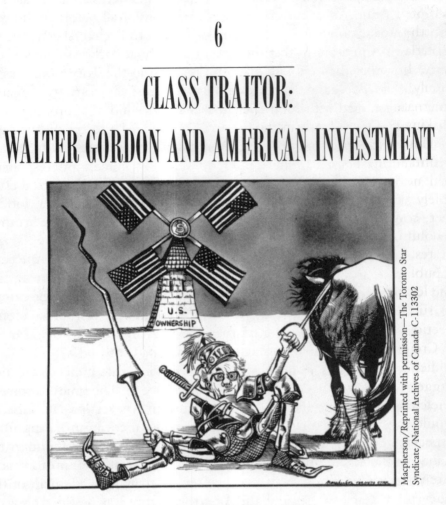

A little wounded but not slain

Macpherson/Reprinted with permission—The Toronto Star
Syndicate/National Archives of Canada C-113302

Tall and gangling, Donald Creighton of the University of Toronto peered down from the lectern at the crowd assembled to hear his presidential address to the Canadian Historical Association. It was June 1957, just a few days after John Diefenbaker's Progressive Conservatives had unexpectedly put an end to twenty-two unbroken years of Liberal Party rule, and Creighton's subject was Canadian history, presented as only the master could. The Liberals under King and St Laurent, he said with his caustic voice dripping with sarcasm, "acting like a dutiful child that has learned to like what its parents think good for it," had "actually accepted American continentalism. . . . had even been sold the idea of North American community fellowship, which may be said to be the Rotarian version of Manifest Destiny." North America, he went on bitterly, humorously, was that psychologist's ideal—"a great big, happy family, in which all the members were perfectly adjusted. It was a gigantic international Elks convention where all the delegates went around handshaking and back-slapping and exuding cordiality at every pore."

This was all dangerous drivel, the biographer of John A. Macdonald maintained with some justice. "The simple truth was that . . . Canada had never broken with Europe; Canada had never identified herself solely with the Western Hemisphere. British North America had, in fact, consciously stood aloof from the familiar, commonplace western revolutionary movement, which had been originated by the United States, and faithfully copied by every duodecimo South American republic." Canada instead had struggled to preserve its identity against the levelling impact of American continentalism and, to a large extent, its success had been attributable to the maintenance of her vital connection with Britain and Europe.[1]*

Creighton's anti-American words must have heartened those in the audience of historians who agreed with him, and Diefenbaker's election suggested very briefly that the clock might yet be rolled back. But Diefenbaker, a weak reed, would be gone by 1963, and the Liberals would regain power once more. If the United States administration had expected the Canadian weather to calm, however, this was not to be. Canada was caught up in a new and self-conscious nationalism and, as so often was the case, Canadian nationalism equalled anti-Americanism. The new Liberal government's Minister of Finance, with some Creightonian elements in his make-up, was setting the tone. Walter Gordon, his plans and budget papers at the ready, was set to take on Wall Street and Washington.

---

* One of Creighton's public lectures in March 1957, ostensibly on Macdonald, had been so anti-American in its attacks on current American policy that the United States Embassy in Ottawa felt compelled to report on it to Washington out of fear that it was "a portent of things to come." Quoted in John English, *The Worldly Years: The Life of Lester Pearson 1949–1972* (Toronto 1992), 191.

* * *

Born in 1906 "with a silver adding machine in his hands," Walter Gordon was an unlikely man to rally the country against American investment. His parents were Toronto aristocrats, his father the leading figure in Clarkson, Gordon, English Canada's major accounting firm, and a stalwart of the militia. Gordon himself attended Upper Canada College and the Royal Military College, the key establishment schools of the era, and he joined the family firm in 1927, eventually branching out into consulting. During the Second World War, he worked in Ottawa for the Foreign Exchange Control Board and, as an aide to Finance Minister J.L. Ilsley, he was instrumental in devising the federal-provincial formula that let Ottawa find the revenues it needed to fight the war. His friends in the mandarinate were also gratified by his stewardship of the Royal Commission on Administrative Classification in the Public Service, a complex name for a commission whose main intent was to raise the salaries of the most senior public servants.

Gordon became a very wealthy man in his own right after the war as his consulting business grew rapidly, and he was prominent enough to be asked to join the Cabinet of Louis St Laurent in 1954. He had declined the proposal, however, because it was clear that no senior portfolio was on offer and because he would not be able to advance issues dear to his heart in a Cabinet dominated by the "Minister of Everything," C.D. Howe, the American-born millionaire who had been in control of Canadian economic and industrial policy since 1940. The issue that had come to concern Gordon, an issue that did not upset Howe, was the extent of American investment in Canada, particularly in the years after the Second World War.

In the late 1940s and early 1950s, Gordon had begun to be troubled by the "complacency with which Canadians were witnessing the sell-out of our resources and business enterprises to Americans and other enterprising foreigners," and he decided to join the debate on the question, hitherto spearheaded by the Labour Progressive Party to which little attention was paid. He drafted an article calling for a royal commission to inquire into the nation's economic policies for the *International Journal,* the quarterly journal of the Canadian Institute of International Affairs, but sent it to friends in Ottawa before publication. The article was destined never to appear in print, but it resulted in the Liberal government asking Gordon to head the Royal Commission on Canada's Economic Prospects in April 1955.

Drawing on the assistance of specialists in government departments, the Bank of Canada, and academe, Gordon marshalled an array of data and evidence as he attempted to forecast the future of Canada's economic growth and development. For a Liberal government, in power since 1935 but increasingly under attack on a host of fronts, Gordon's Commission held out the prospect of new policies and political renewal. The *Preliminary Report* was delivered to the Cabinet in December 1956 and made public early the next month.

Gordon's Report offered recommendations on a host of issues, including university education, energy policy, and tariff policy, and inflammatory suggestions that the Atlantic provinces were not economically viable and might face depopulation. What struck the most sparks, however, was what he had to say about foreign investment. Canada had historically welcomed foreign investment and had benefited from it. But the amount of money pouring into the country was worrisome, particularly its concentration in certain key sectors of the economy, in which decision-making could easily fall into the hands of non-Canadians. Foreign companies in Canada were subject to domestic laws, and there was little evidence they were acting against the nation's best interests, but circumstances could change.

Gordon's solutions seemed as mild as his analysis. He wanted foreign-owned companies to employ Canadians in senior positions and to give full disclosure of their Canadian operations in financial statements. He wanted the larger Canadian subsidiaries to sell a substantial interest (say 25 percent) of their stock to Canadians and to be denied tax concessions if they failed to do so. And he proposed higher withholding taxes on dividends paid by foreign subsidiaries to their parent corporations. He expected foreign corporations to include Canadians on their boards, and the continuing Canadian control of banks and insurance companies had to be guaranteed.

Appearing just months after the Pipeline debate* had highlighted the St

---

* The St Laurent government had committed itself to finance at least half the cost of a transcontinental gas pipeline—"that obscene parody of the trans-Canada rail lines," nationalist writer Dave Godfrey called it—owned by three US corporations, providing shares were offered to Canadians. The issue, thanks to C.D. Howe's attempts to ramrod it through Parliament in May and June 1956 with the use of closure, became one of the most rancorous debates in parliamentary history and an enormous *cause célèbre* that contributed greatly to the public perception of the St Laurent government's arrogance and too-close links with American capital. See William Kilbourn, *Pipeline* (Toronto 1970); D. Godfrey and Mel Watkins, eds., *Gordon to Watkins to You* (Toronto 1970).

Laurent government's apparent economic subservience to US interests, the Gordon Report met a cool response from senior Liberals and, predictably, from the American interests that might be affected by it. The

"Hi, there . . . we're taking over your resources . . . know of any in this area which have been overlooked?"

American Embassy in Ottawa summarized its contents for Washington and reported bluntly that "the Commission's proposals would principally affect United States investment in Canada. They are not only discriminatory but appear unrealistic and impractical."[2]

That view seemed to be generally shared by business circles and the press across the country. John Deutsch, the former senior official in the Finance Department who had almost pulled off a free trade agreement with the United States in 1948 and who in 1957 was a professor of economics at the University of British Columbia, privately called the proposals "half baked."[3] The *Winnipeg Free Press* spoke of the Royal Commission's "apparent determination to find at all costs some ways of hitting at American investment," and denounced the proposed tax treatment of foreign corporations as "fundamentally illiberal in principle." The *Globe and Mail* argued that there was not "enough market in Canada to absorb one-fifth or one-quarter of the combined shares of all the subsidiaries." Even the *Toronto Star* found the proposals "pretty stiff," and the *Winnipeg Tribune* called them arbitrary. The representatives of the Canadian financial élites, in other words, pronounced the Gordon recommendations a threat to the way Canadians had come to do business in a world dominated by Wall Street.

American Ambassador Livingston Merchant was not backward in his comments either. In an interview with the *New York Times* on January 23, 1957, he said that the problem of foreign investment was one of Canada's own creation. He added reassuringly, "there is no sinister and no governmental design behind either our exports or our investments in Canada." More to the point, the US Embassy reported authoritatively that the Liberal government's reaction to the study it had commissioned was lukewarm. St Laurent and Howe were opposed to discriminatory measures, and the latter, "it is understood, has taken violent exception" to many of the recommendations.[4] So did some senior civil servants who, echoing the *Globe and Mail*, told embassy officials that measures such as Gordon suggested would place Canada in the "banana republic" class.[5]

The problem of foreign investment would soon be Diefenbaker's to manage, as the St Laurent government fell from power in 1957 and the Progressive Conservatives took office with a minority government. The Tories in opposition had loudly sounded the nationalist note, their instincts stimulated by the favourable reaction their attack on the Liberals during the Pipeline debate had received. While still in Opposition in Parliament, Diefenbaker had seemed to support the Gordon proposals, using them as a stick to beat St Laurent's ministers who had so pointedly refrained from endorsing them. The Conservative Party's research office, while applauding the *Preliminary Report*'s "sound recommendations," noted that "it is not a report which the Conservatives would wish to make their own."[6]

Certainly, the Diefenbaker government did very little to enhance Canadian ownership or to resist US investment in its six years in office. In 1957 Diefenbaker put in place a tax on advertising in split-run editions of American periodicals but, in the face of protests from Washington, he cancelled it the next year. He made a speech or two that talked of the extent of American investment, but in policy terms his government did little other than forbid foreign takeovers of domestic insurance companies, perhaps reflecting the anti-nationalist policies espoused by his Finance Minister, Toronto MP Donald Fleming. There was, moreover, as the polls suggested, substantial public support for foreign investment (54 percent on January 22, 1958), and almost no opposition to it (only 3 percent).

In 1959 the Conservative government cancelled production of the CF-105, the Avro Arrow, replacing this high-powered and Canadian-designed jet interceptor with US-made Bomarc surface-to-air missiles and eventually also with American CF-101 Voodoo jet fighters. The Arrow's cancellation led to the break-up of a first-rate design and engineering team, to the layoff of 14,000 workers in Toronto, and to an extraordinary nationalist uproar at this sacrifice of Canadian military technology that, amazingly, persists to this day in plays, poetry, fiction, and in pseudo-histories, replete with absurdist charges that the Americans were responsible for killing the project because the Arrow was able to shoot down their high-flying U-2 spy aircraft. (The only American role was to refuse to buy the aircraft, because their own fighters were equally good and American firms wanted the business.) Diefenbaker had made the correct decision—the Arrow was too expensive for a small country to build on its own and probably not as effective as its proponents claimed—but it damaged the government's purported nationalist credentials.

The same point was made in 1961 when the government moved to force out the Governor of the Bank of Canada, the independent-minded and ardently nationalistic James Coyne. He had been speaking across the country in support of the bank's anti-inflationary policy of high-interest rates and attacking the domination of the country's economic activity by foreign corporations. In an address in his home town of Winnipeg early in 1960, Coyne had denounced the nation's "growing deficit in our international balance of payments, a large excess of imports . . . over our exports, increasing reliance on foreign resources to finance (directly and indirectly) both capital projects and consumption, and a great increase in our foreign debt." In other talks, he referred to "foreign domination," and called on Canadians to live within their means: "a country which has reached Canada's stage of development can make better progress, and retain more control over its own destiny, by relying on its own savings to provide the necessary capital." Coyne did not single out American investment, but everyone understood what he meant, given the high percentage of US ownership in key sectors of the economy. At once horrified and bemused by the Governor's calculated outbursts, Walter Gordon told Liberal leader Lester Pearson that Coyne's talks amounted to the bluntest, most outspoken and devastating critiques of government policy ever made by a civil servant in Canada.[7]

Finance Minister Donald Fleming appeared to agree. He could not abide Coyne's nationalist proposals and criticisms, but, in an attempt to make foreign investment in Canada less attractive, his 1961 budget imposed a 15 percent withholding tax on dividend and interest payments to non-residents and subjected the profits of unincorporated American corporations to the same levy. Nonetheless, once the Bank of Canada directors increased Coyne's pension to half his salary, Diefenbaker and Fleming seized the moment and moved to sack him. Coyne resisted the government's clumsy attempts to suggest that he had acted in an underhand way, and the affair caused a huge uproar in Parliament and the press. The Liberal opposition gleefully exploited the ruckus, although it did not share all of Coyne's views. After a Senate committee hearing concluded that he had acted with complete propriety on the pension question, Coyne resigned office, vindicated. He left the Diefenbaker government on the ropes, its stewardship of a Canadian economy wracked by slow growth and high unemployment very much in question.

Conservative bungling provided the ideal opportunity for both Pearson and Gordon. The two men had been friends since the mid-1930s, and when Pearson made the jump from the safety of the senior civil service into the uncertainties of politics in 1948, Gordon raised money in the private sector to make up for the loss of Pearson's public service pension. In 1958, after the Diefenbaker victory of June 1957, Pearson decided to seek the party leadership in succession to St Laurent. He did nothing to organize his campaign, however, seeming to assume that his recent Nobel Peace Prize guaranteed him the post. Again Gordon stepped in to find the money ($3000 was all it took, he wrote) and to organize the troops to secure the leadership for his friend. It turned out be a poisoned chalice in the short term as the Liberals were smashed in the 1958 election and reduced to forty-nine seats. Inevitably, Gordon found himself drawn into active politics as he worked to restore Canadian Liberalism.

For Gordon, Liberalism in the 1960s could not be nearly as continentalist in economic and diplomatic policy as it had been in the 1950s. The Pearson party, the eventual Pearson government, had to be nationalist and pro-Canadian. "I am unhappy about the gradual economic and financial take-over by the United States, or rather the owners of United States capital," Gordon told Pearson in March 1960, and "I would wish to urge some modest steps to counteract" it.[8]

Deeply indebted to Gordon for his personal financial security and his party leadership and more expert in foreign than in domestic policy, Pearson agreed that this thrust was necessary. He had been one of the few St Laurent Cabinet ministers to support Gordon's Royal Commission recommendations, and now he accepted Gordon's direction of the party's economic policy when the Toronto consultant agreed to enter active politics. Gordon's memorandum of their conversation on July 14, 1960, noted their bargain: "He said he agreed *completely* with my ideas. He repeated this two or three times saying that this is exactly how he feels on these various issues." "I was against a continental approach, which I believed would lead to our political absorption by the United States," Gordon added later. "Pearson assured me that he agreed with this conclusion and I believed him."[9]

Gordon took his views public when he published a short book in 1961, *Troubled Canada: The Need for New Domestic Policies*. "Frankly polemical," as Gordon later admitted cheerfully, the book denounced the Diefenbaker government for its economic policies, not least its failure to do anything about the increasing foreign control of the economy. Foreign investments in Canada totalled $22.3 billion in 1960, Gordon noted, and American interests in 1958 controlled 44 percent of all manufacturing, 69 percent of the oil industry, and 51 percent of the mining industry. Worse, the percentages of foreign control had increased over the last decade, thanks in part to the favourable tax treatment the United States gave its investors for their operations abroad. Gordon acknowledged that foreign investment was not all bad—it had developed Canada faster than its own citizens could have done; it gave the country scientific, technical, and managerial knowhow; and it provided assured markets for some Canadian products.

He maintained, however, that there were serious disadvantages in Canada's dependence on American capital. US corporations in Canada were expected by Washington's policy makers to conform to US laws, and there was always the risk that the parent company might object to its Canadian subsidiary seeking export markets that could compete with the plant in Pittsburgh or Los Angeles. The real concern, though, just as he had stated in his Commission report, was that American investment "might lead to economic domination by the United States and eventually to the loss of our political independence." The Diefenbaker government had done nothing to deal with this concern,

Gordon wrote, probably because opinion in the Progressive Conservative Party and in the country was divided on the worth of foreign investment. As he admitted, some economists and government officials "do not think the increasing control of Canadian industry is actually or potentially a bad thing." Some argue that "a greater integration of the economies of Canada and the United States is desirable and in any case inevitable in the long run."* Gordon certainly did not agree, for he firmly believed "that Canada as a separate and independent nation will be able to do more for its own citizens . . . and more for the world at large than she could do as a dependency, even a semi-autonomous dependency of any other country." *Troubled Canada* made clear, though without much detail, that a Liberal government should move to redress the advantages foreign capital enjoyed in Canada, and to offer tax incentives for Canadians to invest in Canada and for corporations to expand. Gordon also proposed a National Development Corporation to invest in long-term large-scale economic projects that might not produce a return for some time. Above all, he attacked the Diefenbaker government for its timidity, its fears "that any move to reverse the present trend would provoke protests from those affected and from the United States authorities."

When the Liberals came narrowly to power in April 1963 after the Diefenbaker government collapsed, Gordon, the leading architect of Pearson's minority government victory, became Minister of Finance, and Pearson willingly handed his friend the chance to implement his policy prescriptions. Gordon would have the opportunity to test the willingness of Canadian business and of Washington to accept a program of economic nationalism.

*   *   *

There is little reason to believe that Walter Gordon was anti-American when he became Finance Minister. He knew the United States well and

---

* In fact, most Canadian economists believed that foreign investment was a good thing for Canada and many had vigorously opposed James Coyne's policy speeches. Harry G. Johnson, one of the "towering figures in Canadian economics," noted in 1965 that he believed that "closer integration of the two economies into one continental economy would be beneficial in both countries, and would involve no loss of any Canadian nationalist objectives worth pursuing." Quoted in Stephen Clarkson, "Anti-Nationalism in Canada: The Ideology of Mainstream Economics," *Canadian Review of Studies in Nationalism* 5 (Spring 1978): 47.

liked Americans. He appreciated the generosity the United States had shown its friends in the Lend-Lease Act of 1941 and the Marshall Plan in 1948, and he understood how dependent Canada was on the Americans both for its defence and its economic well-being. More than two-thirds of Canada's trade was with the United States, moreover, and Gordon's general support for freer trade indicated that he was no advocate of closed borders. But he was acutely aware of all the cultural, economic, political, and military influences exercised by the superpower with which Canada shared the continent, and he worried about the extraordinary dynamism of that acquisitive society as its citizens and corporations pressed ever outwards, invariably backed by the full weight of their government in Washington. Gordon feared that many of the key figures of his generation, the leaders of Canadian corporations, no longer believed that Canadian independence could exist in the face of such American power, and, in his view, many no longer even fretted about this outcome. Gordon did. He was a Canadian, not an American, and his task as Minister of Finance, as he perceived it, was to enhance national independence wherever he could, to preserve what still could be preserved of Canada's ability to decide its fate for itself. In other words, as novelist Hugh MacLennan put it, Gordon's attitude was one of "no cheap anti-American tirades, but a firm and dignified determination to do the best we can."[10] Whether this would be good enough, whether this attitude could survive his time in office, remained to be demonstrated.

Certainly Gordon's time as Finance Minister was troubled. The Pearson Liberals came to power crowing about their experience and their decisiveness, the characteristics that would set them apart from and above the appalling dithering that had characterized Diefenbaker's government. To showcase this trait, the Liberals had campaigned on the promise of "Sixty Days of Decision," a pledge to implement major policy changes within two months of taking office. The Liberals had also portrayed themselves to the electorate as a highly competent team, one that could manage the affairs of state in a businesslike manner. Walter Gordon, the successful businessman, was the epitome of this approach.

But Gordon was the first minister to fall. To help prepare his budget within the sixty-day limit, Gordon brought in some outsiders to assist the Finance Department staff in whom he had little confidence; once it became known, this apparent violation of the strict rules of budget secrecy opened the Minister to a vicious assault from the opposition that greatly weakened Gordon's reputation for omniscient competence.

The budget had been cleared with the Prime Minister and presented in only a bare-bones fashion to Cabinet, in keeping with the practices of the day. Although civil servants had criticized some of its provisions before it was presented to Parliament on June 13, the fifty-third day of decision, and Louis Rasminsky, Governor of the Bank of Canada, had warned that the nationalist measures it contained might provoke "massive attempts at liquidation" of foreign investments,[11] no one seemed to have anticipated the fierce storm that broke.

Gordon's budget consciously set out to begin the process of rescuing Canada from foreign control—most particularly, American control. The Minister levied a heavy 30 percent takeover tax on sales of shares in Canadian companies to non-residents; reduced the 15 percent withholding tax on dividends paid to non-residents by 5 percent for companies that were at least one-quarter Canadian owned, and increased the tax by 5 percent for those with a lower proportion of domestic ownership; and improved the depreciation allowance for companies with more than 25 percent Canadian ownership. The gauntlet had been thrown in the face of American investors.

The immediate response to the budget was relatively benign, even favourable, but the storm of protest began within a few days. Canadian business leaders denounced the budget measures that threatened to impede their plans to sell corporations to American interests or to interrupt the flow of foreign investment northwards. On June 18 the president of the Montreal Stock Exchange, Eric Kierans (later a notably nationalist federal Liberal Cabinet minister), declared that the takeover tax was "based on a serious error" and "complete and utter nonsense," adding for good measure that "the financial capitals of the world have had enough from Canada." Kierans's intemperate comments and his implicit urgings to stockholders to sell short their shares in Canadian corporations threw the stock markets into near panic, and the next day a rattled Gordon withdrew the takeover tax because of what he euphemistically termed "certain administrative difficulties." It had become startlingly obvious that Gordon had neither the business élite—his own class—nor the press behind him. On June 20 he offered his resignation to the Prime Minister. Out of loyalty, Pearson refused to accept it, although he sounded out possible successors before making up his mind. Thus, still saddled with the duties of his office, Gordon was obliged to withdraw or change additional budget measures by July 8. Battered and bruised, his authority and prestige in tatters, the Minister had been transformed from the unchallenged powerhouse of the government into a liability. The heralded Sixty Days of Decision had ended in disaster.

The Kennedy administration was furious with Gordon's budget provisions, in substantial part because Canada had not advised Washington what was coming. Pearson and Kennedy had met in May at Kennedy's home at Hyannisport, Massachusetts, and, while the Prime Minister had said that some measures on investment were being contemplated, he had not given the impression, one senior State Department official later wrote, "that any measures were contemplated which would affect United States investment so directly."[12]

While not conclusive, the evidence strongly suggests that the Americans decided to teach the Pearson government a lesson, much as they had been obliged to do to his predecessor when the State Department's press release in January 1963 brought down an already wounded government. When the Kennedy administration proposed in July that restrictive measures be applied to foreign borrowing in the United States, measures designed to confront their growing balance of payments deficit, the Canadian government had to scramble desperately to deal with a policy that threatened to have calamitous effects on the national economy. While the *Globe and Mail* on July 20 proclaimed that the American measures created "confusion, uncertainty and fear" in government and business circles, the US government played its hand quietly. There was no retaliation here, the State Department told the Canadian Ambassador with a straight face, only the need to meet an urgent domestic situation. Of course, the United States had shown great restraint in its reaction to Gordon's budgetary measures, the official felt obliged to add.[13] Facing the certainty of a financial crisis and the almost certain devaluation of the dollar, a humiliated Gordon had to send officials south to plead for an exemption. The Americans graciously conceded after listening to the delegation's urgent requests. The appropriate lessons were drawn. As the Assistant Deputy Minister of Finance told a meeting of both countries' officials, Canadians had been "seriously disturbed by this reminder of dependence" on the United States.[14] Gordon himself later noted ruefully that "we had been given another sharp reminder of Canada's dependency upon the United States." Like Diefenbaker, he had discovered that Canada's independence was constrained by its position in North America.

This succession of débâcles in the first months of the new government inevitably weakened support in the Liberal Party for economic nationalism, but Gordon hung on as Finance Minister into 1965, trying to restore his political fortunes. Although he raised the Canada Development Corporation idea again in the 1965 budget, his fiscal prescriptions after 1963 generally tended towards the orthodox. Nationalist principles went out the window when the government, trying to implement the recommendations of a 1961 royal commission to control the amount of Canadian advertising printed in split runs of American periodicals in Canada, had to exempt *Time* and *Reader's Digest*, the two most powerful and profitable, from its legislation. In Gordon's view, this kowtowing resulted from the extraordinary pressure exerted on behalf of the two publishing empires by the US government, most notably a threat by *Time*'s Henry Luce to use his influence in Congress to block the agreement on automobile trade reached early in 1965 between Canada and the United States. "I did not like the *Time* exemption any more than they did," Gordon bluntly told the Liberal caucus, "but this was the price we had to pay to get approval of the automotive agreement."[15] Journalist Peter C. Newman wrote to a friend that "Walter Gordon told me that the pressure Time and the Digest put up against any laws that would have endangered their magazine monopoly here was just fantastic. Nothing, not even if we'd sent tanks armed with nuclear warheads to Castro, could have got the Americans madder. And significantly, the Canadian government backed down before the power of Time Inc.!"[16]

The Auto Pact, a modified free trade agreement covering automobiles and auto parts, came into effect in 1965. Gordon was happy with the deal's potential impact on the country's balance of payments and employment prospects, but much less pleased at the degree of continental integration in a critical sector. As Gordon's biographer noted, "The paradox was that this undoubted economic gain tied Canada more intimately than ever to the American economy and further reduced her bargaining power." The possibility, never realistic, of an indigenous auto industry was gone for good after the Auto Pact.

What finished Gordon politically was not his economic policies but his partisan advice. His strong urgings to Pearson for an election in 1965 produced yet another minority government, with an increasingly erratic but skilful Diefenbaker remaining in opposition ready to disrupt the government's efforts on every score. Gordon accepted the blame for his faulty advice, resigning his portfolio. With Gordon gone, the economic nationalist cause within the Liberal government was grievously weakened. In his place as Finance Minister was Mitchell Sharp, a Toronto MP and former senior public servant who shared few of Gordon's sharp reactions to continentalism.

Gordon was not yet finished with active politics. He still had his supporters in the Liberal caucus and party, men and women who remembered his critical role in rebuilding Liberalism after the defeats of 1957 and 1958 and who shared his nationalist agenda. In another book, *A Choice for Canada*, written in 1966 while he was sitting restively on the backbenches, he reiterated his views on foreign investment, calling strongly for more independent Canadian policies. "We still have a choice," he wrote. "We can do the things that are necessary to regain control of our economy and thus maintain our independence. Or we can acquiesce in becoming a colonial dependency of the United States, with no future except the hope of eventual absorption."* He also carried his message across the country, striking responsive chords in university audiences with his call for Canada to reduce the percentage of foreign control in its principal industries to one-third or less by the year 2000.

Unlike his audience, Gordon was relatively moderate on foreign investment. More in tune with student attitudes was Cy Gonick, the editor of the leftist monthly *Canadian Dimension*, who was cheered at a Montreal conference in March 1967 when he argued that Canada should copy Fidel Castro's tactics and take over the whole American-owned complex without compensation. George V. Ferguson of the *Montreal Star*, present at the session, noted in his newspaper on March 6, 1967, that similar enthusiasm greeted a comment that Canadians had other aims than crass materialism. "They better have," he noted, "if this tack is ever seriously pursued."

The Liberal Party itself was badly torn on nationalist questions. At a party policy conference in October 1966, debate focused on a series of economic nationalist resolutions that Gordon had prepared. Perceived by the media as a battle between Gordon on one side and Mitchell Sharp and Robert Winters, the Minister of Trade and Commerce, on the other, the convention proved a major defeat for Gordon and his friends. Sharp noted later that his views were more acceptable "because they better reflected the attitude of Liberals throughout the country. Liberals are a

---

* Writing in 1966, John T. McLeod said of Gordon's book that it had "caused a fuss disproportionate to its merits; as someone said, there's less to this than meets the eye. Gordon says our problem is American broccolli [sic]. I say it's spinach, and I say the hell with it." "Moses with a Maple-Leaf," *Saturday Night* (July 1966) 24.

patriotic lot. Not all of them, however, equate patriotism with economic nationalism of the kind espoused by Gordon and his followers."[17]*

Disheartened by his defeat at the conference, Gordon prepared to resign his seat in Parliament. Pearson, however, was warned that losing Gordon, the party's pre-eminent nationalist, one of its few members who could reach young people and who had active supporters among younger Liberal MPs, would send the wrong signals at a time when the New Democratic Party was gaining strength. In January 1967 Pearson prevailed on Gordon to re-enter the Cabinet as President of the Privy Council. At Gordon's insistence, the Prime Minister gave him responsibility for supervising the preparation of a

* Ironically, Sharp would later oppose the Mulroney government's Free Trade Agreement, while Donald S. Macdonald, a key Gordon supporter, would be one of its main proponents.

task-force study on foreign investment in Canada—"to be debated and then followed by legislation," Gordon noted. "Mike realizes the importance of the foreign control issue (he has always been a nationalist at heart)." The government "would have to mean business—and we would have to hurry if we are to offset the NDP and the Tories on this issue."[18] The subsequent "Watkins Report" of January 1968, named after economist Melville Watkins of the University of Toronto who as chair shepherded eight economists into a unanimous report, demonstrated the very substantial extent of American economic control. (Contrarily, Watkins also showed that the country's dependence on foreign investment had been declining as domestic savings increased.) Very little would come of the report, however, but the reception it received from the nationalist left in the Liberal and New Democratic parties played into the powerful sense of Canadian nationalism fanned in English Canada by the well-funded Centennial celebrations of 1967— everything from arenas, statues, and some 300 subsidized books to the highly successful Expo 67. As well, there was growing opposition to the United States' role in the Vietnam War.

Gordon also involved himself vigorously in the fight over the Mercantile Bank, a small Dutch-owned bank that had been purchased by the Rockefellers' giant Citibank, the First National City Bank of New York. Canadian banks did business in the United States and elsewhere, but the domestic market was their private preserve. Mercantile was the only foreign-owned bank in Canada, a tribute to the substantial power exercised by the Canadian banks in protecting their monopoly position. As Finance Minister, Gordon had tried to keep it that way, warning off the Americans in no uncertain terms. Confident of its power, Citibank decided to proceed, and it purchased all of Mercantile's shares. Gordon then included provisions in the decennial revision of the Bank Act to prevent Mercantile's growth so long as Citibank owned more than 10 percent of its shares. But the revisions to the act had died on the order paper when the 1965 election was called. Mitchell Sharp, who claimed to understand that "one of the greatest threats to Canada's freedom of action is our dependence on massive imports of foreign capital,"[19] nonetheless lacked Gordon's emotional and political commitment to keeping the Rockefeller interests out of Canadian banking.

The US government, through the Secretary and Undersecretary of the Treasury, made strong representations to the Canadian Embassy, and the American Embassy in Ottawa vigorously lobbied on Citibank's behalf when the Bank Act revisions again were under consideration. In negotiations with Sharp around the time of his return to Cabinet, Gordon made a deal that, he believed, would see Mercantile hamstrung. Sharp reneged, in Gordon's view, but the Cabinet supported the President of the Privy Council. The Finance Minister nonetheless let Mercantile violate the Cabinet decision. Only a "flaming row in Cabinet,"[20] Gordon wrote in a private memorandum at the time, restored matters to the agreed position, and the Bank Act was revised to constrain Citibank's operations north of the border. Gordon had won the day—for the time being only, since the Trudeau government would soon allow Mercantile to operate under limited restrictions—but the astonishing support that Mercantile had been able to muster demonstrated anew the strength of powerful American interests.

Such struggles over Canadian economic independence increased Gordon's concerns about the power exercised by the United States in Canada and elsewhere in the world. The Vietnam War saw the United States steadily increasing its military involvement (while Canadian factories cashed in on the fighting by selling ever more war *matériel* to the US armed forces). Gordon had long been worried by what he saw as the aggressiveness of American foreign policy. In 1960 he had told a conference in the United States that Canadians were "unhappy about the Far Eastern policy of the United States. We think it is too inflexible."[21] Vietnam brought those concerns to the fore again more pointedly, and Gordon's confrontations with American power after 1963 had heightened his concerns over the course the United States was pursuing in Southeast Asia.

Gordon decided to go public. On May 13, 1967, he told a Toronto audience that the Canadian government had to press the United States to halt its bombings of North Vietnam and its offensive operations in the South. If Canada did not do everything it could to pressure the Americans, "we must be prepared to share the responsibility of those whose policies and actions are destroying a poor but determined people. We must share the responsibility of those whose policies involve the gravest risks for all mankind." The press shouted that Gordon "threw a political haymaker" by "denouncing" American policy in Vietnam and "deploring" Canada's attitude to it. Although Gordon claimed that Pearson privately agreed with "ninety-eight percent" of what he had said, the Prime Minister slapped the unrepentant Gordon down both in private and in public. At least, "we can now hold our heads up which is worth something in itself," Gordon said in a private memorandum that revealed his frustration at what he believed was Canada's craven attitude to the Americans' brutal, bloody war. Surprisingly, Pearson did not force Gordon from the Cabinet, perhaps because comment from citizens' mail and the press was so positive.

As a result, Gordon felt free to question Canada's continued membership in the North American Air Defence Command and to raise questions in Cabinet and with officials of the Department of External Affairs about the character of the country's role in NATO. Gordon's nationalist critique had thus broadened from foreign investment to key aspects of Canada's American-oriented foreign policy, and when the government decided in February 1967 to renew the NORAD agreement by a simple exchange of notes with the United States, Gordon resigned his portfolio: "I could not in good conscience approve the NORAD extension in the light of what is happening in Vietnam and . . . I resigned as soon as the Watkins report came out to underline the fact that that was all I was staying for."[22]

Pierre Trudeau succeeded Pearson as prime minister in the spring of 1968. But Trudeau was a convinced anti-nationalist, and his government initially proved less sympathetic to economic nationalism than the previous administration. Not even the preparation of yet another Cabinet study of foreign investment, the Gray Report of 1971, moved him towards action.* Frustrated and angry (in part because he had

---

* A copy of the Gray Report, a Cabinet memorandum entitled "Domestic Control of the National Economic Environment: The Problems of Foreign Ownership and Control" and dated May 1971, fell into the hands of the *Canadian Forum*, a small nationalist and left-of-centre monthly then edited by Abraham Rotstein. The *Forum*, with foolhardy courage in the face of the Official Secrets Act (I was a member of the Editorial Board and my recollection is that I was the only one who had ever heard of the Act!), decided to publish the document and devoted the entire issue of November 1971 to this purpose. The November issue was turned into a book, *The Gray Report* (Toronto 1971), which appeared shortly thereafter. The resulting furore made headlines and put substantial pressure on the Trudeau government, though the administration took no action against the *Forum*. The resulting publicity caused such a flood of subscriptions that its creaky administrative machinery almost collapsed. I well remember three or four of us spending a weekend opening hundreds upon hundreds of letters with cheques and trying to process subscriptions. That probably set back the *Forum*'s administrative processes even further.

Rusins/The Citizen/National Archives of Canada C-143279

endorsed Trudeau in the belief he was sympathetic to controlling foreign investment), Gordon, along with Peter C. Newman of the *Toronto Star* and University of Toronto economist Abraham Rotstein, threw himself into organizing the Committee for an Independent Canada, a strongly pro-Canadian—but not overtly anti-American—extraparliamentary group that drew adherents from all parties. The CIC was financed mostly with Gordon's money and boosted as well by support from the increasingly nationalist *Toronto Star*, with which he had close connections. "I wrote the CIC's manifesto at my editor's desk," Newman said years later, "and *shamelessly* used the paper to promote our cause." The committee secured some 170,000 signatures in a few months and increased the public perception—or so opinion polls suggested—that American ownership of Canadian corporations was a "bad" thing. A poll in October 1970 showed that 46 percent of Canadians wanted to "buy back" control of foreign-held companies. Some writers carried the argument further still. Toronto businessman Glen Frankfurter wrote in 1971 that "Canadians should constantly remember that in negotiating with the only nation that has repeatedly attacked us on our own soil and daily exerts the crudest kind of pressure on our Government, the pistol is always on the table alongside the brief. We had better have a little powder of our own handy and make sure that it is dry."[23] Walter Gordon, who could count troops and assess power, would never have shared those perfervid sentiments.

The Committee for an Independent Canada lasted a decade and helped to create the atmosphere in which Trudeau's government established the Canada Development Corporation in 1971 to "buy back" Canada, the Foreign Investment Review Agency in 1973 to ensure that foreign investment would be beneficial to the country, and the National Energy Program in 1980 that tried to take control of the oil and gas sectors. Certainly FIRA did not satisfy the furious Gordon, to whom it was a "repudiation" of the Gray Report and an agency completely inadequate to deal with "the Canadian independence issue." Nor did he seem much more pleased with the government's "Third Option," a program introduced by Mitchell Sharp, now of External Affairs, just prior to the 1972 election and designed to enhance economic links with the European Community and Japan and to reduce Canada's dependence on the United States. The program failed, done in by apathy on the part of business, which found Americans easier to deal with than Europeans or Asians, and the profound lack of interest of the public service.

The simple fact was that, by the 1960s and 1970s, most of the Canadian political and business élites did not see American control as an impediment to their operations or their profits. In precisely the same way it had seen Diefenbaker's anti-American foreign policy as harmful, business viewed the nationalist policies put forward by the Liberals as foolish protectionist efforts that pandered to the anti-Americanism of Canadians. Corporate hostility would eventually override the nationalists in government. As Gordon put it, "we seem destined to lose our independence and eventually to become part of the United States. Most Canadians do not

want this," he added, confident that opinion polls supported his assertion.* "But our leaders seem quite unable to comprehend the implications of trends that, if not soon reversed, will lead inevitably to the
break-up of our country."[24]

Implicit in Gordon's lament for his nation was the thought that
American economic control and Quebec independence sentiment
seemed to intersect. In the 1960s and 1970s anti-Americanism was a
marginal presence in Québécois thinking, especially on economic and
foreign investment questions. That was one difference between francophone and anglophone Canada. Then, American economic and cultural dominance in Canada had so weakened the national identity that
English Canada, profoundly unsure of what it was, seemed unable to
answer Quebec's increasingly particularist and nationalist demands effectively. What Ottawa was to Quebec, in other words, the United States
was to Ottawa. Perhaps it was simply that American control had left
Canadians with an inferiority complex that hindered any serious attempt
at a resolution of the Quebec question. Perhaps the American (and
English–Canadian) control of industry in Quebec had kept francophones
out of the top corporate positions, thus fostering the sense of grievance.
And just as the Canadian government was unwilling or unable to tackle
the problem of American investment in English Canada, so it could do
nothing to resolve it in Quebec. The result was a widespread demoral-
ization at being controlled by foreigners; Quebeckers, of course, had had
that problem longer than their English-speaking compatriots, and the
Quiet Revolution under Jean Lesage had begun the process of securing
political and economic control for *Québécois de souche*. In the process,

---

* Opinion sampling showed that those saying Canada had enough US capital
increased from 46 percent in 1964 to 67 percent in 1972, while those who
thought US ownership of Canadian companies was "bad" for Canada rose from
34 percent in 1969 to 47 percent in 1972. Support for the "bad" choice rose
from east to west. Cited in J. Fayerweather, *Foreign Investment in Canada*
(Toronto 1974), 14; J.A. Murray and M.C. Gerace, "Canadian Attitudes toward
the US Presence," *Public Opinion Quarterly*, 36 (Fall 1972): 390. There were
polls and polls, however. *Maclean's* published one on June 6, 1964, which
demonstrated that while large majorities all across the country (from 60 percent
in the Maritimes to 80 percent in Quebec) wanted to restrict American takeovers
of Canadian firms, 65 percent nonetheless favoured economic union between
Canada and the United States!

Canada frequently seemed on the verge of splitting apart. The Anglos, Québécois seemed to be saying, could allow themselves to be turned into Americans, but not us.

Disappointed and saddened by his experiences in politics, Walter Gordon was never a conventional anti-American, though the policies he advocated fed the sentiment in many others who were less balanced than he. His attitudes were and remained liberal and Liberal, and he came from the class that had never suffered from any shortages or had any reason to fear capital, Canadian or American. But Gordon had repeatedly come up against the economic and political power of the United States, and the beatings he sustained when he was Finance Minister had toughened his rhetoric to the point that it sometimes verged on conventional anti-Americanism.

He did not blame the United States for its position of predominance in Canada, and he continued to reject the label anti-American. As he told one correspondent, "It is our fault, not that of the Americans, that they have been encouraged to acquire so much of the resources of this country and the influence that goes with it."[25] In yet another book, *Storm Signals,* he wrote that Canadian foreign policy "never should be permitted to take on anti-American overtones. The Americans are our friends and allies. We are lucky indeed to have them for our neighbours," but "this does not mean we should allow them to dominate us in the economic or any other fields." For Gordon, Canada's situation was much as the "people's poet," Joe Wallace, had described it years before: "Ours is a sovereign nation/ Bows to no foreign will/ But whenever they cough in Washington/ They spit on Parliament Hill."

The policies he supported might have been anti-American in their intent, but Gordon was not a typical Canadian anti-American. Nonetheless, because he had political power and tried to use it to enhance Canada's independence, he became an icon to those who wanted to resist the increasing influence exercised by the United States over Canada, and a class traitor to the great majority of his friends who had already aligned themselves, their businesses, and their investment dollars with the new continental economic and power realities. Gordon's attitudes and policy prescriptions, along with his ability to push significant elements of academe, the Liberal and liberal left, and the *Toronto Star* in the direction he wished to travel, had come to threaten the interests of the wealthy in Canada. So complete was the shift in the financial élite's needs and desires in the half century since the reciprocity election of 1911 that the Toronto politician, standing all alone, was left exposed to the combined assaults of business and the financial press. Inevitably, his attempt to check the incoming tide failed. Walter Gordon was the last survivor of the corporate nationalist and protectionist spirit of 1911, and his nationalist efforts were the final ones to emerge from the Canadian élite. Henceforth, Canada's leaders would press their sometimes reluctant population towards the south.

7

THE ARRIVAL OF THE ANTI-AMERICAN AMERICANS:
THE VIETNAM WAR AND DRAFT DODGERS

Macpherson/Reprinted with permission—The Toronto Star Syndicate

Jake was a draft dodger who had come to Canada to seek refuge from the Vietnam War. He was, in theory, a refugee from the ethos of America and, hence, a quintessential anti-American. But this character in Heather Robertson's novel *Igor* was unhappy with Canada, too. "Jake found Canadians infuriatingly un-American. Canadians were too fucking quiet. Canadians were too fucking clean. Canadians were too fucking conservative. Canadians were too colonial ('They still worship the Queen, for God's sake!'), too critical ('The US can't do anything right!')

and complacent ('What the hell are they doing about Vietnam?').'' Then there was the exasperating differentness of Canada. "Canadian money was printed in bright colours, like some African nation, and the French Prime Minister, Trudeau, had a Caligula haircut. 'Like this place is nowhere, man,' Jake said. 'I met a Canuck today who hadn't heard of Allen Ginsberg. He *hadn't heard* of him. Can you believe it? Where the hell are we, Bongo Fucking Bongo?'''

Paradoxically, Jake was bothered by the fact that Canadians in Robertson's novel (if not in life) cheered for the Viet Cong. "'Don't they understand those gooks are killing *Americans*?' Jake asked. 'Maybe that's why the Canadians are cheering,'" said his girlfriend, Jennie, also American. Jennie knew "what was really bugging Jake": "He had run away. Was he afraid to die? Was the whole Vietnam resistance just a lot of bullshit? Abbie Hoffman was on television. Jake was watching television. Even some of the guys in Nam were on TV. The guys in the green body bags were on TV. Jake was in Toronto. Nobody in the States had ever heard of Toronto. Jake was a traitor. He was a coward. He was nobody."[1]

Robertson's credentials as an anti-American are impeccable ("I confess to a desire to toss a hand grenade into every American camper I pass on the highway," she wrote in *Maclean's* in April 1975 of the big vehicles full of holidaying Yanks that come north into Canada every summer). Still, her unlikeable character Jake, eventually destined to spy in and on Canada for the Central Intelligence Agency, expressed much of the culture shock that American draft resisters and deserters experienced when they came to Canada in their tens of thousands during the long, divisive, and destructive Vietnam War. Canada seemed very much the same as the United States at first glance, but soon the differences became apparent. Moreover, the dodgers and deserters were not always welcomed, a reflection of divided Canadian opinion on the war and the burgeoning nationalism and anti-Americanism that gripped the country in the 1960s and 1970s. Many Canadians who opposed the war against North Vietnam became ambivalent at this sudden explosion of anti-American Americans in their midst.

* * *

The Cold War had obliged Canada to integrate its defences with the United States, to cooperate in manifold ways to help defend North America and Western Europe. Prime ministers as different as Mackenzie King, Louis St Laurent, John Diefenbaker, Lester Pearson, and Pierre Trudeau came to understand that if Canada did not cooperate, the United States—in its own self-interest—would do the job itself, with potentially serious consequences for Canadian territorial and political sovereignty. The fall of John Diefenbaker in early 1963 after a brutal nudge from the White House was an example of what might befall those who interfered with the Americans' priorities.

Canada could operate on the margins, stretching its wings and cultivating such independence in policy as it could. During the Korean War, for example, Canadian diplomacy had moved well ahead of Washington in its search for an armistice in the war the United Nations, under the lead of the United States, was waging against North Korea and China. Dean Acheson, the Secretary of State in the Truman government whose father had been a Canadian, became exasperated enough with Pearson's preaching to write scathingly of Canada as "the Stern Daughter of the Voice of God." To Acheson, Canada had turned into a nation that never failed to tell those who were bearing the burdens and paying the price in casualties how best to fight wars.

When Pearson became Prime Minister in April 1963, his initial task was to restore relations with the United States, a job he tackled at a meeting with President John F. Kennedy at Hyannisport soon after he came into office. The battles over nuclear weapons were ended at once, Pearson agreeing to take warheads for the Bomarc and Honest John missiles and to arm Canada's CF-104 fighter-bombers in NATO with atomic weapons. There were also difficulties over foreign investment and economic policy between the two countries, and these, as we have seen, were harder to resolve. Soon, there were major problems over the war in Vietnam.

Part of French Indo-China, Vietnam had erupted in a Communist and nationalist rebellion against French rule, a war that pitted lightly armed peasants against the sophisticated army of what was then considered a major power. By 1954 the rebels had won and, after the Geneva Conference of that year, French Indo-China was no more, replaced by the new nations of Laos, Cambodia, and a Vietnam divided in two—North and South Vietnam—with nationalist Communists holding sway in the north until such time as promised free elections unified the country. The elections never came: the North began to aid Communist and nationalist uprisings in the South; and the United States, fearful that the dominos of Asia were beginning to topple towards Moscow and Beijing, began a long effort to prop up the government of South Vietnam. After John Kennedy's assassination in November 1963, President Lyndon Johnson came to believe that freedom was at stake, and he increased the American commitment step by step, eventually reaching a peak troop strength of 542,000 in early 1969.* As the US forces grew in number, so too did the steady flow of body bags home. In return, the Americans pressed their allies to contribute to the war effort, and countries as disparate as South Korea and Australia sent troops to fight with the Americans.

Not Canada, however. At the Geneva Conference of 1954, Canada had been asked, along with India and Poland, to join an International Control Commission to monitor the truce in the three successor states in Indo-China. This was peacekeeping, even if it was not under the United Nations' aegis, and the heavy commitment of military men and diplomats began at once. In Laos and Cambodia, the commitment did not prove especially long-lived or onerous; in Vietnam, where the anti-colonialist war continued in a different guise, the task was frustrating and costly, but there was one saving grace. How, Canadian officials told their American friends, could Canada send troops to fight in Vietnam and still be a peacekeeper on the ICC? The logic was compelling, even if Canada did feel free to give small amounts of economic assistance to South Vietnam, and Canada was let off the hook of its dependent military status. The sigh of relief in the bureaucracy in Ottawa and across Canada was profound. Membership on the ICC, one columnist observed, was "worth its weight in gold."

The Vietnam War nonetheless had its impact on Canada. Contrary to

* Unlike "provincial" Canadians, Robertson Davies wrote, Americans are "beguiled by the notion that the fate of mankind and human culture" lies wholly in their hands. They are "natural-born crusaders, forever in the right, even when they are least aware of what they are crusading about." *Murther & Walking Spirits* (Toronto 1992), 302.

popular memory, the American war effort was supported, though some-times tentatively, by Canadians through almost all of Lyndon Johnson's time in office.* Moreover, the Canadian government, thanks to its Defence Production Sharing Agreement with the United States, actively encouraged Canadian defence contractors to sell as much as they could to support the American war machine and to reduce Canada's balance-of-payments deficit to the south. The Department of Defence Production's annual catalogue, *Canadian Defence Commodities*, circulated widely in the United States, enough so that critics labelled it "The Warmonger's Shopping Guide." Canadians, in other words, made profits and had jobs thanks to the war.

The Vietnam War left its mark on Canada: a growing sense in Ottawa and among the public that yet again the United States had somehow become the world's bullyboy and had lost its way. The war also led to the arrival in Canada of around one hundred thousand young men (often with their wives or girl friends in tow) who had fled the United States to avoid conscription into the armed forces or who had deserted from the US military to protest the war or avoid being sent overseas.

There was a widespread sense not only in Canada but in the United States that the Americans had come adrift from their professed ideals as a result of the war in Vietnam. Walter Lippmann, the distinguished and influential US columnist, said as much in 1967 when he wrote, "There is a growing belief that America is no longer the historic America, that it is a bastard America which relies on superior force to achieve its purpose, and is no longer providing an example to the wisdom and humanity of a free society."[2] The Pearson government, acutely conscious of the ways in which Diefenbaker's government had fallen into difficulties with Washington, seemed to agree with Lippmann's view by 1967, but it felt obliged to play its hand cautiously.

For example, when Secretary of State Dean Rusk asked Pearson in

* Opinion polls show the tenor of opinion. On May 21, 1966, the Canadian Institute of Public Opinion reported that 35 percent of Canadians approved of President Johnson's handling of the war, compared with 34 percent who disapproved. A year and a half later (November 29, 1967), 61 percent said the United States was fighting to stop Communism in Vietnam, and on February 24, 1968, 35 percent expressed gratitude for US efforts, while 37 percent wanted Canada to dissociate itself from the American effort. Not until four years later (February 5, 1972), did 51 percent say that sending troops to Vietnam by the United States had been a mistake, with only 27 percent disagreeing.

1964 to have a first-rate diplomat assigned to the International Control Commission who could convey to Hanoi "warnings about its present course and hints of possible rewards in return for a change," Pearson agreed. Rusk, however, understood that "in light of present Canadian attitudes," Ottawa would not countenance its representative being used to threaten the North Vietnamese. Perhaps that was an overreaction on Rusk's part, for when Pearson and President Johnson met in May 1964, the Prime Minister's only concerns seemed to be that nuclear weapons not be used. The "punitive striking of discriminate targets by careful iron bomb attacks" was a different matter entirely, and the Canadian government made clear repeatedly that, in its view, North Vietnam was the aggressor and that in a contest where China, Hanoi's backer, apparently was facing off against the United States, Canada most definitely supported its neighbour and friend.

Only the New Democratic Party in Parliament seemed to disagree. In March 1965 H.W. Herridge, the Member of Parliament for Kootenay West, sarcastically defined Canadian foreign policy as follows: "Don't rock the United States boat. Don't do anything to annoy our neighbours to the south. Don't take any initiative without their prior consent. Don't do anything about the idiotic, dangerous and hopeless war in South Viet Nam." His British Columbia colleague Colin Cameron referred the next month to the "shame and horror" Canadians felt over the Americans' war, and berated the government for acting like "lickspittles" to the United States. For his part, James G. Endicott of the Canadian Peace Congress pronounced the Americans' war "one of the ugliest, most brutal and most hypocritical wars of aggression in history."

Once the American "iron bomb" attacks began in 1965, the huge B-52 bombers dropping their massive payloads onto the countryside, Canadian government opinion began a slow process of change. In the United States, as a strong peace movement began to take shape, students burned their draft cards and two pacifists immolated themselves in protest at the war. In Canada, criticism on television and in the press, in Parliament, and in the universities was increasing, and Pearson formed the opinion that the Americans' war in Vietnam was the wrong war in the wrong place. When he was invited to speak at Temple University in Philadelphia in April 1965, he took the occasion to utter some cautionary phrases on the need for a pause in the bombing so that negotiations might begin. His words were exquisitely qualified and measured: "There does appear to be at least a possibility that a suspension of such air strikes against North Vietnam, at the right time, might provide the Hanoi authorities with the opportunity, if they wish to take it, to inject some flexibility into their policy without appearing to do so as the direct result of military pressure." Paul Martin, the Secretary of State for External Affairs, had protested against Pearson's plan to speak out even in this oblique fashion. At Camp David the next day Lyndon Johnson, literally grabbing the Prime Minister by his lapels, told Pearson in no uncertain terms that he did not like it when Canadians came into his country and "pissed on [his] rug."[3] In Parliament, John Diefenbaker asked on April 6 if President Johnson had found the suggestion of a bombing pause "refreshing." "He was very interested in it, Mr Speaker," deadpanned Pearson.

"Ohhh, those Canadians, they're so clever," Johnson complained at a lunch for the West German and Canadian ambassadors. "They can come into [our] own backyard and tell us how to run the war. They're so clever."[4] In fact, the President had a point. It was surely extraordinary for Pearson to make his speech on Johnson's turf, and journalist Bruce Hutchison castigated his old friend for "the worst breach of international manners in his long, impeccable career," one which had "grossly and unnecessarily offended" the President. Pearson's method, Hutchison wrote in the Ottawa

Macpherson/Reprinted with permission—The Toronto Star Syndicate

Journal, "was simply incredible and bitterly resented in Washington."

Pearson's speaking out did not win him credit either with the opponents of the war in Canada. Vietnam was the first conflict to be televised, and each night horrific scenes flickered on the black and white screens across the country as the full weight of a technologically rich superpower was directed against a small, impoverished Asian peasant society. Appalling phrases and even more horrifying practices such as "free fire zones" and "body counts" were put into force and transmitted over the airwaves. Church and women's groups, students, and the political left became genuinely revolted by the David and Goliath struggle.

Popular musicians reflected the antipathy to the war that was developing in Canada. Singers like Bruce Cockburn, Neil Young, and Joni Mitchell, popular in Canada and the United States, all wrote and sang anti-war messages, frequently in an explicitly anti-government vein. Similarly, television shows became increasingly critical of the way the war was being waged, featuring interviews with anti-war activists from the nonagenarian Bertrand Russell to draft dodgers, while skits on "This Hour Has Seven Days," the top-rated CBC show of the 1960s, lampooned the Americans with unaccustomed savagery. So sharp was the criticism that opposition leader John Diefenbaker, hypocritically wearing his pro-American hat whenever it suited him to criticize the Pearson government, complained bitterly about the CBC's "brainwashing the Canadian people" by denigrating the Americans "who are dying over there for you and me, for that is what they are doing."[5] "Seven Days" also drew White House criticism when presidential aide McGeorge Bundy denounced the distorted editing of an interview he had granted, and the State Department actually declared the CBC "untrustworthy" and banned it from access to official sources. Although the CBC brass duly objected to the "misleading" anti-Americanism of "Seven Days," the show drew huge audiences until the national broadcaster finally closed it down.

The anti-war and anti-American anger in Canada continued to grow slowly and to reinforce each other. The government suffered continued attacks for the "quiet diplomacy" that kept it mute on matters involving American global policy—although, Ottawa claimed, Canadian representatives vigorously presented their views in private sessions with its officials. Such practices amounted to "complicity," critics claimed, charges fuelled by defence industry profits and revelations that Canadian officers with the International Control Commission had actively collected information for the United States when their duties took them to North Vietnam. In April 1965 the Prime Minister received a delegation of university academics, representing "313 Canadian university professors of all political persuasions" who wanted Canada to press for immediate negotiations in Vietnam without preconditions. The Prime Minister listened but, as he said in Parliament, "did not . . . see eye to eye with them in their entire assessment of the responsibilities and reasons for the present situation." Nor did most Liberal, Conservative, Social Credit, and Créditiste MPs, to judge by the debates in Parliament. Nonetheless, a May 26 letter from Montreal professors—including one Pierre Elliott Trudeau, then a member of the Faculty of Law at Université de Montréal—was blunt in its appeal to "reason and human decency" and its denunciation of Washington's "tendency to judge all political changes in terms of its own over-simplified definitions of what is Communist and what is not Communist." The American intervention in the Dominican Republic that same May, occasioned by fears of a Communist takeover abetted by Castro's Cuba, fed public concerns about a rogue giant running wild around the hemisphere and the world.

Perhaps the most scathing comment of all came from poet and editor Dennis Lee. In the biting phrases of his epic poem "Civil Elegies," Lee defined Canadians as a "nation of losers and quislings":

> In a bad time, people, from an outpost of empire I write
> bewildered, though on about living. It is to set down a nation's
> failure of nerve; I mean complicity, which is signified by the
> gaseous stain above us. . . .
> And the consenting citizens of a minor and docile colony
> are cogs in a useful tool, though in no way
> necessary and scarcely
> criminal at all and their leaders are
> honourable men, as for example Paul Martin. . . .
>
> The humiliations of imperial necessity
> are an old story, though it does not
> improve in the telling and no man
> believes it of himself.
> Why bring up genocide? Why bring up
> acquiescence, profiteering? Why bring up, again,

the deft emasculation of a country by the Liberal party of Canada? . . .
    Doesn't the
service of quiet diplomacy require dirty hands?[6]

By 1967, as the war continued to escalate and the Centennial celebrations
fed nationalism, the focus of public concern in Canada seemed to switch
to the $300 million in annual arms sales to the United States. In January,
360 professors from the University of Toronto petitioned the Prime
Minister to stop the sales. They made little headway, though Paul Martin
did ask his department to consider how and if such a move could be
made. In April, political scientist Gad Horowitz called for Canada to
develop a strong nationalism of its own, excoriating the state for its "relationship with the United States . . . analogous to the relationship of
Finland with the Soviet Union." In effect, Canada was Washington's kept
woman. No one in Ottawa paid attention to this insulting rhetoric, nor
should anyone have listened to the secretary of the Board of Evangelism
and Social Service of the United Church, Reverend J.R. Hord, who at the
end of November 1967 urged Canadians to demonstrate against
Canadian companies selling arms to the United States. Hord put his
protest in explicitly anti-American and anti-imperialist terms: "We, of
course, have to see the Vietnam conflict . . . within the overall picture of
American economic investment in and military domination of South East
Asia. Americans have always claimed that they were innocent of old-style
geographic imperialism. . . . But actually they have developed a stranglehold on the nations of the world through economic expansion."
    This view of the innate imperialism of the United States seemed to be
becoming more widespread in Canada in the age of television. Picketers
demonstrated regularly in front of the US Embassy in Ottawa and at US
Consulates-General across the land, and their complaints were taken seriously by the media. University teach-ins featured prominent academics,
including the nationalist and conservative philosopher George Grant,
author of the immensely popular *Lament for a Nation*, which was published in 1965 (see below chapter 9). Grant seemed increasingly weighed
down with despair over the war and the belief that the English-speaking
world had reached its moral nadir. Meanwhile, Canadian industries
exporting war material to the United States faced difficulties in getting
their job recruiters onto university campuses. The rhetoric was hot in the
1960s, the calls among the young for revolutionary change and the

demands that the United States get out of Vietnam—and Canada—fuelled by the heady combination of marijuana and, thanks to the birth control pill, the sudden collapse of sexual restraints.*

Pearson's government tried to toughen its position on the American war by a process of gradualism, its obvious aim being to keep the lid on and to avoid alienating the Johnson administration any further. But the Cabinet was divided, and Walter Gordon, the President of the Privy Council, denounced the war in an address in May 1967. A few days later, on May 25, President Johnson flew to Canada for United States Day at Montreal's World's Fair, Expo 67. The American flag raised at the ceremony unaccountably had a hole in it and had to be replaced, while embarrassed dignitaries sat in silence. The President's perfunctory speech was almost shouted down by teenage protesters chanting, exactly as their counterparts south of the border, "Hey, hey, LBJ, how many kids did you kill today?" The chill in the air was noticeable.

Criticism of US policy emanated from the political mainstream, too. The next month, three university principals, the former senior public servants Douglas LePan, Escott Reid, and A.F.W. Plumptre, all close associates in External Affairs and friends of the Prime Minister, echoed Gordon's call for a bombing halt and increased Canadian efforts to pressure the United States to that end. On September 28, 1967, the Canadian government finally called at the United Nations for a halt to the bombing.

No one in Washington listened, and the war raged on. The assassinations of Martin Luther King and Bobby Kennedy, the black uprisings in the great ghettoes of many American cities, and the police riot in Chicago during the Democratic Convention of 1968 all suggested that American society might be reaching a crisis point. The new Liberal government of Pierre Trudeau tried to keep its distance from the Americans and their war, though the Prime Minister spoke darkly about the possibility of violence spilling over the border. The Trudeau government, however, said nothing in April and

---

* Not all the young shared in the prevalent anti-American mood. Substantial numbers of Canadians served in the US military during the war, estimates ranging from 12,000 to 40,000, and some one hundred were killed in the fighting, including the son of General J.A. Dextraze, later the Canadian Chief of the Defence Staff. In 1995 the Canadians' service in Vietnam was finally commemorated when a monument, built by four Michigan men at their own expense, was unveiled in Windsor, Ontario. *Toronto Star*, July 2, 1995.

May 1972 when President Richard Nixon extended the bombing of the North to cover the entire country except for Hanoi and Haiphong. Negotiations for a truce dragged on until, in December 1972 and January 1973, Nixon escalated the bombing once more, this time specifically targeting the cities that had been spared.

The reaction in Canada was apoplectic. The minority Trudeau government, dependent after the 1972 election on the New Democratic Party for its majority in the House of Commons, found itself pushed towards the most explicitly anti-American act of a Canadian government at least since 1911. To cheers from the left, on January 4, 1973, Parliament approved a government motion condemning the prolongation of hostilities in Vietnam. The Nixon administration, furious at this betrayal, put Canada alongside Sweden on its "shit list," and Canadian diplomats were frozen out, barred from seeing their American counterparts in their offices.

Canada had its uses, however. When the US–North Vietnamese truce negotiations finally bore fruit in late January and the two countries struck a deal to end the war, Canada found itself pressed by the Americans to join a new International Control Commission to police the armistice. Reluctantly, Ottawa agreed, this time imposing time limits and conditions on its participation. The freeze in Washington was effectively over in less than a month.

The war took longer to wind down. Without American troops to bolster their resolve, the South Vietnamese army collapsed in 1975. The long struggle in Vietnam ended in a complete victory for the Communists, who unified the country under Hanoi's control. Vietnam would need years to recover from being bombed and fought over; the United States, defeated for the first time in a major conflict, would also need years to recuperate.

Canadian official and public attitudes to their neighbours and their policies had been battered by the war. The Korean War had begun the process of chipping away at Canadian confidence in US leadership in the global struggle, but Vietnam dramatically advanced the unease. Trust in American leadership had seemed to make sense so long as leaders like Roosevelt, Truman, Eisenhower, and Kennedy were in charge, presidents whose popularity in Canada rivalled or even exceeded that in their own country. The same was never said of Johnson or Nixon, chief executives whose style and actions almost always received critical appraisals north of the border. The Canadian willingness to follow the United States' lead began, for the first time since 1945, to weaken in a dramatic way. Was this anti-Americanism in combination with nationalism? Or was it simply a disagreement over policy that reflected Ottawa's ability to assess a world problem and formulate its own response? Or, more likely still, was it excessive Canadian moralism, a desire to criticize the Americans, those bearing the free world's burdens, while not carrying a fair share of the load?

*   *   *

"Many young Americans' first acquaintance with Canada began with a letter from the United States government," wrote historian Robert Bothwell. "The 'greetings' conveyed by Uncle Sam stimulated reflection," and thousands of draft-age Americans headed for the Canadian border. With a total American immigration to Canada of almost 175,000 between 1965 and 1974, estimates of the number who had fled the war range from 50,000 to 125,000. This was the first period in decades that the emigration of Canadians to the United States had been exceeded by the immigration of Americans to Canada. "The New Refugees," the "Refugees from Militarism," and "The New Exiles," as they were called in some of the books published about the influx, flooded into Canada in the years after 1965. As fugitives from the draft, they were cutting their ties with their homeland, for all faced arrest if found in the United States. Those who had been accompanied to Canada by spouses or girlfriends, however, could use them as "couriers" to keep up contact with friends and family back home and even to bring their belongings into Canada.

There were also deserters from the US armed forces, men already inducted into the military and indicted by the courts, who came to Canada, again sometimes accompanied by spouses or friends. Deserters had to reckon on long terms in harsh conditions in military prisons if caught; they too were in Canada for good. Only an amnesty, which did not seem likely in the late 1960s under Presidents Johnson or Nixon, could permit these draft evaders and deserters to return to their families and friends. (President Jimmy Carter's amnesty to draft evaders in January 1977 opened America's gates once more; for deserters, the options—a less than honourable discharge followed by an individual review—were somewhat less palatable.)

There was a certain irony in the arrival of war resisters in Canada. The United Empire Loyalists had left for Canada rather than become citizens of the new United States. There was no parallel with the new migration, Richard Lemm, a draft resister, wrote, "but there is the irony that the earlier migration was away from the visions held by the American rebels, while the present migration is away from the violation of those visions by the rebels' successors, away from the increasing cleavage between those founding visions and the intentions of established America." For so many to have renounced their homeland "implies a general diminution of their attachment to the American experience."[7]

The draft dodgers were overwhelmingly middle class and well educated, according to most studies. While more than 90 percent of draft evaders had some college training (64 percent with completed degrees), only half the deserters (generally younger than the dodgers) had college experience, much of it community college training. In other words, if dodgers were college educated and unable for some reason to secure the deferments that were generously handed out to university students, most deserters were not; if dodgers were middle class, most deserters were lower class in origin. Even so, by a substantial measure, American draft-age immigrants to Canada, whether evaders or deserters, were likely the best-educated immigrants Canada had ever received in wholesale quantity.

The dodgers fell into two broad categories, the politically active and the apolitical. The former capitalized on "feelings of disappointment" in the country of their birth. These were the men running exile organizations

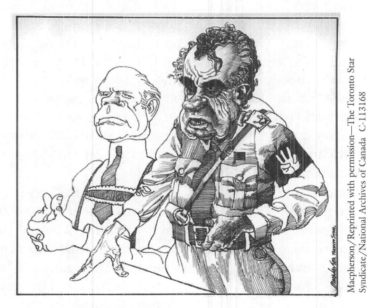

Macpherson/Reprinted with permission—The Toronto Star Syndicate/National Archives of Canada C-113168

order
"Law and morality are threatening the presidency,
now here is mein game plan—"
my

183

and demonstrating "in front of the American consulate (possibly shouting 'Fascist pigs!' at the top of [their] lungs)." These were revolutionaries who saw Canada as "a regrouping area of sorts, a haven from which to wage some kind of war, even if only a verbal one, on the United States. . . . the bodies of the self-conscious exiles may be on this side of the border, but their heads are not." Douglas Fetherling, too young to be drafted when he came to Canada but a refugee nonetheless from "the great American virus" of "republican brutality and hatred of culture," echoed many of the dodgers in his rejection of "the institutionalized violence, the purblind worship of stupidity and all the rest" that characterized Behemoth.[8]

The apolitical, on the other hand, came to Canada simply to make a new life and to forget the United States, and this kind of war resister was happy whether he lived in a city or on a commune in rural British Columbia, content that he had in effect beaten Uncle Sam. Political or apolitical, the anti-American Americans, the first in almost two centuries, had arrived as a large and growing group of new immigrants who vigorously rejected the policies of the United States and some of its works.

The influx of Americans had begun at roughly the same time that the Johnson administration escalated the war in Vietnam in 1964–65 and increased its draft calls. The Canadian official response was cool but proper. The Deputy Minister of Manpower and Immigration made clear that there was no provision in the Immigration Act against admissions of persons "seeking to avoid induction into the Armed Services" and, therefore, if they met immigration requirements, they could not be barred. As well-educated young men, the dodgers met Canadian immigration requirements, and particularly so after the Immigration Act was altered in 1967 to feature a points system that rewarded youth, education, and fluency in French or English. Deserters, ordinarily less educated, had more difficulty reaching safety north of the border.

In Parliament, meanwhile, John Diefenbaker and others pestered the Pearson government with questions of two kinds: why were the Royal Canadian Mounted Police cooperating with the Federal Bureau of Investigation in searches for draft dodgers in Canada? And why should "these people, not being willing to assume the responsibilities of their own citizenship," be welcomed as good citizens here?[9] The government tended to deny any cooperation with the FBI, and the Prime Minister noted that "we would certainly not do anything to encourage admission to Canada of this category of United States citizens."[10] That qualified response probably reflected the government's ear to the ground—opinion polls demonstrated that ordinary Canadians supported the war and were not well disposed to American war resisters. A poll in 1968 found that 58 percent would have banned what one correspondent of the Minister of Manpower and Immigration called "the dreadful horde of Yankee trash coming into our country, to evade the responsibilities of citizenship in their own." Only 28 percent wanted to let them enter Canada.[11]

Still, the government did nothing concrete to discourage the flood of evaders, deserters, or "political refugees," as they thought of themselves, until a further change in immigration regulations in 1972 obliged applicants for landed status to apply at a consulate in the United States or by mail to Ottawa. The process took some six months and effectively eliminated deserters as a category of immigrant. Nonetheless, in the period of open immigration between 1965 and 1972, the one substantive, if irregular, check on deserters and dodgers was the immigration officer at the border. While many were sympathetic to the Americans, others, often veterans of the Second World War, were much less so, only too willing to interpret the regulations as harshly as possible to deny entry to Canada. Indeed, in 1968, Ottawa had reminded the border stations that "personal qualities" were a discretionary category of the points system that could be used to bar entry to deserters; significantly, draft dodgers went unmentioned. In 1970 five students from York University's Glendon College, each posing as US Air Force deserter William John Heintzelman, tried to secure entry to Canada at five different border crossings; all were denied entry, a result that provoked an outcry in the press.

Those Americans who made it over the border perceived Canada and Canadians with varying eyes and differing degrees of perception. Some had an idealized view of Canadian reality. "Ah, Canada: no more draft, no aggressive policies, sweet little big country of the northland where children laugh, women can be on the streets at night without fear, policemen are still polite to you. Yes," Dee Knight, a 1968 arrival, wrote, "Freedom, you're pretty!"[12] Toronto was a large city of immigrants without poverty or ghettoes, yet another said, and there was no unthinking support for government in Canada as there was in the United States. This draft evader, arriving just before the October Crisis of 1970, saw his rose-coloured view of Canada survive even this event, with its overwhelming public support for the federal government's massive effort to crush separatist terrorism and the civil rights of suspected *felquistes*. Not even the call by the mayors

of Montreal, Toronto, and Vancouver for the use of the War Measures Act
against radicals, in general—and in Vancouver, draft dodgers were mentioned in the same breath—seemed to upset his relief at being in Canada.
Others, however, and particularly those young Americans who had ended
up in Montreal or other parts of Quebec, saw the October Crisis as a
"wake-up call." Canada could be as repressive as any other country. There
seemed to be only a weak tradition of dissent to get Canadians out on the
street to protest the abrogation of their rights.

Most of the American arrivals believed that Canadians generally treated
them well, despite the cautionary message of the opinion polls. All across
the land, student organizations formed to assist the draft evaders. The
Student Union for Peace Action had come into existence to help
American resisters and to protest the war, and one of its off-shoots, the
Toronto Anti-Draft Programme, published the *Manual for Draft-Age
Immigrants to Canada*—which sold tens of thousands of copies and led
to the RCMP investigating its authors and bugging the organization's
telephones. Despite the welcome, or perhaps because of it, the new
refugees found that Canada "looks so much like America that they can't
quite believe they've arrived some place else," Robert Fulford wrote.
"The Canadians they meet aren't quite sure that their own country exists
and the newcomers are profoundly confused. It's hard enough growing
up with the Great Canadian Identity Crisis; think how much harder it is
to be forced to adopt it."[13]

The resisters, in other words, had left their own country but arrived
. . . where? Instead of landing in a totally foreign country, one resister
noted, "They find themselves in cities where people speak English, drive
American cars, drink coke, smoke dope, read *Time* magazine and do a lot
of disconcertingly American things which were bad enough back home,
and seem even worse in Canada."[14] Another recalled the culture shock
he felt—Canadians read the same books, listened to the same music, and
spoke the same language, yes; but the decisive factor was that the
Vietnam War was different for Canadians, who were onlookers, not par-
ticipants. "This is Little Brother country," another said as he began to get
a sense of the Canadian situation. "Canadians envy Big Brother to the
south . . . They seem to sense that power has its unfortunate obligations,
and so try to let Big Brother bear the responsibility while they garnish the
rewards of American investment." This duality troubled many of the new
arrivals. One US Navy deserter promised "to start a nationwide drive to

completely block out all US ties, a boycott of all US goods. . . . I think Canada should wake up."

Another put it more bluntly: "The only thing you beat when you cross the border is the Selective Service Act. You come over here to the same bullshit system. And we react to it in the same way." That attitude upset many Canadians, conditioned to take a generally benevolent view of the United States, however fierce their occasional anti-Americanism. "It started becoming clear to me," one evader wrote, "that more people were suspicious of me not because I was so disgustingly *American*, but because I was *un*-American. I didn't honor GM, Esso, Jackie Kennedy and the rest."

Nonetheless, the American war in Vietnam remained the resisters' primary target. Exiles' organizations sprang up with great rapidity from Halifax to Victoria—and usually died as quickly—factionalism shattering the temporary unity that arose solely from being American resisters in Canada. In October 1967, for example, several hundred young Americans marched in a Toronto anti-war parade under the banner "We Refused to Go," and the next year the Union of American Exiles took shape, dedicated to creating radical dissent against the Vietnam War and the American system. "The establishment of a collective identity in a nation that would like nothing more than to absorb these exiles into her middle class quietly," one article in the union's magazine said, "will be a difficult and perhaps dangerous task. The establishment of an exile politics is altogether likely to result in repression." Perhaps the most important product of the bitterly divided union was its baseball games. One US reporter wrote drily that "they have the only baseball games in the world where both teams are the dodgers."

Many dodgers saw Canadian nationalism and Canadian opposition to the United States as pitifully weak. Charles Campbell, writing in *AMEX*, a resisters' magazine in 1970, noted his hopes that a large influx of "young, vigorous and, hopefully, politically-aware Americans as immigrants will give the Canadian nationalist movement the righteous indignation and anti-imperialist perspective it needs to succeed." Those poor Canadians. Even in creating their own nationalism they needed the benefits of American knowhow.

In the face of this ugly Americanism, the Canadian nationalists and the members of the student movement who had initially seized on the dodgers as "potential 'movement' heroes" began to change their attitude to the American influx. The exiles, dodger John Sandman wrote, "began getting a reputation in many quarters for displaying the same arrogance in flaunting their American-ness that Yankees have been famous for around the world." The evaders and the deserters came to be viewed by many on the nationalist left as "hopelessly professional Americans who are detached from the mother country in name only, and do nothing to assimilate themselves into Canada, remaining closed to everyone but a small coterie of other draft dodgers and deserters."[15] The American radicals, warned James Laxer, a student movement veteran, were inappropriate guides for Canadian students because they sprang from the heart of the empire rather than from a dependent country. Moreover, they challenged domestic organizations and institutions. While it was right to do so in the United States, it results in Canada "merely in a further softening-up of this country for American takeover." The Canadian anti-anti-American Americans had sprung into existence.

Not surprisingly, one of the first to take up the pen against the evaders (invaders?) was Robin Mathews, the Carleton University professor of English who had galvanized the opposition to the influx of American professors into Canadian universities (see chapter 8). Mathews, a believer in the tradition of sanctuary and an early supporter of the draft dodgers, wrote in *Canadian Dimension* in early 1970 that Canadians could not "turn a blind eye to the implications of the draft-dodger in Canada—the draft-dodger and US imperialism." The new American arrivals understandably were passionately involved with US issues, Mathews wrote, "and they tend to turn any discussion among groups in Canada to the morality or immorality of US internal and external policy. (Separatism, many of them believe, is the Canadian expression for the partition of North and South Viet Nam.)" The American dream is dead in the United States, he quoted one dodger, but the new exiles hope to keep it alive in Toronto. More seriously, Mathews argued that if the United States had to jail the estimated 60,000 dodgers and deserters then in Canada, the costs would be at least $300 million a year. The incarceration of so many dissidents would increase pressure against the war. Speculating that Washington realized this danger, Mathews argued that the "freedom train" to Canada was "a necessary safety valve if the war is going to continue without serious civil disruption." Moreover, the war resisters in Canada had increased the acceptability of American radicalism in Canada. He cited an American professor who had addressed the Canadian Humanities Association's meeting in Calgary as if he were speaking to his fellow Americans.* The most important issues facing students today, the visitor had said, were "Vietnam, the draft, race, poverty, the nature of higher education, the function of scholarship." Doubtless, Mathews complained, "He has never heard of or is indifferent to moral problems in Canada created by the francophone fact, national survival, alien takeover and so on."

No one, the angry Mathews claimed, ever mentioned that Canada was a good nation to belong to or that dodgers and deserters owed a special obligation to Canada and Canadians, not least to learn about the country to prepare themselves for eventual citizenship. The Americans were contributing to the "colonization of Canada" without fulfilling their moral obligation to the country. "When are they going to begin asking what they can do for Canada, for *Canada's* primary problems, because the Vietnam War is not the only nor even the primary Canadian problem?" When, he asked, would resisters organize a benefit performance to raise money for scholarships for Canadian students as a gesture of thanks?**

Mathews had raised points that struck responsive chords. In December 1970 the *Toronto Star* ran an article about one exile organization and noted unfavourably that its fifth priority—"to try and fit into Canadian life"—ought to be its first, or else "they risk arousing a growing hostility and suspicion among Canadians."[16]

Much later, Margaret Atwood's novel *The Robber Bride* had as one of its characters a dodger, Billy, who takes advantage of the woman to whom he is assigned by a draft resister support group—living with her, impregnating

---

* Of course, given the data collected in Mathews's voluminous writings on the Americanization of Canadian colleges, the visitor might well have been addressing a majority of US citizens!

** Paul Hollander's standard modern work *Anti-Americanism: Critiques at Home and Abroad, 1965–1990* (New York 1992), 426ff, notes that 31 percent of those Canadian academics replying to his 1989 survey on anti-American attitudes were born in the United States, many of them Vietnam-era draft resisters and critics and many whose self-description was "radical" and "radical-liberal." This, he postulates, might explain "the highly critical attitudes toward the United States" he discovered. In other words, the anti-Americanism of those draft resisters and critics of the Vietnam War who came to Canada and took university posts seems to have remained intact. As Hollander also noted, "The Canadian intellectuals . . . were for the most part united in regarding American policies and influences [as] harmful to Canadian national and economic interest and culture" (439).

her, and then betraying her for another woman. A domestic spat, to be sure, were it not for Atwood's anti-American sentiments, sentiments perhaps strong enough to make Billy a symbolic figure. The same theme of betrayal is apparent in Linda Spalding's novel *The Paper Wife*. "Her draft dodgers are flower-power-tripping dropouts with little ethical fibre," one reviewer commented. Spalding said that the dodgers she knew "weren't particularly heroic or wonderful people—or even activists. They were ordinary people who didn't think the war was proper."

Some dodgers could see the truth that underlay the concerns expressed by the critics. There was a concentration on the United States, inevitably so, in the draft resisters' organized and individual activities. Rick Bebout, writing in Jim Christy's *New Refugees*, accepted Mathews's point, but refused to agree with him. "I am disturbed that he seems to insist on a person's citizenship being a more important factor than his beliefs and intentions. A draft dodger who comes to this country with no more than a dedication to living as happy and as free a life as he can," he wrote, is "far less an agent of American imperialism than a solid Canadian citizen who takes a management position with Esso or Reader's Digest or Coca-Cola." There was arguably much truth in that, and in Bebout's next shot: "Mathews and some of his fellow Canadian nationalists have a preoccupation with the United States which is perhaps as great as that of anyone in the American exile community."

It was not only Robin Mathews who was affected by the war and the atmosphere of the era. In November 1970 the distinguished University of Toronto political scientist James Eayrs, for years a faithful Cold Warrior, told a Columbia University audience that "the identity of basic aims" between Canada and the United States had been shattered. The Americans had betrayed Canada's trust, wearing their anti-Communism as "a protean disguise . . . behind which American oilmen as well as American airmen could go about their stealthy business." The situation had changed, Eayrs said, and now "the main strategic threat to Canada comes not from [the Soviet Union] but from our south," from "a new generation of American imperialists."[17]

The Vietnam War, obviously, was far less traumatic an experience in Canada than in the United States, but the war and the influx of resisters had its impact on the country as a whole and on its politics. Reflecting on the draft dodger phenomenon in 1990, Robert Fulford observed: "I think their impact on Canada was to make us feel our separateness from the US more than we had felt at any time since the Second World War. . . . One thing that helped . . . Canadians to see themselves as separate . . . was their consciousness of the Vietnam War and their deep desire not to be involved in it. That was fed by the draft dodgers."[18]

The amnesty of 1977 allowed many of the Americans who had come to Canada to escape the war to return home, duly "Carterized." How many did is unclear, though estimates do not usually go above 15 percent of all those who had come to Canada. One, at least, a successful painter in London, Ontario, waited until amnesty was offered before taking out Canadian citizenship. He had wanted his choice of Canada to be one he could make when there was the possibility of returning home.

The evaders and the deserters, too, had assimilated into Canadian society, taking citizenship, marrying, raising hockey-playing kids, and reading the Canadian newspapers. All that betrayed their American origins was a different accent and, perhaps, a warier eye on the United States than that of their native-born compatriots.

8

ANTI-YANKVILLE: ROBIN MATHEWS VERSUS THE AMERICANIZATION OF CANADIAN UNIVERSITIES

"SOH, I WANT YOU TO HAVE THE BEST AMERICAN PROFESSORS AVAILABLE—SO I AM SENDING YOU TO A CANADIAN UNIVERSITY"

Shane/National Archives of Canada C-143293

"It's practically an American university," the professor at the University of Ottawa told his old friend from graduate school days. "We call it the American University of Ottawa, but not when Canadians are around." The friend was uncomprehending. "How come?" The reply was straightforward: "In psych, sosh, poly sci, economics and anthropology, there's more Americans than anything else. We run the place." The friend was still confused. "But what about Canadians? Don't they hire them? Don't they want the jobs?" "Oh, they hire some," came the reply. "But Canadians aren't very good."

Weren't there any Canadian books? the friend queried, continuing to be puzzled. "Oh, yeah, they've got some books and journals. They study the Eskimo, and they study their own elections, and they write some history. But they don't have any literature, and the kids all study American history and government." "But they must study *something* of their own besides that," the friend probed. "Well, I guess they do," came the grudging response. "Most departments keep a few token Canadians, usually drunks or World War Two veterans or guys who couldn't get a PhD—sometimes all three at once. They teach little Canadian courses. People are nice to them. But nobody pays them much heed."

Robin Mathews's "Kingsmere," from which this conversation is taken, was a short story—fiction, of course. But in the late 1960s and early 1970s, Mathews and many others, both faculty and students, in Canadian universities believed that the situation was almost exactly as related by the imaginary Ottawa professor to his friend. Whole departments in virtually every university in the country were overwhelmingly American in composition, and Canadian courses were thin on the ground. The issue of the Americanization of Canadian universities, coming as it did at the same time as the Vietnam War and the height of the concern over American investment, helped to raise the temperature. Anti-Americanism had been discredited by the left in the 1950s and by Diefenbaker in the early 1960s, but in the super-charged atmosphere that energized Canadian nationalism during and after the Centennial, in 1967, it came to life once more.

*   *   *

Robin Mathews was a thirty-seven-year-old assistant professor of English at Carleton University in the fall of 1968. He had been born in the small town of Smithers in the interior of British Columbia in 1931, his mother an English war bride from the Great War, his father a piano teacher and a cultured man. He graduated from the University of British Columbia in 1955, and did his MA in English at Ohio State University. Mathews began, but did not complete, his doctoral work at the University of Toronto, where he studied from 1959 to 1961, then he took a job at the University of Alberta which lasted until 1966. After two years' teaching and lecturing in Europe, still without a completed doctorate, he took up his post at Carleton in the fall of 1968.

During his time in Edmonton, Mathews had become exercised by the corruption that seemed epidemic under the regime of Mayor Hawreluk, and he had led a long, bitter struggle that captured headlines. He and three companions were arrested, jailed, charged with a variety of offences and subsequently acquitted. All four then sued the mayor, the police chief, and the city solicitor for false arrest and malicious prosecution, but their case was lost in the Alberta Supreme Court. Mathews had also, to judge by a 1965 controversy in the pages of the *Canadian Forum*, become concerned about the numbers and the political attitudes of American members of the political science department at the University of Alberta, a department that had vigorously opposed his anti-Hawreluk campaign. The reform drive in Edmonton ultimately unseated the mayor for breach of public trust and, most important for our story, began the process of turning Mathews into both a public figure and an anti-American.

It was not until November 1968, however, that Robin Mathews became a widely-known and controversial figure, when he and his new Carleton University colleague James Steele, an associate professor of English, launched a campaign to have the university's faculty association consider ways in which the imbalance of Canadian to American faculty at their university could be redressed. They urged their colleagues to support a motion that "it will be the general policy of the University to employ enough Canadians to ensure that Canadians remain, or become, a clear two-thirds majority of full-time faculty members in each Department." They proposed that if a department fell below this "desired minimum," the department would have to demonstrate that it had actively sought "well-qualified Canadians" through advertising before recommending the appointment of a non-Canadian. Moreover, Mathews and Steele wanted academic administrative positions, such as chairs, deanships, and presidencies, to be limited to Canadians. They urged the national organization of the professoriate, the Canadian Association of University Teachers, to secure information on the nationality of faculty across the land and to formulate a policy on the matter.

The two English professors bolstered their case with a memorandum setting out the situation as they viewed it. "Foreign scholars are always welcome in Canadian universities," they began. "Nevertheless, it is a matter of concern that in recent years the proportion of Canadians on academic faculties has been rapidly diminishing." In 1961, approximately 75 percent of the 8779 male faculty in Canada were Canadian-born and thus, likely, citizens. After a half-dozen years of heavy immigration of faculty, ranging from 539 in 1963 to 1986 in 1967, their estimate—Steele, the duo's statistician, discovered there were no hard data—was that Canadian faculty in Arts and Sciences across the country had dropped to just under 50 percent. At their own university, again based on partial data, Mathews and Steele suggested that 58 percent of faculty had their first degree from a Canadian university and were likely Canadian citizens; of the non-Canadians, they speculated, no more than 10 percent had adopted Canadian citizenship. Carleton was likely better off than some other institutions, they added. The new Simon Fraser University in British Columbia, according to an internal survey, had 68 percent of its faculty as non-citizens in 1967–68—a figure that assuredly meant most were Americans.

Why should anyone care about the citizenship of faculty? The two professors argued that "teaching and research are not ordinarily conducted by disembodied minds in a metaphysical world of learning. They are carried on by particular men, in particular places, about particular problems and in the context of particular communities." The fact of the matter, they maintained, is that American and other scholars teaching and researching in Canada worked on and taught about subjects they knew. Very few, the implication was clear, knew anything about Canada.

Mathews and Steele placed the university situation in a broader context: it "is only one aspect of a much larger crisis which Canada is now undergoing," they said, pointing to foreign ownership of key sectors of the economy and the waves of American culture flowing over the border. This overall situation made it necessary for Canada to have "scholars committed, aware and working as Canadians for intellectual excellence." There were available then and in the foreseeable future, they said much more dubiously, "a much larger number of Canadians well qualified for university teaching than there are posts to be filled."

The response at Carleton and elsewhere to this statement was sharp—indeed, almost hysterical. The Carleton faculty association initially refused to consider the motions put forward by Mathews and Steele, and a petition began to circulate at the university supporting "the principle of an academic community of excellence, dependent upon criteria of professional and academic performance, and not criteria of race, gender, nationality, or any like basis. Specifically we unequivocally *reject* the notion that there be a quota on appointments of Americans, or any other foreign nationals." When the faculty association did eventually meet to discuss the Mathews-Steele Canadianization motions, all were defeated by huge majorities, and there were claims (subsequently demonstrated to be incorrect) that the motions violated Ontario's Human Rights code and that they had been incorporated into "the most reactionary document . . . since the Weimar Republic." It all smacked of "McCarthyism."

More telling was the comment on CBC Radio of Carleton University historian Blair Neatby who, while arguing that Canadian universities would not be worth preserving if chauvinism became more important than academic competence, stated that "it would be more constructive if we concentrated on defining what is uniquely and distinctively Canadian about our universities. Most of the American professors that I know," Neatby added, "would lean over backwards to respect our identity if we could tell them what it is. If our universities become American it will be because we don't know what makes our universities Canadian."

Just two decades after the end of the Second World War and Nazi genocide, anything that suggested application of a national—not even a racial—test was viewed by many academics as a threat. Working for a majority of Canadians in Canadian universities was seen as the thin edge of the wedge towards a quota system, and it had been only a few years since Canadian universities applied quotas on, for example, the number of Jewish students allowed into engineering or medicine.* No one wanted to return to that era. Moreover, scholarship, the pious refrain within the university went, was international, and excellence was the only criterion that mattered. The fact that, only a decade before, historian Harry Crowe had been driven out of Winnipeg's United College when a private letter critical of the administration found its way into the president's hands remained fresh in the professoriate's memory. That assault on academic freedom, the right of scholars to write and speak their minds without fear, had led to the formation of the Canadian Association of University Teachers. Were there

---

* Times change. By the end of the 1980s academics were quietly acquiescing to quotas to allow minority students entrance to law schools; quotas to control the number of Chinese students in dental, pharmacy, and medical schools; and eagerly accepting rules for faculty hiring that effectively gave preference to women candidates, and particularly women from minority groups. Ontario universities also acquiesced in the NDP government's employment equity law that imposed racial, gender, and disability numerical goals—but never quotas, the Rae government claimed—on the faculty and other employees of universities as well as all other large concerns in the provinces. One of the first acts of the Progressive Conservative Harris government in Ontario in fall 1995 was to repeal Rae's employment equity legislation.

now to be national tests to ensure that foreign scholars spoke only Canadian truths in their classrooms?

All Mathews and Steele had wanted was for Canadians to have fair opportunity in Canadian educational institutions and for Canadians to be able to learn about their own country, Mathews remembered a quarter-century later,[1] and, instead, they were being denounced at every turn. The two English professors were shaken by the assault—the calm, rational, and cerebral Steele lost ten pounds through fretting—but they did not fold their tents. It was like living "in an Orwellian world where you say one thing and you are represented to the whole world as saying something else," Steele said. Their response was to make themselves as expert as possible on the Americanization issue and, paid or unpaid, to speak anywhere in Canada where people would come to hear them. "We became the best informed people in Canada on the subject," Mathews later bragged a little, "prepared to risk a great deal if not all. And we were merciless debaters. We had to be better than our enemies who were legion and the powerful."

Inevitably under the attacks they attracted, their rhetoric and argumentation broadened and toughened. Mathews wrote to one of his critics at Carleton that "the US teaches many social philosophies that are peculiarly the substance and the product of that nation. . . . Some of the most serious threats to the survival of the Canadian community . . . come from US power, US influence, US takeover. To strive for a majority of excellent Canadians on Canadian faculties is simply to try to keep the doors open to Canadian students, that they might be able to know their own culture." To strive for the existence of Canada, he said, "is not to be anti-American, but pro-Canadian. I am not ashamed to be pro-Canadian. If *any* nation lay along our border and was seriously threatening our existence, I would fight for our existence. If that means a hotting up of feeling between Canada and the US I am very sorry."[2]

*   *   *

The Mathews-Steele controversy was part of a great crisis in Canadian education. In the 1960s Canadian university attendance increased and increased again. In 1954–55, there had been 68,000 university students; ten years later there were 178,000, and in 1967–68, 261,000—a staggering increase of almost 400 percent in little over a decade. To serve this enormous and sudden influx, new universities took shape, some grafted onto small religious colleges, others carved out of farmland. In Ontario alone, York, Brock, Laurentian, Lakehead, Trent, Waterloo Lutheran (later Wilfrid Laurier), Windsor, and Waterloo universities joined the few colleges that had been sufficient to serve the small percentage of post-secondary students hitherto going on to higher education. The same situation existed in every province as the barriers of class (and, some might say, high standards) fell. Unfortunately for Canada, this rapid expansion was an international phenomenon—new "red brick" universities in the United States, Britain, and France similarly sprang up overnight, creating an international sellers' market for professors.

The sad truth was that at the beginning of the higher education explosion, Canadian university faculties were tiny—in 1950–51, for example, there were only 30 political scientists teaching in all Canadian universities; fifteen years later there were some 200, and in 1973–74 there were an estimated 750. In sociology, in 1960–61, there were 61 faculty teaching in Canadian universities; by the mid-1970s the number teaching had ballooned to 917. Quite clearly, that explosion in staff simply could not be met from the very few Canadian graduate schools that produced a tiny number of PhDs each year—from 1960–61 to 1970–71, for example, only 27 doctorates in political science were awarded by Canadian universities, while in sociology, in the same decade, only 29 PhDs were completed. Graduate education in some fields had scarcely been developed, and for years Canadians had gone to Britain, France, or the United States to do their advanced studies.*

Universities, new and old, tried to attract Canadians back home, and many came, often fleeing the disruptions, riots, and violence that plagued American campuses during the Vietnam War. In this sense, the return of Canadians to their native land was a reversal of the "brain drain" that had long sent ambitious Canadians to the greener pastures in the south. In 1963, for example, there were more than fifty Canadians on the medical

---

* I went to Duke University in Durham, NC, to do my PhD in Canadian history in 1963. With a family to support, I was attracted by the fact that Duke offered more scholarship money (the vast sum of $3400, out of which tuition fees swallowed $1200) than any Canadian university. It offered no Canadian history, other than that embedded in its small Commonwealth Studies Center, but that did not seem much of a liability at the time.

faculty of Johns Hopkins University alone. But hundreds of other Canadian-born scholars enjoyed their lives in the United States (or in the United Kingdom), liked the prestige of working in a highly developed field and in top-rank departments, and had no interest in returning to Canada to engage in the arduous, risky task of creating a new or an expanded university. The problem was especially serious as the new universities hunted for senior scholars, men and women to lead their new faculties and departments. Excellent and accomplished associate and full professors, usually in their late forties or fifties with family responsibilities, were scarce and not easily moved to the howling wilderness that was the Canadian university scene.

In the circumstances, all the universities, but most especially the ones created out of nothing, their buildings rising overnight out of muddy fields, did what they had to do in the late 1960s: they looked to foreign academics to staff their faculties. Deans and chairs fanned out to the annual academic meetings in the United States and Britain, setting up in a hotel room well stocked with bourbon or scotch in the attempt to entice new PhDs and established faculty to Lakehead, Lethbridge, or Sackville. Many of the major academic meetings in the US were well-organized hiring halls, their sessions carefully scheduled to take place in the fall or between Christmas and New Year's, precisely the time departmental searches were in full swing; the Canadian Learned Societies, by contrast, bizarrely met in May and June, after hiring for the next academic year had ended.[3] Some of the faculty approached about Canadian jobs were interested; many were not. The resulting situation was—or ought to have been—predictable. G.M.A. Grube, a classics professor at the University of Toronto, spoke only blunt truths when he said that "standards vary a great deal in US universities. Some are *very* good but generally the most highly qualified Americans stay in the US. I suspect if you looked at the university calendars in Canada you would find very few US professors from Harvard, Yale and MIT. The good ones," he said, "stay home." Another academic, John Woods, a University of Calgary philosopher, was blunter still when he wrote a few years later that the best new American PhDs win competition for places in the United States, while "the failures and the unlucky . . . quickly seek out opportunities for employment north of the border. Though there are numbers of exceptions in which we can rejoice, America's answer . . . is the overproduction of locally unemployable comparative mediocrities, the unused supply of

called "promise." There was a chance that they might become first-rank scholars. Of course, letters of recommendation, then as now, were too often half-truths or outright lies. A PhD was considered the equivalent of the union card in a closed shop, and the higher the percentage of faculty with doctorates, the clearer the university's commitment to research and scholarship as the first criterion of its standing. Inevitably, if the choice for a position in history, sociology, economics, or political science was between a very good Canadian with an MA and a so-so American with a PhD, the American was almost certain to be chosen, something that especially rankled those, like Robin Mathews, who had incomplete doctorates. This, Canadian critics claimed, was the "professionalization" of their formerly humanistic disciplines. "Canadian students," Toronto professor Ian Lumsden wrote, "are now increasingly taught by faculty whose academic standing is measured by their 'professional reputation' rather than by their intellectual abilities." That the two in all likelihood were related did not seem to trouble Lumsden.

Naturally enough, the new American arrivals ordinarily knew nothing about Canada, and in their first years north of the border their faculty dinner parties often seemed to be devoted to relief that they were far away from the chaos south of the line induced by the Vietnam War, and to discussions about the quaint customs of the locals and how hard it was to get the *New York Times*. If belatedly they realized that a Canadian or two was present, there would be a slightly abashed momentary silence, and assurances that "you" were different from the rest. More often, the American faculty simply assumed that they were among friends and no notice was taken of the squirming, uncomfortable Canadians.*

More important than these minor social gaffes, the courses offered by the relatively small number of British faculty and the much larger number of Americans dealt with their specialties. It could not have been otherwise. If a political science professor had studied American government, the chances were that he knew all about voting patterns among blacks in

---

* I can still remember such a dinner in Toronto in the late 1960s where my wife and I were the sole Canadians in a group of political scientists. Somehow the Americans, one soon to be a dean and another a chair, had convinced themselves that Canadians served only lamb at their dinners. The lamb disappeared by the 1970s, the American faculty became more cautious in their utterances (or their guest lists), and the overt offensiveness largely disappeared.

Missouri but almost nothing, beyond a cursory understanding of the British parliamentary system, of how Canadian government functioned. If a sociologist understood the problems of the Massachusetts Irish, he ordinarily knew nothing of Quebec's Quiet Revolution and the problems of Canada's status Indians. How could the professor teach courses on Canadian problems in such circumstances? One of Mathews and Steele's critics, the Canadian-born sociologist Bernard Gustin who taught at the University of Chicago, thus missed the mark when he said: "There is no such thing as Canadian sociology as distinct from Cuban sociology as distinct from American sociology. There are various types and techniques of sociological analysis . . . but all these may be applied to the study of Canadian society." The Carleton professors' point, of course, was that there was much too little analysis of Canadian society, thanks to the dominance of Americans in Canadian sociology departments. "Dear old Hugh MacLennan said it so well in a speech," Robin Mathews wrote some years later. "He said Quebec was moving to crisis; things were hellish there, and the students were marching on the Principal of McGill demanding he end the war in Viet Nam; Laurier LaPierre told me a little later that in over 800 sociology papers at McGill about 15 were on Canadian problems, *three on French Canada*. What were the students writing about: why, Congressional voting patterns, and the negro in the small southern town, being urged to do so by the wonderful, lively, US professors who had flooded in during the sixties."* In effect, "in the academic world, the conventional wisdom was continentalist," said Stephen Clarkson and Christina McCall, and in economics, sociology, and political science, the mainstream social science disciplines, the "national school of political economy" created by Harold Innis and others had largely been replaced by newer American models of analysis. Novelist Robertson Davies in 1969 made the same point more gracefully: "These professors see history, economics and literature as Americans see them and, with the effortless superiority of a greater people approaching a lesser, they assume that their view is the right one. In the course of a few university generations . . . it may be assumed that their attitudes will prevail in Canada."

---

* A few years later, McGill students would be in the streets about Canadian and Quebec issues. The university was to be all but torn apart by the campaign to make the old Anglo–Canadian bastion more sensitive to the francophone milieu in which it survived.

All too many of the new arrivals from the United States seemingly sprang full-blown from the pages of "Kingsmere." Political science was a modern discipline in the United States and an old fashioned one in Canada, American critics complained. The issue was not one of Americanization but of modernizing the Canadian discipline, which was "folkloric at best." The critics, as University of British Columbia political scientist Alan Cairns noted, "are unable to consider an argument for any Canadianness to the political science of Canada, because they are unprepared to recognize any Americanness to the political science they view as the instrument of modernity." This was true in other fields as well. Canadian writing and scholarship, except perhaps for Canadian history (which interested almost no one except Canadians, and precious few of those), was held almost by definition to be second rate by global standards in content and/or methodology. Louis Dudek, the Canadian poet and McGill University English professor, noted that compatriots in his department were unable to teach what they wanted "because . . . well . . . whenever you have a preponderance of Americans, the problems and issues will be American." His department had one "anthology" course, he said, "and for three years we succeeded in getting Canadian literature on it. About 1,000 students in that time studied Canadian literature and then it was taken off the course because the quality was said not to be high enough. This is nonsense! But in any case *every* nation studies its own literature—except colonial countries."[5] At Carleton University, located in Canada's capital, the supervisor of graduate studies in the English department, Mathews recalled of his arrival in 1968, was a specialist in American literature, "a US immigrant, former Marine," whose aim was to "reconstruct graduate English Studies to make Carleton University . . . a centre for the study of US literature."[6] This infuriated Mathews— who would be much less likely to be allowed to teach graduate students than those with the PhD—and others who believed that the study of Canadian literature was important.

Some departments scarcely even tried to offer Canadian content. As the data demonstrated, departments in some universities had no Canadians on staff—other than those drunken Second World War veterans without a PhD, noted in Mathews's short story. At York University's sociology department in 1969, there were two Canadians out of twenty-two faculty, and, early in the 1970s, fifteen of sixteen departments in the Faculty of Arts had American majorities. Waterloo's sociology department offered sixty-two courses, none on Canada; the

English department gave two courses on Canadian literature out of some ninety offered. Alberta's sociology department had four Canadians of twenty-three faculty and in 1968–69 offered seventy-nine graduate and undergraduate courses—of which only one, according to the calendar, dealt with Canada. In political science at Alberta, the department had six of thirteen Canadian faculty, but offered only seven of sixty-six courses on Canadian questions, of which only two were open to undergraduates. At Laurentian University in Sudbury, the political science department offered a single half-course on Canadian government, while the English department had no courses in Canadian literature. At Montreal's Loyola College, eleven of sixteen members hired by the English department between 1966 and 1969 were Americans. Only in a few departments, notably history, did Canadian courses amount to a reasonable proportion of those offered, likely because Canadian history had been studied for a substantial period and the graduates, though small in number, were respectable in quantity.

The problem, nonetheless, was very real in the social sciences, despite the claim in the report of the president of the University of Toronto in 1969 that the "cloudy debate" was "one part statistics, and two parts nationalism." The numbers of faculty and course offerings suggested that, even where there were Canadian professors, their interests lay elsewhere than in their own country's problems. In part, this focus seemed necessary for those who wanted to advance their careers. Professional standards in the social science disciplines increasingly had become founded on esoteric dialogue with international specialists rather than on communication with the public. Thus, the prejudice suffered by blacks in the US south as an issue worthy of study was more important to faculty members than the biases keeping French-speaking Canadians out of the highest ranks in the Ottawa public service. And if faculty interests leaned that way, so inevitably did student interests. Political scientists Alan Cairns and Reg Whitaker put the problem in their discipline calmly: "A careful analysis will reveal very precise distortions of Canadian research priorities, most particularly a failure to deal with political problems crucial to Canada but either absent from or of marginal significance to the United States." In essence, a generation of Canadian university students, often the first in their families to secure a higher education, lost the chance to learn about their own country, and Canada was the poorer for it. This concern lay at the root of Robin Mathews's crusade, and all he was doing was calling for Canadian universities to focus on their own culture and society.

"I watched an American professor of theatre on television," he told *Weekend Magazine*. "He said he didn't know the names of the provinces when he got to Canada, or anything about the country for his first five years. I say Canadian students want to know about Canadian theatre, how Canadian playwrights think within the Canadian frame of reference, what influences work on them. I say that in this case Americans positively *obstruct*." His colleague James Steele added it was not what Americans brought with them that was bad, "it is what Canadian students are *missing* that is bad. We are pro-Canadian but we are not anti-American."

* * *

Pro-Canadian, not anti-American: the clichéd phrase was in common usage—John Diefenbaker had dropped it regularly into his speeches—but as the debate over the Americanization of Canadian universities heated up, and as it integrated into the general discussion of Canadian independence, it became difficult to separate one from the other.

Mathews tried with increasing difficulty to maintain the distinction. His preferred term was not "anti-Americanism" but "anti-imperialism." The United States, he argued, infringed on areas of Canadian sovereignty in an imperialist way. To attempt to keep Canada sovereign and independent inevitably involved differences with the United States, and that, he maintained, "is clearly Canadianism. It is also (like it or not) anti-imperialism. And in some areas it must involve anti-Americanism. But in that scale." Those who refused to see the Canadianism, "who refuse to see the legitimate anti-imperialism, are left with anti-Americanism, the least important part."

In other words, the Canadian student had to watch as his country was taken over by an imperial power. "Canadian material is treated colonially, and the Canadian university is becoming a branch-plant brother of Canadian industry. The capitalist élite is rubbed out, the worker colonized, the Canadian student is in the midst of the colonization of the Canadian intellectual community." The "dominant corporate system on this continent" for a Canadian, Mathews said, "is the system of an alien, imperial power." Or, as he put it in an angry open letter to the president of the University of Waterloo in September 1969, "The United States is a republican, racist, imperialistic, militaristic, two-party, chauvinistic, culturally aggressive community," and there were huge cultural differences between Canada and the United States.

From the mid-1960s on, teach-ins were held at universities across the country focusing on issues from revolution in the Third World to the Vietnam War to university governance. At the University of Toronto, for example, the americanization of Canada was the subject of one such popular manifestation, with Mathews debating historian Kenneth McNaught on the "Americanization of Canadian Universities" at one of five sessions (the others being the politics and economics of independence, organized labour, foreign policy, and Quebec–English Canada relations). Harassed university administrators tried desperately to stay one step ahead of the changes occurring on their campuses, changes they often believed were brought north by American professors or "sour Marxian missionar[ies] to the unconverted," in Claude Bissell's testy phrase.

The attack on the Americanization of the universities continued to draw counter fire. "The Jews who were continentalist called us anti-Semitic," Mathews recalled, "but we had also good Jewish allies.* US people called us racist over and over. The Right called us Communist. The Left called us fascist, and when they felt good called us sentimental nationalists. . . . [and] continentalists said we wanted back into the warm embrace of Britain." The philosophically anti-nationalist York University historian Ramsay Cook, teaching for a year at Harvard University, lashed out in the *Canadian Forum*. "Our universities," he said, "are in the process of serious disruption as a result of our local variant of the 'Black Power' movement: the proponents of Canadian Power, the academic nationalists." With few exceptions, Cook went on, "there is no evidence that the people who are making the loudest noises about our national purity have ever made a single significant contribution to the understanding of Canada . . . to dismount the soapbox

---

* "They don't really want justice for all Canadians," Mathews remembered his critics saying; "secretly they want to get Jews, or Hindus, or Italians, or Americans, or High Church Anglicans." Anti-Semitism was the "nastiest charge of the time; so it was used." An interviewer on the CBC labelled Mathews and Steele racist anti-Semites to such an extent that, after Mathews threatened to sue, a second program the next evening was devoted to the subject. This time, the interviewer again attacked with such vehemence that he was reprimanded by CBC management and taken off the air for a week. (Letter, Mathews to author, April 22, 1995.) There is no evidence whatsoever that Mathews was anti-Semitic.

long enough to enter the study in order to fulfil that necessary requirement for the professorial title: publication for the judgment of peers."

Cook's stinging phrases clearly rankled Mathews (who had published relatively little at this time), as did the failure of Canadian leftists generally to see the issue of Canadianization clearly. When he participated in a debate at Convocation Hall at the University of Toronto, Mathews seized the opportunity to strike out at both Cook and the lukewarm Marxists. As he recalled years later,

> I remember . . . a Lefty taking the microphone to ask if I really believed a Canadian non-Marxist was better to teach Canadian history than a US Marxist. I said "absolutely." I said you may not like [historian] Donald Creighton, but he can answer and challenge every point you raise from deep Canadian experience and learning. Having a Marxist US person refer all Canadian questions to US experience . . . might not be the best pedagogy.
>
> I paused. . . . Then I said, "I am so serious about this point I would even prefer a Canadian history course to be taught by Ramsay Cook than a US Marxist." There was great laughter in the Hall, and I was told later that Ramsay Cook was sitting in one of the front rows.[7]

Another among the multitude who tackled Mathews & Company head on was the influential Canadian-born economist Harry Johnson, of Chicago and London School of Economics fame. When Carleton University gave him an honorary degree in 1970 (the requisite committee knowing his views and likely encouraging him to let loose), Johnson used the occasion to fire directly at those "Canadian intellectuals, more gifted in elementary statistics than in economic and social understanding," who "have decried the results of Canada's ability to hire foreign scholars at short notice to teach its rapidly expanding student body." It is true, Johnson said, "that foreign competition prevents third-rate Canadian academics from earning first-rate salaries, and also prevents them from managing second-rate departments in a fourth-rate way; but it is not clear that Canadian students would benefit from having their instruction monopolized by whatever intellectual rag-tag-and-bobtail can qualify itself as genuine Canadian." Terence Crowley, a young Canadian academic trained in the United States, added his view: "Nationalists are, by definition, naive and parochial. They present simple solutions to what they think are simple problems." The Canadian Association of University Teachers apparently agreed, for, in Mathews's later words, "the CAUT did everything it could to frustrate our efforts," attempting to deny the proponents of Canadianization a hearing.[8]

Despite—or because of—the assaults directed at him and his cause, Mathews clearly revelled in being a public figure, his rhetoric blossoming. Look into your heart, he said in the grandly titled "Robin Mathews Replies to His Critics": "What do you see? Stars and Stripes? It's a common colonial condition as well as an incurable imperial disease. It spawns, unfortunately, most of the arguments against Canadianization." The critics, he went on, push for internationalism.

> It's a word that easily disguises imperialism. Scholarship, as we know, is international. Every country . . . looks at the problems that confront the home society and all mankind. Out of the local . . . comes special insight and unique solutions. Moreover, by addressing peculiar problems countries develop ways of looking at world problems. That is internationalism. But our critics really want imperialism. Though almost every country in the world fosters its home scholars, brings them to excellence in order to provide for order and continuity, even in change, our critics sneer at the idea.
>
> Internationalism for them is US "value-free" (read "pentagon-approved") study. Internationalism for them is studying British and US literature, not Canadian. Internationalism for them is the US city. Who else has them? Internationalism for them is science research that moves in the US grants orbit. For that reason they prefer alien scholars who won't rock the gravy boat.

The American "imperialist-scholars," Mathews continued, "tell us to fight US militarism, US economic takeover, but they tell us not to fear US citizens who are conditioned in the American Dream, the frontier theory, Manifest Destiny, oaths of allegiance to the US flag, and other US ideas of 'internationalism.' . . . There can be no denying that the US citizen in Canada today, teaching in a Canadian university, is a part of the general US expansion and takeover of Canada for US uses." Many, of course, did deny any such intention.

Another sign of this takeover for Mathews was the presence of Americans on prestigious award committees. In 1969, for example,

University of British Columbia professor Warren Tallman was named a judge on the panel selecting the Governor General's Awards, the leading Canadian literary prize. Although he had taught in Vancouver for fourteen years, Tallman had remained an American citizen. Mathews attacked Tallman as a "conscious or unconscious" American imperialist, denounced the Canada Council for selecting him as a judge, and called on the professor to do the decent thing and resign. The protest, which became vociferous and featured the picketing of the Canada Council offices, wrote Robert Fulford, "was in all ways unreasonable." Tallman knew the country, understood its literature, and had spent a good part of his life in Canada; Mathews's efforts as "the noisiest proponent of the New anti-Americanism" merely served to "discredit further the whole dubious collection of views with which he is associated."

When writer and editor Dennis Lee warned Mathews that he was in danger of becoming typecast as a "yankeephobe," the Carleton professor responded that he cared not a whit. "Let them say away. . . . given the condition of Canada, whatever is said . . . is going to cause charges of anti-yankville."[9] And that condition? To Mathews, it was all the product of generations of Canadians saying that they were inferior. Historian Frank Underhill, for example, had attacked the Massey Commission on the Arts, Letters and Sciences two decades before by arguing that the "so-called 'alien' American influences are not alien at all; they are just the natural forces that operate on a continental scale." The test of Canadian maturity, Underhill proclaimed, was how we adjust to "American leadership," noting that Canadian history was as dull as dishwater, that Canadians were a "people incapable of tragedy." Underhill's generation had said that "kind of thing over and over," Mathews protested. "Canadians, they said, are inferior. In one way or another, over and over: Canadians are inferior."[10] Historians and two generations of students would vehemently disagree that Underhill, arguably the liveliest historical mind of his time, believed his compatriots to be inferior beings with a boring history. Nonetheless, the distinguished historian Arthur Lower said much the same in a letter to Mathews: "Few Canadians in my experience want to be Canadians: they want to ape the great and the rich and simply do not understand you when you speak of being themselves."[11]

* * *

That historians like Lower and distinguished writers like Hugh
MacLennan* had enlisted in Mathews's Canadianization crusade was an
indication that his campaign for the nationalization of the universities had
made substantial headway. In the first place, Mathews and Steele legit-
imized what many Canadian students, eager to learn about their own
country *and* the world, believed was wrong with their university education—they could find out little other than what came to them filtered
through an American lens.[12] Those students were likely voters; certainly
their largely middle-class parents were. Although William Davis, in 1969
the Minister of University Affairs in the Ontario government, had initially
been sharply critical of "the anti-American tone" of Mathews and Steele's
efforts,[13] by 1973 the Davis-led government created a Select Committee
on Economic and Cultural Nationalism and held hearings on the
Americanization of the province's professoriate and universities. The
committee insisted that the universities reveal data on the percentage of
non-Canadians on their staff, a demand that the Council of Ontario
Universities rejected because, its Executive Director said, it would breach
the right to confidentiality. Such a request, moreover, violated the
Ontario Human Rights Code. The Minister of Colleges and Universities,
Jack McNie, said that Ontario would urge the federal government to
make the immigration of foreign professors more difficult. Ontario universities needed professors "who know what they're talking about on
Canadian subjects." A rising nationalist sentiment had begun to win the
notice of politicians, including those to the right of centre.

The Minister's argument and the committee's efforts were assisted by
two cases that stirred public concern. The first was the January 1973
sacking of five Canadians on one-year contracts at the University of
Western Ontario's sociology department. The department had thirty-six
members, with eleven Canadians; five of the eleven were being let go
because of shortfalls in student enrolment. This fact was presented to the

---

* Hugh MacLennan had been raised in an extraordinarily anti-American atmosphere. His father, biographer Elspeth Cameron wrote, "was so anti-American
that he had refused to buy what he thought was the best kind of car, a Pontiac,
for the simple reason that it was named after an *American* Indian." *Hugh
MacLennan: A Writer's Life* (Toronto 1981), 8.

Legislature Committee by professors Paul Grayson and Craig McKie of Western Ontario, and their revelation produced shouting matches in departmental corridors, inaccurate responses by Western's President, the decision by the sociology department to give the one available tenure-track job to an American political scientist, and student protest meetings addressed by the "85 Percent Canadian Quota Campaign," a new organization led by Barry Lord, an art historian at Ryerson Polytechnical Institute.[14] The next year, the University of Toronto sociology department made eight appointments, none of them Canadians. The chair, Irving Zeitlin, a Princeton-educated US citizen, told the *Toronto Star* that Canadians had not been hired because "either they didn't have Canadian research interests or they were inferior to the non-Canadian applicants. . . . No one is going to sacrifice competence to hire Canadians." The open arrogance, the assumption that Canadians, and especially those trained in Canadian institutions, were inferior academically, was appalling. The Toronto university's action was duly censured by the Canadian Sociology and Anthropology Association on a motion moved by Paul Grayson, by then employed at York University.

There would be more instances like those, but the tide had already turned. Mathews was talking about public institutions supported by Canadian tax dollars, and the children of the middle classes, especially, had an interest in the universities. The Progressive Conservative government in Ontario had recognized that a problem existed, and this was the first sign that Mathews's cause was all but won. Another was that Peter C. Newman, then the influential editor of *Maclean's* and a key figure in the Committee for an Independent Canada, spoke in favour of universities having two-thirds of their faculty Canadian so that the country's colleges could "start reasserting themselves as uniquely Canadian institutions." In 1972 the Commission on Post-Secondary Education in Ontario urged institutions, government, and society "to pay close attention to the special role of post-secondary education in the Canadian intellectual tradition," a goal it wished to achieve without "quotas or restrictive controls."

The next landmark came with the March 1976 release of a report by Trent University's founding president, T.H.B. Symons, called *To Know Ourselves*. The Commission on Canadian Studies, with Symons as its sole member, had been created in 1972 by the Association of Universities and Colleges of Canada, the umbrella organization of the country's universities, "to study, report, and make recommendations upon the state of teaching and research in various fields of study relating to Canada at Canadian universities." The AUCC had first tried and failed to secure Ramsay Cook to do the study (an idea that utterly horrified Mathews), so it settled for Symons, whose report was late, expensive, and no model of scholarly rigour. Nonetheless, it pointed to old-boy networks, academic snobbery, and foreign scholars "blinded to the possible merit of scholars raised in another tradition with academic interests that related to their own country" as favouring the employment of Americans over Canadians. One American-born chair of a sociology department actually told Symons that his department would not hire Canadians: "once one hires a few then they will be pushing for more and more." The commission similarly found that curricular offerings, much as Robin Mathews and others had charged years before, short-changed Canadian subjects. In fact, by the time Symons reported, most universities had begun to offer a wide range of Canadian content in almost all disciplines, and Canadian studies programs, slapping together courses from a variety of disciplines, had sprung into existence all across the country, frequently with more money at their disposal than traditional departments. As a sociologist conceded in the mid-1980s, in words that might well have been uttered of any discipline, the Americanization debates had been "salubrious because they forced the realization that 'Canada' was a social phenomenon in its own right, the study of which had a legitimate place." Home-grown nationalism—pro-Canadian, but not necessarily anti-American—had had its effect on faculties, professors, and students.

Once Symons' report was published, governments began to use immigration regulations to make the hiring of non-Canadians more difficult. In 1977 the federal government required universities to demonstrate that they had advertised widely before making appointments; four years later this practice was strengthened with a requirement that advertisements must first be placed in Canada before universities could search abroad. In 1983 the government put into place a complex system that required universities to consider the dossiers of Canadian candidates for positions before opening the files of foreign applicants. If an American applicant, say, was offered a job, then governmental approval would be required, with the university being obliged to demonstrate that candidate's superiority over domestic applicants. The litany that "in accordance with Canadian immigration requirements, this advertisement is directed to Canadian citizens and permanent residents" began to appear in every job advertisement. (Cynics and Americans phrased it differently: "No competent candidates need apply.")

The resulting enhanced public awareness of the problem and the impact of government regulation had quick effect. The percentage of professors who had obtained their first degrees in Canada, usually a reliable indicator of citizenship, rose steadily. So too did the citizenship of full-time faculty (about 74 percent in 1977–78) and the percentage of new appointments going to Canadians. The problem—if there was one—had evaporated, though there would be occasional storms over the place of teaching versus research in higher education, the latter always being viewed as a key determinant of Americanization. Research was as Canadian as maple sugar, though many of the Canadianization proponents seemed blissfully unaware of the fact.

By the early 1980s, however, rapid university expansion had long since ground to a halt in both Canada and the United States, and hirings in most fields were few. The Americans in the Canadian professoriate, safely tenured and utterly immoveable, remained in their posts. Many gradually adapted to Canadian society and, whether or not they opted for citizenship, their lives blended into the norm. (Some ensured that their spouses retained their US citizenship or, when the United States began to allow dual citizenship, carefully sought the restoration of their original citizenship—just in case a job opened up in a "good" university to the south.) A small number remained radically disconnected from Canada, continued to be deeply involved in every twist and turn of American politics and society, and remained dependent on CBS, NBC, and the *New York Times* for their daily and Sunday fixes of US content.

The Americanization of Canadian universities, insofar as the citizenship of professors and the content of courses was an indicator, had been checked. Whether the quality of Canadian universities was affected by this process—for good or ill—is much harder to determine. Whether Canadian students knew more about their country was similarly uncertain. Novelist Graeme Gibson noted in *Quill & Quire* in January 1994 that "at most Canadian universities, one can get a BA, an MA, even a PhD in literature without taking a single course in Canadian writing. It follows that students in other faculties, in medicine, law, engineering, in history, or business . . . will have little or no chance of encountering their own literature, their own imaginative heritage. It boggles the mind." So it does, but the situation is even worse: a student can also graduate with degrees in history or political science at virtually every university in Canada without ever taking a Canadian course in those disciplines.

What may have changed, perhaps, is that as the level of anti-Americanism in the universities increased and as national origin became a factor to be considered in higher education, so too did other characteristics such as sexual orientation, gender, and race. Political correctness, a term that had not even been invented in the late 1960s, had entered academe in the wake of anti-Americanism with consequences that still remain to be determined. The man who had begun this change in Canadian reality was not T.H.B. Symons, however much he appeared to monopolize the attention of the public and to bestow on the Canadianization cause the establishment's seal of approval. Instead, the frequently reviled Robin Mathews had done the trick.

Mathews's subsequent career saw him move determinedly to the left on all issues. In the early 1970s he joined the Waffle, a nationalist and socialist faction within the New Democratic Party, and in 1978 briefly became the leader of the National Party of Canada on a platform that was, he said disingenuously, neither on the right nor on the left of the political spectrum but devoted wholly to attacking foreign control of the economy, institutions, and culture—in effect a policy of broad-based anti-Americanism. His political efforts also included a race for Parliament in the 1980 federal election that went nowhere. In 1987 he took early retirement from Carleton University and returned to his native province to teach part-time at Simon Fraser University, where he continued to crusade for the hiring of Canadians and to publish his poetry, plays, fiction, and essays. In a curious way, Mathews had become the late-twentieth-century equivalent of Colonel George Taylor Denison, the anti-American and pro-Canadian crusader of the late Victorian era whose causes, all taken on with equal enthusiasm and conviction, ranged from Canada First to Imperial Federation to anti-reciprocity.

History, however, has not treated Mathews any better than Colonel Denison. Mathews's literary works, though of good quality, never seem to be published by mainstream journals or to secure mention in literary histories. Politically, it is much the same. As he noted with bitterness, writing in his characteristic third person, "Mathews and Steele have been dropped from history. The *issue* has been erased. Check the *Canadian Encyclopedia*, check *The Oxford Companion to Canadian Literature*, check the source books. Nothing." There is some truth in that plaintive

cry and in Mathews's exaggerated assessment of his own place in the
resurgence of post-Centennial Canadian nationalism:

> The truth is Mathews and Steele appeared December 11, 1968, gave
> the impulsion, occupied the press and TV screens. After came the
> Waffle, the National Farmers Union, the Confederation of Canadian
> Unions . . . the League of Canadian Poets, the Association for
> Canadian and Quebec Literatures, the Canadian Artists Registry—
> the huge blossoming of post-1967 developments concerning
> Canadian sovereignty and self-respect. We did not create those
> things, of course, but we were first and supportive in every direction.
> If we had not been born we would have had to be invented.[15]

To this day, Mathews maintains that he never was and is not now anti-
American. "I am not antiamerican at all," he wrote to one critic in the mid-
1980s, "I am an anti-imperialist. The people of the United States may be
what they want to be. When they tell us that we must be like them, they
introduce a political question, and that is where I react."[16] All too often,
however, Mathews saw this issue—indeed, every issue—in starkest black and
white. In one of his academic articles, he quoted T.C. Haliburton's Sam
Slick, the Yankee clockmaker and pedlar of aphorisms, that the United States
was "a great whirlpool—a great vortex; it drags all the straw and chips and
floating sticks, drift-wood and trash with it." It is difficult not to see
Mathews's own view of the dangers of Americanization in that quotation.
The choice to him, as Alan Cairns put it so caustically, seemed only to be
between service in "the academic army of American imperialism or the academic branch of the people's army of Canadian independence." To most
Canadians inside—and outside—the universities, that was no choice at all.

Yet Mathews had won his battle against the Americanization of the universities, and had done so largely by his gritty hard work and his charismatic
speaking, aided by a small army of vocal supporters and the shrewd seizing
of a brief historical moment. Fifteen years later, Mathews likely would have
gone nowhere with his cause; in the nationalist late 1960s and early 1970s,
in an era shaped by the Centennial, the Vietnam War, and the struggle
against American investment, he was the man on the spot. Where arts
groups, periodical publishers, and broad-based nationalist movements
largely failed, he succeeded. His success was one of the very few after 1911
that anti-American nationalists had in any area of Canadian life.

9

IMAGINING CANADA: ACADEMICS, ARTISTS, WRITERS, AND THE CULTURE OF ANTI-AMERICANISM

Gable/The Leader Post

The celebrated novelist, writer, and "professional anti-Canadian" Mordecai Richler stands out from his compatriot writers for many reasons. He is successful both in Canada and abroad, and he makes a good living from his art. He is unafraid to tackle hard subjects, to expose himself to political fire. He has made something of a career mining the rich vein of the Canadian and Québécois inferiority complexes. *Oh Canada, Oh Quebec,* his viciously witty attack on separatism and francophone anti-Semitism, created a furore in Quebec in 1992. But he is even more unusual in that he has frequently and unhesitatingly poked a sharp stick in the eye of the Canadian nationalist beast, enraging it again and again.

In 1971, for example, Richler wrote in the *New York Times Book Review* about the Canadian mood of the day, focusing on Quebec separatism and English Canada's "militant nationalism, its most vitriolic expression being anti-Americanism." English Canadians, he argued, had been painted by Québécois as "quasi-Americans," and when Canada began to scrutinize its soul, the upshot was "self-discovery, rancid self-discovery, and a sharp (and convenient) turning against the other America. Suddenly, there was a sea-change. If, as French Canada scornfully charged, we were in fact spiritually puny, the fault, then, was most happily not in ourselves, but in the stars and stripes. America, America. Washington, ever our rapacious landlord; Wall Street, the usurious shop where we pawned our ore and oil." The result, Richler noted, was the creation of a Committee for an Independent Canada, a "fistful of militant new publishing houses and magazines," a Canadian Film Development Corporation, a National Arts Centre, and, in the universities, the proliferation of Canadian literature courses and a rebellion against the hiring of American professors. All of Canada's problems were blamed on the Americans, "most of whom are blithely unaware of Canada's existence, let alone that it is presently ridden with problems other than the rising cost of fishing licenses."

Given his position, his dark eye perpetually turning its focus on Canadian excesses, it came as no surprise during the 1988 general election when, in the face of virtually the entire Canadian cultural community, Richler was one of a small handful of artists who endorsed the Free Trade Agreement in a large advertisement in the *Globe and Mail*. What was surprising, however, was the venom with which Richler was singled out for attack. Farley Mowat, another Canadian writer of international reputation, called Richler a "non-Canadian." Richler "has his own sense of identity. It's his Jewish identity and it's his little neighbourhood identity. He has no sense of Canadian identity at all." Almost no one reacted to this outrageous characterization until John Metcalf, a critic every bit as acerbic as Richler and, like him, a man who had made a fine career out of attacking the nationalist pretensions of the practitioners of CanLit, singled out Mowat's attack. Such remarks, he noted, "reveal an almost instinctive conviction that Jews are not really part of Canadian society. There exists for Mowat . . . a Canadian identity to which Jewishness is inimical. The implication of Mowat's remarks is that a Jew can't be a 'real' Canadian." If he were a genuine Canadian, Mowat seemed to be saying, Richler would be against the Free Trade Agreement, opposed to American imperialism, and taking a stand as an outright anti-American. After all, how could a Canadian artist, forced to live in a world dominated by the cultural flood from south of the border, not be anti-American? Anything else was positively unCanadian.

Metcalf disagreed, noting that "the anti-Americanism of cultural nationalism and its self-absorption sadly diminished us and delayed our entry" into the international culture of which Canada was part.[1] Were Richler and Metcalf right? Or was Mowat, stripped of his unpleasant anti-Semitic overtones, correct in his anti-Americanism? Was Canadian culture such a fragile flower that overt resistance to America was essential if it was to survive at all?

In the dark era before Canadian culture began to flourish and the Canada Council changed the cultural landscape, survival of publishing and the arts could never be taken for granted. Yet government intervention was not unknown. Did American wire services dominate the distribution of news to Canadian newspapers? Ottawa would help create the "Canadian Associated Press," the forerunner of the Canadian Press. Were Canadian magazines fearful of American competition that entered Canada without duty and for one cent a pound in postage? They could receive special postal rates and privileges and, under the Conservatives in the 1930s, tariff protection. Was the development of radio threatened by the emergence of networks in the United States and their wish to establish outlets in Canada? Royal commissions would convene and the Canadian Radio Broadcasting Commission, the ancestor of the CBC, would be put in place. Was high culture being throttled in the cradle by American imports? The federal government would establish a royal commission to investigate the arts and culture under future Governor General Vincent Massey and, in response to the flood of Americanizing influences noted in the submissions and in the commissioners' report, create the Canada Council to foster the development of the arts. Was magazine advertising being drawn away to split-run American publications that milked the Canadian market? Ottawa would risk the anger of Washington to try to intervene to protect local periodicals.

"Better the state than the States," Prime Minister R.B. Bennett was said to have remarked when his Conservative government created the national broadcasting system in the 1930s. That attitude was a constant until the money—and the will to sustain a nation—all but ran out in the mid-1990s, a casualty of the bond markets and of Liberal and Conservative governments intent on creating a level playing field on which Canadian exporters could compete for market share against American and Mexican firms.

Did state intervention work in protecting Canadian culture? The answer is both yes and no. The trends that were glaringly apparent in the first two or three decades of the twentieth century have continued to develop: Canadians are ever more American in their popular tastes and attitudes, in their reading matter, in their movie-going and television-watching, and in the books and magazines they read. Nonetheless, even in the straitened circumstances of the present, Canadian theatre, art, music, dance, and literature thrive, greatly assisted by government grants and subsidies. Still, no sector of Canadian life today is more overtly nationalist and anti-American than the arts. In culture, the weather along the Canadian–American border is always stormy.

*   *   *

The most sustained critique of American influence on Canada by a cultural figure came from the Red Tory philosopher and professor of religion George Grant. Born in 1918, Grant was a child of the Canadian establishment. His mother was a Parkin, the daughter of Sir George Parkin, the leading Canadian proponent of the Divine Mission of the British Empire to spread civilization around the globe and the foremost critic of those, like Goldwin Smith, who called for annexation. Parkin was Principal of Upper Canada College, Toronto's upper-crust private school, and later the administrator of the Rhodes Scholarships. George Grant's father was W.L. Grant, the son of G.M. Grant, the Principal of Queen's University who had turned that small Presbyterian college into a leading Canadian educational institution. W.L. Grant became Principal of Upper Canada College a month after his son was born.

George Grant's antecedents were the best Canada could boast, and his academic career tried hard to live up to them. He was educated at the family schools, Upper Canada, Queen's, and Oxford on a Rhodes Scholarship. He spent the war years in Britain as a conscientious objector, his sister married a senior Canadian diplomat, and he knew Vincent Massey, the High Commissioner and a cousin by marriage. His sympathies were with the Labour Party, and he was the very model of a 1940s Anglophile Canadian.

In 1945 he began study towards a DPhil. in theology from Oxford, which he completed in 1950; he married in 1947 and began his teaching career at Dalhousie University in September of that year. From 1961 to 1980 he taught at McMaster University, and once more at Dalhousie from 1980 to 1984, when he retired. His philosophical writings were worthy, though slim, but what made him a public figure of note was what Mordecai Richler called his "succinct but bitchy" *Lament for a Nation: The Defeat of Canadian Nationalism*, published in 1965.[2]

Provoked by the nuclear crisis of 1962–63 and the defeat of Diefenbaker's government by Pearson's Liberal Party, aided by the Kennedy administration's devastatingly effective press release, *Lament for a Nation* combined political polemic and political philosophy into a scream of rage against Canada's absorption into the American empire and against those who had presided over the nation's demise. The Liberal Party, the agent of American imperialism, was the chief villain: Liberals "were in office during the years when the possible basis for nationalism disappeared. It was under a Liberal regime that Canada became a branch-plant society; it was under Liberal leadership that our independence in defence and foreign affairs was finally broken," Grant claimed. "The Liberals failed to recognize that the real danger to nationalism lay in the incipient continentalism of English-speaking society, rather than in any Quebec separatism. Their economic policies homogenized the culture of Ontario with that of Michigan and New York." How any Canadian could pretend that Quebec separatism was a chimera in 1965, *la belle province* already five years into the Quiet Revolution, was more than a little extraordinary.

Grant was a man who, in his youth and especially during the Second World War, had believed that Canada was instinctively American, but the emergence of the United States as a superpower dismayed him. He believed as early as 1945 that the dominion had to remain part of the British Commonwealth if it was to have any hope of resisting absorption by the great republic. By 1956 his views had crystallized further, and he was infuriated that Canada followed the United States' lead during the Suez Crisis. This was Lester Pearson doing what he did best—a lot of moralizing without responsibility, Grant believed. Canada's Suez policy was part of the process of Americanization, of homogenization, of the seizure of political, military, and economic dominance over all North America by Washington. By turning away from Britain, Canada had driven itself into the arms of the United States, to become a satellite not unlike Bulgaria on the borders of a great empire.

This was the key. Grant had long believed that Canada's only defence against the Americanization he despised and feared lay in the conservative tradition in which his grandparents and parents had lived and in which he had been raised. The values of Upper Canada College, in other words, were the values that ought to have prevailed in Canada—if only every Canadian could have gone to UCC!* The Tory tradition embodied by that school was not simply Loyalism, not just a long-lived complaint against the winners of the American Revolution. It was a genuine, philosophical distrust of individualism and bourgeois notions of Lockean progress, of a society that celebrated the profit motive as its greatest good. Canada, as created by its founders, was different, Grant maintained. It was a society with "a greater sense of order and restraint" than the United States, a society that was willing on occasion to employ the powers of government to control private intrusions on public interest. Thus the Canadian National, Ontario Hydro, and the Canadian Broadcasting Corporation. Moreover, unlike the Liberal Party, which saw the British link as an impediment to the development of Canadian independence, Tories saw the Crown as the "font of constitutional government." Red Toryism, in other words. And, though Grant did not say so, whatever might happen and whoever might come to live in Canada, the Anglo-Canadians presumably still ruled the roost.

By 1965 this was all gone, Grant argued. The Canadian state no longer had either the desire or the capacity to control big business, in substantial part because American capital and branch plants had achieved such dominance over the Canadian economy that the greater part of the élite now identified its interests with those of the American corporations. The election of Diefenbaker, the last champion of Canadian nationalism, had been the final chance to reverse this process, but the opportunity had been squandered. As Grant's biographer noted, *Lament* is a systematic indictment of Diefenbaker's government. "His administration . . . was confused and inconsistent; his response to the Canadian predicament bewildered." That was fair enough, and Grant was later even more blunt: "My book is not a

---

* "One can argue that UCC," the nationalist political scientist and UCC old boy Stephen Clarkson said in a book on the school, "as the pre-eminent private school in English Canada, has had a large impact on the country. In my judgment it has been largely negative." Clarkson cited Michael Wilson, Brian Mulroney's Finance Minister, as personifying the UCC graduate "who is very comfortable with the values of the new empire. He can take the American prescription for what is good for Canada the way earlier generations . . . would have taken the British prescription for what was good for Canada. . . . Canada has come to the position where the only thing it can do is tag on to the economic and political system of a declining American hegemony. I see Upper Canada College as a microcosm of the problem." In James Fitzgerald, *Old Boys: The Powerful Legacy of Upper Canada College* (Toronto 1994), 100–1.

defence of Mr. Diefenbaker. . . . Before the Defence Crisis I saw nothing in his favour, just nothing. . . . Over the Defence Crisis, I see the hero of this book as Mr. [Howard] Green [Secretary of State for External Affairs], not as Mr. Diefenbaker" (which says very little for Grant's understanding of foreign policy). Even so, Grant did argue that the crisis of 1962–63 revealed Diefenbaker's "deeply held principle for which he would fight with great courage . . Nothing in Diefenbaker's ministry was as noble as his leaving of it."*[3] No one who understood the events of the nuclear crisis ought to have been able to overlook the most salient facts: that Diefenbaker's government had bought the weapons systems and agreed to take the nuclear warheads needed to make them effective, and that the United States and NATO had very good reason for being angry that the government, and especially its leader, had begun to wobble. The Cuban crisis of October 1962 had demonstrated how serious that could be. Grant was a pacifist who hoped to see Canada leave NATO and rid itself of its defence alliances with the United States. Diefenbaker himself would not have agreed with that; nor would Tommy Douglas, the New Democratic Party leader, who had voted against the Tory government in February 1963, helping to drive it from power.

Thus, Grant believed that his *Lament* had left him all but alone, however many chords his little book stirred in Canadians.** He foresaw the

* When Diefenbaker died in 1979, Grant wrote a long appraisal of the Chief in the *Globe and Mail*. "Diefenbaker's principles were grounded in primary loyalties," he wrote, "and loyalty is the great virtue for political leaders"("Diefenbaker: A Democrat in Theory and Soul," August 23, 1979). I well remember the Progressive Conservative leadership convention in 1967, when Diefenbaker spoke of his loyalty to the party that was overthrowing him and to its leaders. John Bracken and George Drew, his predecessors, sat on the stage behind Diefenbaker and both, as one, rolled their eyes into their heads at Diefenbaker's words. The Chief had been a notoriously difficult, not to say disloyal, subordinate since his arrival in Parliament in 1940, and he backstabbed his own successor, Robert Stanfield, at every opportunity.

** *Lament for a Nation* was "the most important book I ever read in my life," socialist academic James Laxer gushed. "Here was a crazy old philosopher of religion at McMaster and he woke up half our generation. He was saying Canada is dead, and by saying it he was creating the country." Quoted in Charles Taylor, *Radical Tories: The Conservative Tradition in Canada* (Toronto 1982), 148. In the introduction to the reissue of *Lament* (Toronto 1971), viii, Grant recanted his gloom slightly, apparently stirred by the new nationalism of Canadian youth.

disappearance of Canada, its absorption into a universal and homogeneous state, its annexation by the United States, a nation in the grip of the homogenizing power of modernity in its purest form, "the only society on earth that has no indigenous traditions before the age of progress."[4] Moreover, he saw the country's disappearance as necessary. "Canada's independence," Grant's biographer William Christian summed up, "no longer served anything the world thought good. Formal annexation by the United States would eventually come, and when it did it would have only a minor impact. It was fated because most North Americans accepted the modern understanding of what was good for human beings."[5] The struggle to preserve an independent Canadian state in North America was over, Grant told Christian. "I was talking about the *end* of Canadian nationalism. I was saying that this is over."[6] Was Grant a pessimist? the biographer needlessly asked. Was there nothing Canadians could do? "Of course not. The one thing needful was always possible. It was always open to any human being at any time or place to orient his soul to God."[7] The soul of Canadians might be saved, in other words, but their nation was gone, a victim of technology and continentalism. Moreover, given English Canada's surrender to its American fate, Grant asked if "the French [of Quebec] are not best to be separatists in the face of the North American situation." Was not English-speaking culture merely "a Trojan horse for the 'rationality' of the North American monolith?"[8] No bleaker vision of Canada's imminent demise had been written in the modern era (except perhaps Goldwin Smith's *Canada and the Canadian Question* in 1891), certainly none that was so widely read and so generally praised by reviewers across the country.* As Canada's survival teeters dangerously in the 1990s, the worst of it is that Grant may turn out to be right.

* In 1965 I lent my copy of *Lament for a Nation*, a book that had greatly impressed me, to the distinguished historian Charles Stacey, for whom I was working at the Directorate of History, National Defence Headquarters. When he returned it, I can still remember Stacey saying that the book was "pure hate" against Americans. Not all published reviews of *Lament* were favourable. F.H. Underhill was characteristically blunt: "George Grant is as violently and neurotically anti-American as John Diefenbaker himself or as Tommy Douglas," and parts of the book have "a good many passages . . . which strike me as emotional drivel." *Journal of Liberal Thought*, 1 (1965): 101.

* * *

Northrop Frye's place in the pantheon of Canadian letters is secure, and he was above the venomous anti-Americanism that sometimes characterized historians like Donald Creighton. Nor was he given to much in the way of overt Canadian nationalism or to the style of critique that moved George Grant. Frye was conscious of both the east-west or Laurentian links in Canadian literature and art and, as a Maritimer by birth, of the north-south tendencies. The pull exercised by "the Boston states" was always strong in the Atlantic region, however much loyalty had developed to Confederation, and he was all too aware that "Canada is in the American orbit and will remain so for the foreseeable future. Canadians could not resist that even if they wanted to." Nonetheless, Frye pointed to the differences between Canadians and Americans that seemed to be reflected in Canadian literature. "As for the USA," he noted,

> there is a political separation from that country which a Canadian feels as soon as he goes outside Canada. Politically, Canada ought to be one of the small, observant countries in a new world of continental powers, much as, say, Switzerland has been in Europe. A Canadian going to the United States to teach in a university there is often asked by his American students if he notices any difference. They expect the answer to be no, and nine-tenths of the time it is no, but the tenth time there is some point of discussion that suddenly makes him feel like a Finn in Russia or a Dane in Germany. His students have been conditioned from infancy to be citizens of a vast imperial power; he has been conditioned to watch, to take sides in decisions made elsewhere.[9]

Canadians are voyeurs, waiting to take sides in decisions made elseand frequently carping about them, is a brilliant formulation of the
an psyche and Canada's history. There is much more of that
l waiting in the mainsprings of Canadian writing than there is of
l," Margaret Atwood's formulation of the dominant theme in
literature.

twood's is undoubtedly the central thesis for Canadian literary
ts. A brilliant polymath, Atwood is a poet, novelist, critic, and,
the author of the poetry collection *The Journals of Susanna*

Moodie (1970), consistent anti-American (despite, or because of, her graduate work in the United States). To her, Canadian literature has the same sort of binding myth that unites cultures elsewhere. For this country, it is the "basic victim positions" that Canadians, "exploited" and an "oppressed minority," adopt in the face of American power. There are "cultural side-effects" of the "colonial mentality," she says, but the "root cause" of them is economic, Canada's domination by American capital. The "key critical book of the period" (or so Robert Fulford called it), *Survival* examines, among other types of victimization, the political. The literature Atwood admired was that naming "real causes of victimization, not displacing the causes onto Fate or the Cosmos. And unlike most other books, they include political realities—the United States as an imperial master—among the causes of victimization." The stories she wrote at length about (Ray Smith's "Cape Breton Is the Thought Control Centre of Canada" and Dave Godfrey's "The Hard-Headed Collector") show their heroes as powerless and trapped or doomed to failure and death. These results occur "not because the author's literary tradition demands a failure but because failure is consistent with the conditions depicted in the stories. A successful revolution in the present is not imaginable. . . . And it's at points like these—when literature names situations we can recognize—that writer and reader connect in an area we can call real life; it's *our* situation that's being talked about."[10]

Scattered throughout Atwood's extensive essays, novels, and poetry are innumerable indications that she herself put this "real life" principle into her own work. A few examples only: Atwood's essay "Nationalism, Limbo and the Canadian Club" talks about her schooling, and how she emerged from high school knowing almost nothing of Canada other than a "very little about Louis Riel, W.L. Mackenzie and Quebec, except that they all lost." What might have been more useful, she added, "were the disadvantages of being a colony, political or economic, and the even greater disadvantages of being an Indian." At graduate school in the United States, however, she had discovered that "They," the Americans, "had been taught that they were the centre of the universe, a huge, healthy apple pie, with other countries and cultures sprinkled round the outside like raisins. 'We' on the other hand had been taught that we were one of the raisins, in fact, *the* raisin, and that the other parts of the universe were invariably larger and more interesting than we were." Then, in her poem "Backdrop Addresses Cowboy," a "Star-spangled cowboy/ sauntered

out of the almost-/ silly West," is as "innocent as a bathtub/ full of bul-
lets." The cowboy invariably shoots first, leaving behind a "heroic trail of
desolation," and the poem ends with Atwood declaring, "I am the space
you desecrate/ as you pass through." Atwood's bleak futuristic novel,
The Handmaid's Tale, with its Republic of Gilead in the grip of right-
wing religious fanatics and its women reduced to breeding stock, surely
offered the author's view of where America might be heading.* Finally,
Tony, the improbable woman military historian in *The Robber Bride*, tells
her friends that Canada's military and economic alliance with the United
States inevitably meant that the country would have to participate in the
Gulf War against Iraq's Saddam Hussein. "Our attendance will be
required," Atwood's character says. "If you take the king's shilling, you
kiss the king's ass. We'll be there, us and our falling-apart, rusty old
navy." But as David Staines has noted, very often the antagonists, the pol-
luters, the killers, the targets of Canadian hate in Atwood's fiction turn
out to be Canadians, not Americans. "Again and again in her fiction,
Atwood castigates Canadians for their willingness to blame the enemy, be
the enemy American or any foreign nationality, rather than accept any
responsibility." Anti-Americanism, in other words, however justified it
may be, "must also be seen as a potent evasion of responsibility, an easy
method for Canadians of embracing political and literary maturity" while
accepting none of its obligations.[11]

The country's most important non-academic critic, Robert Fulford, is
one of the legion of admirers of Atwood's writing, but he is markedly less
enthusiastic about her politics or her frequently "wildly overstated" accounts

---

* Set in the United States. *The Handmaid's Tale*, at least one critic has charged, rep-
resents the breakdown of "many of Atwood's own working distinctions between
Canada and the United States." Moreover, the absence of political activism in the
novel *Cat's Eye* is demonstrated by the uncaring attitude of her main characters to
"issues of Canadian nationalism." "So much for Atwood as anti-American freedom
fighter," one reviewer observed. Shannon Hengen, *Margaret Atwood's Power*
reviewed by Lawrence Mathews in *Literary Review of Canada* (September 1995)
9–10. Atwood's anti-Americanism, which I take to be unalloyed, appears to have
had no effect on her substantial sales in the United States. It may well be that her
militant feminism, every bit as strong as her anti-Americanism, overrides any negative impact her views on the United States might have on American readers. It is
also quite possible that many of her American readers simply assume that she is one
of them, yet another anti-American American.

of Canadian culture. In the mid-1970s, as he recollected in his memoirs, *Best Seat in the House*, Atwood said to him on one occasion that "there's a lot of paranoia about the Americans going around. The other day somebody told me *you're* a CIA agent." Fulford claimed to be understanding, noting that while he was thought to be a radical in some circles, in others "I was seen as a moderate at best and a sellout at worst." After all, he admired American democracy and culture, and "those opinions in themselves aroused suspicion. And when I deviated from the official line in Canadian nationalist circles—Canadians Good, Others Bad—my political allegiance was called into question." Never Atwood's, Fulford said. The "purity" of her nationalism "has always been beyond doubt," and she remains "the most articulate and forceful exponent of cultural nationalism."

Surprisingly, over time Fulford came to agree that Atwood and "the new nationalists" were largely right. The anti-nationalist Fulford had been sharply critical of "Cancult," the process by which Canadian literature and art became a crutch for Canadian nationalism. Cancult exacted a price, Fulford had said in 1961. "The price is anti-Americanism—or as some anti-American Canadians say, 'pro-Canadianism.'" Most countries supported the arts because culture was a good thing. But not Canada, he went on. "Cancult demands that we justify the tax money used . . . by saying it prevents something from happening. That something is the further spread of American culture in Canada." In essence, Cancult was anti-cultural, even Philistine. "It is Philistine because it holds that in a contest between art and nationalism, nationalism is more important. That's Cancult."[12] But Fulford eventually changed his tune: "Canadian culture had always been a kind of resistance movement against American domination," but the younger writers now argued that the resistance had not been strong enough in the past and, if it were to succeed in future, it had to be better organized. In *Saturday Night*, he wrote that while he had been against the reflexive anti-Americanism that so often characterized Canadians, "what we didn't realize was that if you *weren't* a nationalist, in some sense at least, then somebody else's nationalism would roll right over you."[13] That didn't turn Fulford into the male anti-American Atwood, but it at least recognized the force of her position. Cultural anti-Americanism at last had been made respectable by the mainstream *Saturday Night*.

Virulence similar to Atwood's can be found in Graeme Gibson's fine novel *Gentleman Death*. Gibson's ruminations on the United States' harmful influence on Canada are every bit as bleak as Atwood's, his spouse. Writing about the Free Trade Agreement, one of Gibson's characters reflected on "our wretched prime minister trumpeting 'FIRE SALE! FINAL CLEARANCE!' like Crazy Abner on late-night television. 'Everything must go!' And so it does. And so it will. Crazy Brian. Crazy Crosbie and ill-tempered Simon [Reisman] the Negotiator." These men were "handmaids to the merchants who traffic in Canada," the Canadian version of Scottish lairds who exchanged clansmen for sheep to pay for their own incompetence, their lack of vision, and their "arse-licking greed for all things English." It made no difference which party was in power. "Grit or Tory. The dismantling of my country has been going on for years."

If Gibson sounded like the army brat he was, raised to believe that a good dose of parade square discipline would bring the country back to its roots and its senses, his anti-Americanism paled by comparison with that of the American-born Douglas Fetherling. His memoir, *Travels by Night*, was a superb piece of writing about Fetherling's misspent youth in West Virginia and his journey to Canada in 1967, significantly not as a draft resister. Its anti-Americanism was all-pervasive. By the time he was eighteen, his ambition was to be a last-generation American and a first-generation Canadian. In the United States, "there was no moral commitment because there was no civilization worth the name, and no civilization because there was no education, no humaneness, no sense of the necessity of ongoing improvement." That was mild by comparison with his vitriol in an interview:

> I believe in original sin, not in a religious sense but in the demographic sense. I'm not naive, I've never believed that I should be considered the equal as a human being of anybody who was born in Canada or anybody who was born in some third place. . . . I don't think there is a statute of limitations on having been born in the United States. Not to be over-dramatic or to compare the Americans to Nazis, but I think that in the younger generations . . . that carries much of the same baggage of the past as I think younger Germans feel for their own country.

The nature of America and its pernicious influence on Canada was Fetherling's obsession.[14] But the violence of his anti-American beliefs was so un-Canadian, so *American*, as to make him nothing so much as the literary equivalent of a "Right to Life" crusader who supports capital punishment.

Another notoriously anti-American writer was Farley Mowat, the internationally known author of many volumes of popular natural history and of some of the finest writing anywhere on the Second World War. Mowat has an exuberant personality, and sometimes he allows his words to run away with themselves. There is no doubt, however, about his near-contempt for and fear of the United States. In 1969, he wrote of a Canada without "a snowball's chance in hell of escaping ultimate ravishment at the hands of the Yankee succubus." The blame lay with C.D. Howe, the "Minister of Everything" in the King and St Laurent governments. Howe had sold out Canada on a national scale, but now "every single province is trying to conduct its own sellout, in direct competition with the Ottawa salesmen." If that spread the blame around, there was still no doubt where it truly resided—in a United States that was ever-motivated to "accept wholeheartedly the duty and opportunity as the most powerful and vital nation in the world," as *Time* magazine founder Henry Luce put it, "and in consequence to exert upon the world the full impact of our influence, for such purposes as we see fit and by such means as we see fit."[15]

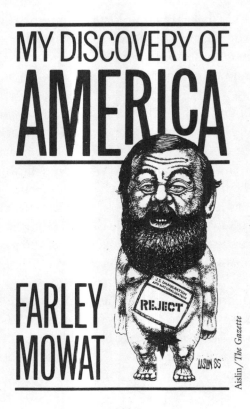

Aislin/The Gazette

More puckishly, Mowat denounced the United States in 1985 for barring him from the country to promote one of his books. The reason, it appeared, was that in 1968 Mowat had "turned down the command of something called the Col. J. Sutherland Brown Volunteer Brigade whose purpose . . . was to defend Canada against an invasion by US Strategic Air Force bombers carrying out simulated attacks at the 500-foot level every fifteen minutes over the Saskatchewan prairies." Mowat was quoted in the press at the time as saying he had refused command of the brigade because, though he had fired his .22 at SAC bombers flying over his house in Newfoundland, the Volunteers were going to use only blanks. Buster Brown had been the Director of Military Intelligence and Operations in the 1920s (see chapter 3), preparing plans for Canada to launch pre-emptive strikes against US targets in the event of an Anglo-American war. In the 1960s, Mowat said, he shared Brown's uneasiness about American intentions, but the Volunteer Brigade idea was farcical and intended only to make a nuisance of itself, not to fire at B-52s on practice runs. Still, the rhetorical flourishes brought Mowat to US notice, and he hooted at the fuss his banning from the United States had caused. He was quick to get in the last word, too: "We Canadians are hardly more than house slaves to the American Empire. Of course, we are better off than the field slaves of South America."[16]

*　　*　　*

"Questions of aesthetics in the age of imperialism are questions of politics," Gail Dexter wrote in *Close the 49th Parallel etc.: The Americanization of Canada* in 1971, a book that drew much of its inspiration from George Grant's work. "It is important to understand American art because it is imperialist art. And Canadian art, like Canadian industry, is no more than a branch plant of the American." Dexter added that "because American art is imperialist, Canadian art, if it is to evolve a national style, must be overtly anti-imperialist. In other words, it is my firm belief that the creation of a Canadian style of painting is nothing less than a political act." Robert Fulford in effect conceded the force of Dexter's point when he wrote that Canadians believed with good cause that Canadian art was dominated by American influences and that the "hegemony of New York in the art world is seen as a form of unconscious imperialism."[17] A few years later, Fulford added that "we were swamped by the Americans and totally unable to develop our own views." It was all right for him to learn about art in New

York at the Museum of Modern Art, he wrote in his memoir, "but it was not all right for me to spend the next decade or so judging all of contemporary art with a sensibility trained by the Americans. Nor was it all right for most of the abstract artists in Canada to believe . . . that the final judgement on all their work would be made by New York."

No artist better embodied Dexter's conception of an anti-imperialist and pro-nationalist art than Greg Curnoe. Indeed, the phrase "Close the 49th Parallel etc." was lifted intact from one of Curnoe's most famous works, a series of lettered panels he called *The True North Strong and Free.** It formed the theme of his Dadaistic, satirical, and hilarious thirty-seven-point 1970 manifesto, "Amendments to Continental Refusal/Refus Continental" (the title was a deliberate reference to Paul-Emile Borduas's *Refus global* of 1948):

1. That we the Citizens of the 2nd largest country in the world should sever all connections with the smaller country immediately south of us.
2. Electric shock treatment to be used on all businessmen . . . politicians . . . musicians etc. who have US content in their heads . . . more than 2 percent. . . .
5. All Canadian atlases must show Canada's southern border to be with Mexico. . . .
9. No animals . . . germs . . . insects . . . spores . . . seeds etc to be allowed to pass between the two countries. . . .
21. American accents to be banned from all media.
22. Use of American spelling of words to be punishable by strapping. . . .
29. All American art in Canada to be exhibited in a degenerate art exhibit & then to be auctioned off in the States.[18]

Born in 1936 in London, Ontario, Curnoe attended the Ontario College of Art, which failed him in his third year because, his friends said, he "refused to submit to the imported criteria of the New York School in the classroom."[19] The imperial centre was not his centre, and he rejected absolutely

---

* Historian Ramsay Cook noted, correctly, that "Close the 49th Parallel, etc.," could "have been painted in the 1850s as easily as in the 1960s, though the style would have been British Imperial rather than American Pop." "Imagining a North American Garden," *Canadian Literature* (Winter 1984): 12.

the notion that art that failed to emulate the art of the metropole was by definition provincial, imitative, idiosyncratic, and, therefore, minor. Returning to his home town, as his wife later put it, "he understood what happened and he was determined to turn it to his advantage and wage his war against them," the "them" being an all-inclusive Diefenbakeresque collection of establishments whose values he rejected. To Curnoe, a proponent of the idea of regionalism, Canada was a federation of local and regional cultures, and creative life had to be anchored in the source of one's experiences. He recognized that for some Canadian artists—painters like Jack Bush and William Ronald who had been influenced by New York critic Clement Greenberg—the source was New York. For him, it was London, Ontario. And if the internal enemy of regionalism is provincialism, wrote Pierre Théberge of the Montréal Musée des Beaux-arts in the 1982 catalogue for a retrospective show of Curnoe's work, "its external enemy is Americanization."

No pan-Canadian nationalist, then, Curnoe's searing anti-Americanism was all the more noticeable because many of his paintings featured block-printed messages. "THE LIBERALS SOLD US TO THE U.S.A.," said one painting; "CANADA ALWAYS LOSES," shouted another; "THIS IS TRULY GREAT ART BECAUSE IT WAS NOT MADE BY AN AMERICAN," was lettered into an image; a proposal for a mural encouraged Canadians to do a good deed by telling Americans to go home; a slogan reproduced on the University of Western Ontario's Business School quarterly proclaimed that "IMPOTENT ONTARIANS ALWAYS PROSTRATE THEMSELVES TO THE UNITED STATES"; and one painting even posed a referendum question for all Canadians outside Quebec: "WHICH NATION DO YOU WANT TO BE SEPARATE FROM—QUEBEC OR THE UNITED STATES?" "The tendency," Curnoe said, "is for people to put words in my mouth and assume that I'm isolationist. That I'm xenophobic. But I'm only xenophobic about one nation, and that's the United States."*

---

* Curnoe's serio-comic approach was also found in the Nihilist Party of Canada, of which he was one of the founders and presidents—all members of the party were president simultaneously and its program of action on each and every issue was simply "No." He also was a creator of the Nihilist Spasm Band that played "non-music on kazoos, drums, home-made guitars and bass" and held "non-concerts" that aimed to drive audiences out of halls across the land and abroad, apparently with great success. Barrie Hale, "Talking Pictures," *Canadian Magazine* (July 17, 1976): 12; Barry Lord, *The History of Painting in Canada: Towards a People's Art* (Toronto 1974), 227.

"Seldom," wrote critic Barrie Hale, "have an artist's political and creative concerns come so solidly together in his work as they do in Curnoe's."*[20] He, moreover, refused to show his work in the United States.

Curnoe's political/artistic vision became a public issue early in 1968 when a huge 560-foot twenty-six-panel work commissioned by the federal government for permanent exhibit at Montreal's Dorval Airport was ordered to be taken down after US Customs officials, stationed at Dorval to handle pre-clearance of Canadian travellers, protested. The painting was replete with explicit anti–Vietnam War sentiments featuring boxer Muhammad Ali: "MR. MUHAMMAD ALI, FORMERLY CASSIUS CLAY, DECLINED TO TAKE THE OATH FOR THE AMERICAN ARMY. THE AMERICAN WORLD BOXING ASSOCIATION STRIPPED HIM OF HIS TITLE; IT IS NOT KNOWN ON WHAT GROUNDS, SINCE HIS US–SPONSORED FIGHT IS NOT BEING FOUGHT IN A RING, WITH GLOVES, FOR ANY PURSE OR UNDER ANY RULES. . . ." President Lyndon Johnson was painted flying through the air, disgorging bombs, and having his hand chopped off by a propellor. The Department of Transport's decision to remove the work was cheered in Curnoe's home town newspaper. "Anti-Americanism is an unfortunate fact in the life of some Canadians," wrote the *London Free Press*. "It is not, however, a policy of Canadian government, nor is it an attitude endorsed by many Canadian citizens." Curnoe's work was removed, the paper said: "And rightly so."[21]

None of the criticism deterred Curnoe, who waged his battles with great exuberance, becoming the most articulate proponent of nationalism in Canadian art.[22] He was a founder of Canadian Artists Representation in 1968, a national union of artists that worked to protect the rights of artists and to lobby government for both grants and Canadian cultural autonomy. CAR, in Fulford's phrase, made "gallery directors shake with fright" and "even in the universities—which only a few years ago believed nationality had nothing to do with teaching ability—there is now a reluctance to allow

* York University critic Michael Greenwood noted Curnoe's "stubborn parochialism" and remarked that the "occasional intrusion of xenophobic slogans" in his art "is simply part of the game, the semiscared defiance of a beleaguered provincial toward the encroachment of alien mass culture upon local folkways. As the source of all we pretend to despise and reject but are nevertheless cheerfully seduced by, the US is Everyman's instant scapegoat." Michael Greenwood, "Some Nationalist Facets of Canadian Art," *artscanada* 36 (December–January 1979–80): 71.

arts faculties to be dominated by foreigners (usually Americans)."[23] Then, when *artscanada* published a commissioned survey of Canadian culture by an American in its autumn 1975 issue, Curnoe was outraged. He criticized the choice of author, noted that the editor of the magazine was American in origin and relied extensively on American contributors, and mocked the article's emphasis on the problems caused by government funding of the arts when *artscanada* itself was so heavily dependent on subsidies. In the *Canadian Forum*, in May 1976, Curnoe pronounced this a classic case of "cultural colonialism or its other half, cultural imperialism." As he put it bluntly: "*artscanada* has in recent years caused an important part of Canada's culture to be locked into a narrow bilateral (unilateral, really, since it is not reciprocated) relationship with the US so that, far from being isolated by 'narrow nationalism' we are being isolated by those very people who claim to be internationalists (Americans)."

Killed when his bicycle was hit by a car in 1992, Curnoe continued to produce his anti-American art until his death. The National Gallery of Canada displays his construction, *Hurdle for Art Lovers*, at the beginning of the modern Canadian art exhibit. Literally a hurdle, the piece is a "metre-high wooden barricade, painted red, white and blue with erect steak knives, spatulas and knitting needles, [and] stands as a warning to those who would view art with a comfortable sense of detachment." Curnoe's widow, enjoying the irony of this work being displayed, noted: "Maybe they should actually make people jump over it . . . and Americans should have to jump twice."[24] Simply put, Curnoe and the artists who shared his vision refused to accept the premise that American culture was the only valid culture.

What made artists like Curnoe into overt nationalists? Robert Fulford correctly suggested that the reaction to the Vietnam War was one cause. Canadians who rejected the war also rejected the society that produced it.* Moreover, the arrival in Canada not only of thousands of draft dodgers

---

* My own favourite anti-American piece of art is a 1965 untitled graphic by Toronto artist Joyce Wieland that provides her definitive comment on American society. The text reads in successive lines of differing sizes: "Patriotism/ Big Cash Savings/ Canada Si Yankee No!/ Human Missiles/ Marrow Death/ Pesticides/ Orbital Spies/ Genocide/ Pepsi/ C.I.A." and then shows a sailboat, presumably Canada, in four successive drawings sinking further beneath the waves. Wieland was then living in New York City, but returned to Toronto in 1970.

but of some strikingly eminent older Americans, was important. "The most celebrated critic of American town planning in the last decade, Jane Jacobs, moved to Canada; so too did the most eloquent critic of American mass education, Edgar Z. Friedenberg. From people like these," Fulford said, "the Canadian artists heard again and again a single message: don't copy the American style; don't be swallowed up by it; find another way of doing things."*[25]

As late as 1995 the Art Gallery of Ontario replaced its American director with another American. Almost no one complained—except the American-born critic John Bentley Mays, who noted in the *Globe and Mail* on June 3 that "it's business as usual in Canada's cultural institutions, which have been hiring foreign-born executives, especially Americans, since the beginning of time." An artist and definitely no cultural bureaucrat, Greg Curnoe flew in the face of this trend, and in his full-throated anti-Americanism he was representative of a substantial, if not necessarily long-lived, trend in Canadian art. What was different about Curnoe was that he fought his battle with more talent, humour, and wit than his peers.

*   *   *

For all their troubles with Behemoth, Farley Mowat and Margaret Atwood can at least make a good living from writing. Most Canadian authors of fiction, poetry, and non-fiction cannot, despite the support the arts receive from Canadian federal, provincial, and municipal governments. It is a rare Canadian novel or scholarly book, for example, that sells five thousand copies. Poetry in Canada, with average sales of four hundred copies for each title, said poet Tom Wayman, "is like a brain-dead pygmy, kept clinically alive in the academy by an artificial life support system."[26] Canadian writers, indeed Canadian artists of all kinds, claim a very small share of their own country's market.

The problems of Canadian writers spring from many causes.

---

* Friedenberg found his own way of doing things: he instantly became an expert on Canada and things Canadian, writing essays on the country for American magazines. I can still remember reading these pieces, becoming furious at the number of historical and contemporary errors in them, carefully marking each one, and mailing them to Friedenberg. I received no replies; nor did he stop writing!

Competition for readers with American and British books and magazines remains a significant factor. As well, a small population spread across a large territory makes distribution and promotion costly and difficult. Canadian publishers were and remain notoriously inefficient, slow to get their wares out and reluctant to advertise and promote. Moreover, as Fulford noted of his *Saturday Night* (significantly the only Canadian magazine founded before 1900 that still survives), "We had to impress an audience that was used to first-class publications from New York, but we were playing to a population that wasn't a tenth the size of the potential American audience."[27] Even selling prices were largely determined by the US competition, though Canadian publishers lacked the economy of scale of American publishers. Magazines like *Time* and *Reader's Digest*, which had long produced "split-run" Canadian editions, had lower costs than comparable Canadian magazines: most of their material came from New York; there were only a few pages of locally produced Canadian material; and the additional Canadian advertising inserted in the edition was gravy for the American owners. In

Macpherson/Reprinted with permission—The Toronto Star Syndicate/National Archives of Canada C-112977

"One consolation, they are notoriously bad shots."

1993 *Sports Illustrated*, which already had 130,000 Canadian sales, began to produce a Canadian edition and drew shouts of outrage from domestic magazine publishers. "Is Sports Illustrated 'eating anyone's lunch'?" the executive director of the Canadian Magazine Publishers Association asked. "You bet it is: the first so-called 'Canadian' edition has eaten an estimated quarter of a million dollars worth of Canadian advertising that would have likely otherwise ended up in our own Canadian magazines." Fearing a precedent that would open the way to additional US magazines, the CMPA and cultural nationalists dutifully gathered their forces and railed against *Sports Illustrated*, a low-brow magazine that had no Canadian competitor and that appealed primarily to the devotees of its annual swimsuit edition. Tentatively, hesitantly, and obviously frightened of the United States' response, Ottawa in late 1995 imposed a special 80 percent tax on the Canadian income of the publication's split-run edition, effectively killing it. "A bit of a kangaroo court decision," *Sports Illustrated*'s general manager called it, correctly. "This has nothing to do with culture. It's about money."[28] In March 1996, the United States government challenged the Canadian position at the World Trade Organization, the very first case ever brought against Canada there.

Book publishers faced comparable problems with those of the magazine industry. The Centennial in 1967, and the nationalist resurgence it created, had been a boom period for Canadian publishers, who churned out subsidized titles on every conceivable subject. Inevitably, though, the bust had to come. McClelland & Stewart, one of the biggest and oldest Canadian publishers, found itself chronically in financial trouble in the late 1960s and early 1970s, either begging for money from government or being offered for sale. "We will, of course, consider offers from any responsible source," the flamboyant and publicity conscious owner Jack McClelland said in 1971, knowing full well that he was stoking nationalist and anti-American fires, "but this firm was not developed in order to be sold to foreign owners." Foreign ownership, however, was better than receivership.[29] Just a few months before, in December 1970, the oldest Canadian publisher, the Ryerson Press, was sold to US giant McGraw-Hill. Led by the *Toronto Star*, the media painted the fire sale as a national humiliation, the death of Canadian culture. Fulford noted drily that Ryerson Press "had been the source of many of the worst books in Canada . . . a joke." Characteristically, Mordecai Richler expressed delight that the Yanks had "taken the damn thing off our hands." Maybe "the poor fools would like to buy the RCMP musical ride as well."*[30]

Canadian-owned book publishers believed they were under attack, a feeling that reached panic proportions after the Ryerson Press sale. Within months, virtually all the remaining Canadian-owned publishers had left the sixty-year-old Canadian Book Publishers Council to set up the Independent Publishers Association (which shortly charged its name to the Association of Canadian Publishers, or ACP). The industry had subdivided into two warring camps: the CBPC, dominated by American-owned branch-plant publishers; and the ACP, usually on the left, militantly pro-Canadian, and, yes, anti-American.

The financial resources were with the big battalions of the CBPC, but as time went on, and as the nationalist and anti-American rhetoric increased, government found itself pressed into backing the ACP. In 1973 the Royal Commission on Book Publishing, created after the Ryerson sale and established by an Ontario government cognizant that more than 80 percent of Canadian book publishing was based in the province, proposed a system of grants to aid Canadian-owned publishing houses. In a preliminary report, the commission had recommended a low-interest government loan of $1 million for McClelland & Stewart. Much of the argument in the commission report focused on the need for Canadian students to use Canadian texts—a direct offshoot of the Canadianization campaign still being waged in the universities, and the boom in Canadian studies that derived from and fed it.

Soon after, the Progressive Conservative government at Queen's Park began providing publishers with grants through the Ontario Arts Council, the Ontario Development Corporation, and the Ministry of Citizenship and Culture. The federal government was only a few years behind, setting up its own Book Publishing Development Program in 1979–80 to supplement the substantial sums provided for two decades to authors by the Canada Council. That the government largesse went only to Canadian-owned publishers, inefficient in selling books and in paying royalties to authors, widened the split between the ACP and the CBPC, forcing every publisher to take sides and embittering personal relations at

---

* And they did. In 1995 the RCMP sold its promotional rights to Walt Disney— all mugs, statuettes, and other tourist souvenir trash featuring the Mounties and their logo would now be marketed by the creators of Mickey Mouse.

all levels of the industry. Favoured firms, seemingly, had only to report losses and talk of selling out to have loans and grants pressed upon them. But small Canadian houses—new press, Peter Martin, Anansi, James Lewis & Samuel, and, subsequently, Lester & Orpen Dennys, for example—found surviving difficult even with the government funding available to them. Ironically, because of their political stance and because of federal government regulations that restricted foreign purchases, those that foundered either disappeared or were sold to Canadian buyers for relatively little.

The war within Canadian publishing has lasted for a quarter-century and continues still, though the battle is all but over. By the 1990s, foreign firms controlled two-thirds of book sales in Canada and 80 percent of educational publishing, and the population seemed to be increasingly weary of the constant rhetoric. In April 1995, a high school teacher told *Quill & Quire*, the Canadian book trade newspaper, that he was tired of the old nationalist arguments for Canadian texts. "Economics and education don't mix, and they're not talking education; they're cloaking it by waving the old maple leaf, but the fact is, they're talking dollars. Besides," he added, "textbooks aren't that important." The teacher was wrong, but by 1996 there were few genuine Canadian textbook publishers left. The best one could expect in classrooms were Canadianized versions of American texts, their approach barely camouflaged by the substitution of "Ottawa" for "Washington."

Yet Canadians bought Canadian writers, as Canadian literature reached maturity, thanks in substantial part to the government grant programs. Authors such as Richler, Atwood, Robertson Davies, Pierre Berton, and Peter C. Newman had huge sales in Canada for their fiction and non-fiction works; Richler, Atwood, Davies, and latterly W.P. Kinsella, Tom King, Michael Ondaatje, Alice Munro, and Carol Shields developed substantial and enthusiastic followings abroad. But when Berton, a nationalist icon and a long-time stalwart of the McClelland & Stewart stable, decided to publish the second volume of his memoirs with Doubleday, a one-time US-owned firm now under German control, because it offered him more money, there was some shock among his nationalist friends. Berton was unabashed. "I thought about Doubleday's paternity," he said in January 1995. "For about ten seconds. I've done enough Canadian books. I don't have to justify myself." Was Berton's choice a sign of a new maturity in Canadian writers and in publishing? The anti-Americanism so prominent in the 1970s has been muted by a much more international perspective in publishing, ironically thanks to government funding that permitted Canadian publishers to explore foreign markets for the first time.

Franklin/ *Globe and Mail*/National Archives of Canada C-143602

The Free Trade Agreement of 1988 in theory protected Canadian culture, although the United States retained the right to retaliate against any new Canadian initiatives it deemed to be damaging to US interests. ("We thought we had very good language" in the cultural clauses of the FTA, one of the American negotiators boasted to journalist Marci McDonald.) It was in the area of popular culture that the retaliation was fiercest. The United States government and American entertainment industries attacked every Canadian effort to resist the overwhelming power of American popular culture. In 1995, for example, a US country music channel was removed from cable TV to be replaced by a new "Canadian" country station that played nothing but music videos and allocated 30 percent of its air time to Canadian groups, in effect a counterpart to the

Canadian content regulations that had worked on radio to ensure airtime for Canadian musicians.

The American government response was to draw up a "hit list" of targets for retaliation, while the US entertainment industry's reaction was to denounce Canada for hiding a "culture of greed" behind the façade of cultural protection. The American ambassador's phrasing was somewhat milder: "a raw commercial grab." To Ambassador James Blanchard, "Canada and the US need to have a meaningful dialogue on how cultural industries can be both nurtured, protected and allowed freedom of expression and allow for fair trade as well." The two countries, he said, had to get beyond the exemptions for culture in the FTA and in NAFTA.

If he was referring to country music, the ambassador was surely right, and the defenders of Canadian culture badly needed to define their terms. Whether *Sports Illustrated* and country music were culture, let alone Canadian culture, never appeared to cross the mind of those anti-American cultural nationalists who automatically rallied against the interlopers. The principle should have been clear: popular entertainment did not merit government efforts to protect the right of Canadian capitalists to profit in a US-dominated market.

Serious culture, however, was different. Literature, publishing, art, theatre, film, quality television, and especially the CBC, generated relatively small sums in comparison with entertainment, but they were important for the nation's soul and mind and had to be defended.

Take Canadian films, for example. The National Film Board had almost sixty years of history behind it and a deserved reputation for documentary film-making. But its government funding was drying up, and the private film industry had no such history of success. There were good Canadian films, but they could be counted on the fingers of a very few hands. Companies such as Alliance and Atlantis produced high-quality work, though mostly for television, and feature films such as *Mon Oncle Antoine*, *Goin' Down the Road*, *The Decline of the American Empire*, and *Margaret's Museum* were first rate, though each one, separated by years, was hailed anew as the birth of the Canadian industry. The problem ultimately came down to distribution. Here Hollywood had, for years, maintained a complete stranglehold and assiduously lobbied, schmoozed, and thrown its weight around to keep matters precisely as they were. The gregarious Jack Valenti, the movie industry's lobbyist-in-chief, apparently exercised dominance over presidents, congressional representatives, and trade negotiators in Washington. Hollywood mattered in the United States, and, when the movie industry called, the administration was always ready to strongarm Canada into line—as happened to Tory Communications Minister Flora MacDonald's nationalist 1987 film policy. Denounced in Hollywood as yet another manifestation of Canadian anti-Americanism, the policy was received with hostility in Washington and was quickly caught up in the on-going Canada–US free trade negotiations. The result was wholly pre-dictable: MacDonald's policy died a-borning and American films continued their free run in Canada, with over 95 percent of the market. Valenti had won yet again. Still, the various film development programs created by Ottawa were important and had to be maintained. Film was entertainment, to be sure, but it was also culture, and it had to survive in Canada.

So too did the CBC. On radio, the Canadian Broadcasting Corporation's AM and FM networks represented the sole oasis of quality on the dial. Nowhere else were there good news shows, high-quality dis-cussion, music that did not pander to teenagers, and a blessed absence of commercials. CBC television, however, was much more like the wasteland of commercial TV. The necessity for advertising revenues seemed to oblige the CBC's bloated administration to purchase American sitcoms and soaps, something that turned off a large portion of the public network's natural viewing constituency which was devoted to the fine news, public affairs and documentary shows that the CBC continued to do so well. (The all-news channel, Newsworld, was an example of what the CBC did best.) A study commission's (non-starter) proposal in 1995 that the CBC be supported by a tax on cable subscriptions alienated another large block of viewers. In 1996, however, Perrin Beatty, the Corporation's new president, pledged that prime time would feature only Canadian shows. That was promising but, given the declining government funding, problematical.

The CBC was *in extremis*, but, like Canadian film, it simply could not be allowed to perish. The other national networks showed almost nothing but American *schlock*, and the CBC was the sole network that could be counted on to televise nationally major events ranging from provincial elections, to the opening of Parliament, to the almost week-long commemoration of the fiftieth anniversary of VE Day in 1995. The CBC was culture, too, and even if it was fated to be just a Canadian "niche" channel in a thousand-channel satellite universe, that was sufficient to justify its continued existence.

Entertainment, in other words, had no claim on the public purse, but culture did. Many did not make the distinction, mistaking a country music channel for high culture. A spokesperson for the Canadian Conference of the Arts put the position in a straightforward fashion: for the Americans, "it's the entertainment industry. But for us it's the national cultural identity. They can't accept that. It's like we're speaking a strain of Mandarin." Poor Canada. For most of its cultural nationalists, its "achey breaky heart" of a cultural identity seemed to be hanging by a thread and all but dependent on a country music channel.

Even some intelligent media commentators failed to see the difference between culture and entertainment. The *Globe and Mail*'s Jeffrey Simpson, no anti-American, was outraged at the American "culture of greed" argument: "Some greed. Some protection. Nowhere in the world do cultural products struggle so hard to reach a domestic audience as in Canada. . . . That Canada might wish to create space for its own cultural products, while still giving consumers access to an incredible range of US products, has always struck American entertainment moguls as literally incomprehensible." Simpson then imagined an American consumer living in a United States that had suddenly been transformed into a replica of Canada. On TV, virtually all the programs were foreign. In bookstores, US books were not extensively displayed, and where they were, often condescendingly grouped under the heading "Americana." The movies were the same—95 percent were not American. Simpson's consumer settled for a magazine—again almost all were foreign. "That is the life-experience of any English-speaking Canadian, but it is completely beyond the comprehension of any American."[31] Under strong US pressure, the owners of the Canadian country channel capitulated, sold part of their stake to the Nashville-based Country Music Television Inc., and counted on Ottawa to change its rules on foreign ownership to make the deal work.

Country music simply was not worth arguing about, but literature was. Surprising the owners of the US chains who called the action "bizarre" and not about culture, but only about the business of selling books, Ottawa proved itself willing to bar the giant American bookstore chains that were poised to enter Canada in 1996. Canadian regulations required effective operational control of booksellers in Canada to be in domestic hands, and changes to copyright legislation also aimed to oblige booksellers to buy foreign books from Canadian distributors. Here Ottawa was right to act. If book-selling had fallen into US hands, and if US chains began to purchase their books in the United States, Canadian publishing might no longer have remained viable. To the astonishment of everyone (and not least business commentators who railed at the "pathetic cultural nationalism" of the government's "culture police"), Ottawa had acted toughly in defence of culture.

Even so, the wholly predictable outcome of the country music battle and the fears that the US government's Trade Representative might well challenge Canada's "cultural exemption" in the Free Trade Agreement demonstrated perfectly why the owners of Canadian entertainment industries and those who write literature or music or create art so often were and remain anti-American. It also demonstrated how readily anti-American sentiments in the cultural sector could be whipped up by financial interests that were prepared to play the nationalist card to protect their profits. Still, the *tsunami* from the south was almost always able to roll over everything in its path, and the American government, usually with support from members of Cabinet and the bureaucracy in Ottawa, could wash away almost any Canadian government or private initiative that rose above the waves—and threatened the near-total hegemony of the American entertainment industry in Canada.

While governments fought over the issues of popular entertainment and culture, the total indifference of most Canadians was evident. From St John's to Vancouver Island, they happily watched American TV and movies (where they enjoyed the talents of Canadians such as Christopher Plummer, John Candy, Keannu Reeves, k.d. lang, and Pamela Anderson) and read US magazines and books. Canadians had long ago voted with their channel-changers, a switch that largely accounts for the disillusionment of Canadian cultural nationalists. "Continentalism is Treason," wrote Susan Crean in one outburst. "Like other imperialist cultures, US culture conquers, by fair means or foul, chewing up whatever it comes in contact with." She went on to argue bluntly for "a national cultural policy [to] restore Canadian control as its first priority. Because of the situation we have inherited, it must, at least initially and within Canada, be anti-American."[32]

Crean notwithstanding, today the fight against American popular entertainment is irretrievably lost, and efforts to resist the floodtide across the border are all but pointless. To fight to protect serious culture, however difficult it will be, is well worth the effort; indeed, it is utterly essential. The tragedy is that under the weight of debt and deficits, Canadian governments' funding of the arts has begun to collapse. The struggle may be over, bar the shouting, and cultural anti-Americanism little more than a cry of frustration and impending defeat.

10

LAST GASP ANTI-AMERICANISM:
THE FREE TRADE AGREEMENT OF 1988 AND AFTER

Donato/*The Sun* (Toronto)

The two men sat across from each other at a stately table in a high-ceilinged room. The Maple Leaf flag on one side and the Stars and Stripes on the other made for a decidedly formal air, and it was instantly clear that this was an important international meeting.

"Since we're talking about the Free Trade Agreement," one began, "there's one line I'd like to change." A close-up shot of the other man on the Canadian side of the table showed him to be young—well-meaning, sincere, but young.

"Which line is that?" he asked cautiously.

The camera switched back to the other man, definitely more experienced. "This one here. It's just getting in the way." Suddenly, the shot was of a pencil eraser, which began to remove a red line on a map. The map was of North America, and the vanishing line was the Canada–United States border. An overhead camera angle showed the younger man gradually erasing the line, stopping occasionally to wipe away bits of eraser. The older man watched silently, obviously pleased.

A new voice then began to speak, as the international boundary slowly disappeared: "Just how much are we giving away in the Mulroney free trade deal?" The unseen speaker concluded ominously: "The line has been drawn. Which side do you stand on? Vote for Canada. Vote Liberal."

The total time was only thirty seconds. But this election campaign commercial, which appeared on TV screens across the land in late October 1988, struck a chord with Canadians. Within a week of its first showing, and helped by John Turner's effective performance in the leaders' debate, popular support for the Liberals surged. The Grits first caught and then passed Mulroney's Conservatives in public opinion polls. Turner seemed poised to form the government and to destroy the Canada–United States Free Trade Agreement (FTA) recently concluded with the Reagan administration.

The Liberals appeared to have understood something fundamental about Canadians. Portraying the United States as a great power that schemed to swallow Canada whole, a nation motivated by its Manifest Destiny to control the entire North American continent, was a political strategy that still could pay dividends in the late 1980s. The country was vulnerable, the Liberals and others claimed, and the Americans were prepared to exploit that vulnerability. In their long history, Canadians had "never been so threatened," Turner had suggested, and the threat came not from American guns, but from the lure of American dollars. The FTA, agreed to in October 1987 by Prime Minister Brian Mulroney and President Ronald Reagan, was the dominating issue in the 1988 campaign. Amidst the typically overblown theatrics of a Canadian general election campaign, the national drama cast the United States in the leading role and, for many, it was the villain.

Yet the bad guys in the black hats were not without their powerful friends on the Canadian side of the line. In 1988, in marked contrast to the previous reciprocity elections of 1891 and 1911, the business community overwhelmingly supported the Conservatives in their campaign for free trade. Just as in the past, business was motivated by money, and fears about US domination played an important part in the election. But in 1988 Canadians voted to elect a prime minister, a government, and a Parliament which, by a very substantial majority, favoured closer economic ties with Washington. There seemed no doubt that the decision would forever alter the course of Canadian history: the idea and the images of anti-Americanism were no longer the keystone of the Canadian identity.

*　　*　　*

"But what possible retaliatory measures could the Americans take?"

The road to the 1988 showdown over free trade had begun as early as the recession of 1981–82. Pierre Trudeau was still Prime Minister, Ronald

Reagan was the new President and, though relations with the United States under the Liberal government were never intimate, the Liberal Cabinet began to move to the conclusion that closer trade relations with the United States should be pursued. Quite simply, there did not appear to be much choice. Trudeau's vaunted Third Option, a trade and foreign relations strategy designed to create stronger links to the European Community and Japan and to reduce dependence on the United States, had failed, a victim of geography as well as business and bureaucratic indifference. Although three-quarters of Canadian exports went south, and that fraction had been growing steadily since the Second World War, the Liberal government did not try to curry favour with the Reagan administration. The National Energy Program remained in place, for one thing. Supported by many intellectuals and large numbers within the New Democratic Party, for another, Trudeau dabbled with the equivalency theory of the superpowers. The Americans and the Russians were similar, the argument went, and Trudeau, like his academic supporters, often seemed to find the vulgar, threatening capitalist power to the south more frightening than the bear across the Pole. The Reaganites, convinced that the Evil Empire was based in Moscow, were not pleased. The Canadian attitude found no admirers in Washington, but the wisest American officials understood, as Stephen Clarkson and Christina McCall quoted one, that "we would just have to wait out the nationalist mood and the Canadian navel-gazing."

Waiting was good strategy. The difficulty the Liberal government faced, however, was that it could do nothing to switch trade elsewhere, and protectionist pressures all over the globe, not least in Washington, threatened to leave Canadian exporters out in the cold. After a broad review of trade policy, the Liberals proclaimed a "new era in trade relations with the United States" in August 1983. The Trade Minister promised that discussions would soon be initiated to pursue a series of sectoral free trade deals—not a comprehensive treaty, but industry-by-industry agreements that would, in combination, lower trade barriers between the two countries.

The new Liberal initiative built upon earlier sectoral arrangements with the United States that had been deemed successful. The Defence Production Sharing Agreement in 1959 and the Canada–US Auto Pact in 1965 had both given Canadian business access to the American market and helped spur employment and investment. Nonetheless, Ottawa had tended to pursue a multilateral trade strategy under the auspices of the worldwide General Agreement on Tariffs and Trade (GATT). It was easier to deal with the United States on the broadest trade questions in a larger forum than in bilateral trade negotiations, and, in fact, approximately 80 percent of Canada–US trade was free of duty, so effective had GATT been in reducing tariffs. By 1983, however, the United States Congress, worried about foreign competition, trade deficits, agricultural surpluses, and high unemployment in the "rust belt," was contemplating protectionist bills that were certain to cause serious difficulties for Canadian exporters of industrial and agricultural products. Like it or not, the Liberals had decided that they had to secure the best arrangement possible with the Americans to guarantee Canadian manufacturers and producers access to the vast, rich US market.

Peterson,/*Vancouver Sun*

"Frankly, Pierre, not only are we annoyed that there's too much Canadian investment in American industry — we're really hacked that there's too much Canadian investment in Canadian industry . . ."

Little more than a year later, the Liberals' trade plans, like the government that had launched them, had become completely immaterial. First, the

Americans had appeared notably uninterested in the sectoral arrangements Ottawa proposed. Then, Trudeau had gone for his famous "walk in the snow" in February 1984 and retired from politics after fifteen years in power, and his replacement, John Turner, had been promptly and massively trounced at the polls by Brian Mulroney's Progressive Conservatives. Though he had promised to improve Canada–US ties and to open the country to American investors during the September 1984 election campaign,* Mulroney had issued no clear trade program. He had, in fact, argued during the 1983 leadership campaign that chose him as Progressive Conservative party leader that free trade with the Americans would be a dangerous policy for Canada: "It affects Canadian sovereignty, and we'll have none of it, not during leadership campaigns, nor at any other times." But the new prime minister was a pragmatist, and events soon changed his mind.

In March 1985 Canadians watched their new prime minister entertain President Ronald Reagan in Quebec City at the "Shamrock Summit." The two politicians of Irish extraction seemed to get along famously, settling disputes on defence matters and agreeing to discuss environmental issues. Then, as the nation watched a televised gala performance from Quebec City, Mulroney and his wife, Mila, led President and Mrs Reagan onstage for a quartet (with the Reagans grinning in embarrassment through it all) of "When Irish Eyes Are Smiling." This public display of sucking up to Reagan may have been the single most demeaning moment in the entire political history of Canada's relations with the United States.

Reagan brought his ideological commitment to freer trade along for the visit, and that, combined with a growing climate of opinion in Canada that seemed favourable to some sort of trade deal with the United States, was the recipe for a joint pledge to reduce trade barriers. Business in Canada increasingly supported the idea of free trade, for a change, and the issue had hit newspaper front pages in November 1984. Former Liberal Cabinet

---

* Here, at least, Mulroney was as good as his word. His government quickly converted the Foreign Investment Review Agency into Investment Canada, with a mandate to attract foreign investment, and killed the National Energy Program. Both decisions were arguably defensible on policy grounds, possibly even beneficial to Canada; what was utterly indefensible was that Mulroney cancelled legislation hated by American business and received nothing in return from the US government by way of concessions. Canada really was open for business, just as Mulroney had pledged.

minister Donald S. Macdonald, the chair of the Royal Commission on the Economic Union and Development Prospects for Canada, hinted strongly at a meeting of the American Assembly at Harriman, New York, that his Trudeau-appointed commission would likely recommend free trade in its final report. The time had come, he suggested, for Canadians to take a "leap of faith" into free trade. For Mulroney's government the suggestion could hardly have been better timed: ministers and bureaucrats were interested in, but not yet committed to, a free trade strategy. Mulroney himself had become a proponent of free trade. As Paul Robinson, the American Ambassador at the time, later put it, "Brian has no fear of America gobbling up Canada. He sees our closeness as an asset, and he's right—who wouldn't like to be anchored next to the world's biggest market?"[1] Having Macdonald, a prominent Liberal, propose the idea allowed it to be tested publicly. The media reaction to the Harriman statement was mostly favourable,* and Mulroney began to prepare his government for possible negotiations. The Prime Minister later appointed Macdonald High Commissioner to Great Britain.

The free trade idea was fully aired in the Cabinet, and the balloon was floated again across the country by several of Mulroney's ministers. The signs all seemed positive. Western premiers were fully behind the policy, Quebec showed enthusiasm, and public opinion polls indicated that a majority of Canadians favoured a free trade deal with the United States. Other polls, however, contradictorily pointed to potential difficulties ahead: for twenty years, consistent majorities of Canadians had believed that the Canadian way of life was influenced too much by the United States.[2]

On September 26, 1985, Mulroney took his own leap of faith and announced in Parliament that Canada would seek a bilateral trade agreement. Shrewdly, the Prime Minister had waited until the Macdonald Commission had tabled its final report—with its clear endorsement of free trade—earlier the same month. The timing of the free trade

---

* I was a participant at the Harriman meeting on Canada–US relations that November, and I was horrified at Macdonald's announcement which, if it had not been arranged with the organizers, certainly was seized upon by them and used to shape the communiqué the next day. I was not alone in thinking that I had been subjected to a "hustle," but the meeting was so orchestrated that the communiqué, presented for the briefest consideration in the final session, was all but impossible to amend.

announcement also helped to distract attention from a series of never-ending and embarrassing scandals that beset the government's first year in power. Mulroney was convinced that free trade was the policy that would rescue his government's lagging popularity.

Wanting a deal and having one were entirely different matters. The government knew that negotiating an international trade agreement with the United States was a daunting prospect at the best of times, with decision-making power in Washington diffused so widely among bureaucrats, political parties, Representatives and Senators, and the White House. Moreover, a trade deal with Canada was nowhere near the top of the American political agenda. As a result, Canada—with its own free trade negotiating team, led by the cigar-chewing and rough-tongued Simon Reisman, ready and willing—had to wait until May 1986 before the Americans were prepared to sit down to talk. This delay put the Mulroney Cabinet on the defensive, forcing it to support an idea that remained a popular target: easy to criticize, but difficult to defend since nothing had yet been accomplished.

The Cabinet knew what it might be up against in selling the idea. "To the man in the street," Trade Minister James Kelleher admitted in September 1985, "free trade conjures up an image of the United States as a blood-sucking Dracula. Most people do not understand what we are trying to accomplish." Prepared or not, the Cabinet must have been surprised at the growing vehemence of sentiment against any trade deal with the United States. The *Toronto Star*, quickly entrenching itself in its familiar nationalist position of scepticism towards the United States on all things and to free trade in particular, led the charge. Before Mulroney even announced the negotiations, the newspaper claimed on September 21 and 22 that the government was harbouring "secret fears" about the implications of a comprehensive deal. There would be "real risks" to Canadian sovereignty under free trade. The Liberal government in Ontario seemed genuinely anxious as well. Premier David Peterson worried openly about the costs of a deal for his heavily industrialized province, and NDP leader Bob Rae claimed free trade would make Ontario "a modern colony" of the United States. Would factories, especially branch-plant operations, stay in Bramalea and Belleville when their home operations in Peoria or Pittsburgh could readily service the Canadian market?

Cultural nationalists also joined the debate early. Academics Daniel Drache and Duncan Cameron published *The Other Macdonald Report* in September 1985, bluntly claiming that "free trade is only a code word for continental integration." Canada, they argued, was at risk of being swallowed by its giant neighbour. Peter C. Newman was even more florid: Canada was "vulnerable to cultural genocide." National social welfare groups also came out firmly against the negotiations: a Roman Catholic bishop's claim that a free trade deal would result in Canadians "serving the market interests of the United States, including that of military production" was typical.[3] Trade unionists, not least Bob White's new Canadian Auto Workers, which he had led out of the US-dominated United Auto Workers in December 1984, worried about the "gleeful acceptance" of Canadian business at its integration into the American economy and the resulting "permanent insecurity" of workers.[4] At the same time, umbrella organizations opposed to free trade were starting to organize. The most notable of these, the Council of Canadians, was founded in October 1985.

Federal NDP leader Ed Broadbent attacked the Conservatives' trade strategy in Parliament, but opposition leader Turner initially avoided committing his Liberal Party on the issue. Turner was still relatively fresh from his law career serving Toronto's Bay Street business élite, and his caucus was badly divided on how to respond to the Conservatives' trade initiative. Gradually, however, as negotiations began in the spring of 1986, Turner came out in support of the anti-free trade, nationalist cause.

Opposition politicians and others who spoke against free trade in the early phase of negotiations talked candidly about the threat they saw to Canadian sovereignty if a deal were ever achieved. No one doubted that the threat came from the Americans, but critics usually aimed their attacks at Mulroney's Conservatives, most trying to hold to a position that, predictably, could be claimed as "pro-Canadian" rather than "anti-American." More could be gained at this stage by keeping the fight in the family, it seemed, than from gratuitous attacks on the Americans. Even so, Mel Hurtig, the Edmonton book publisher and nationalist, in no way shied away from the historic appellation of anti-American. Those who so labelled him, Hurtig said, were "mental midgets . . . colonial-minded twits" who scarcely merited a response. David Orchard, a little-known Saskatchewan farmer destined to become one of the major critics of free trade as the founder of Citizens Concerned About Free Trade, was perhaps more shrewd when he recognized that "anti-American," like "radical," was a loaded phrase that did serious damage to those so labelled.[5] Interestingly, these two key leaders of the anti-free trade fight came from the Prairies, contrary to the usual academic and popular view that anti-Americanism was largely an Ontario phenomenon. So too did

Marjorie Bowker, an elderly retired family court judge in Alberta whose 1988 pamphlet dissecting the Free Trade Agreement and pronouncing it a disaster for Canadians circulated widely across the country.

By late 1986, the sustained attention devoted to free trade in the media—both positive and negative—was beginning to have an impact on public opinion. According to one poll in November, 42 percent of Canadians believed that free trade would make Canada "better off," down twelve points since December 1984. Those who thought free trade would make Canada "worse off" had grown to 38 percent. At the same time, the polls suggested that most Canadians expected the United States to gain more than Canada if a deal was made.

By early 1987, however, there were few signs of any such deal. Negotiators failed to find much common ground, and Reisman's team complained bitterly that the Americans were unwilling even to propose an opening bargaining position. That this was a deliberate tactic on the Americans' part scarcely seemed to occur to any politician. The American negotiators recognized that Mulroney's Canada was the *démandeur*—the Tory government needed free trade much, much more than the United States did, and they could afford to wait out Reisman and his team. Who knew what offers desperation might lead the Canadians to put on the table? Naturally, the delay did not help Ottawa's efforts to make free trade popular at home—quite correctly, the Canadian public assumed that the Americans were simply waiting to get their way. As one close to the negotiations later suggested, the process was widely interpreted as "the supplicant Canada beaten up by the big American bully."[6] While the summer of 1987 wore on, the Prime Minister appeared to despair of ever getting a deal. Finally, after a strategic—and melodramatic—withdrawal from the talks in September, Canada at last managed to attract some attention from the administration in Washington. The negotiators and trade specialists momentarily stepped aside in early October, and with astonishing haste their political masters were able to agree to a tentative deal after a weekend of harried talks in Washington. The timing was crucial, since American "fast-track" negotiating authority, which allowed the treaty to be presented to Congress without fear of amendment, was on the verge of expiring. What had seemed impossible only weeks before had come to pass: Canada and the United States had a comprehensive free trade agreement.

The Americans, carefully avoiding any public gloating, expressed quiet satisfaction with the result. The agreement won them equal treatment in the areas that mattered to them—foreign investment, energy, and even culture, where the United States now had the right to retaliate if a Canadian government ever took new actions to protect Canada's culture from the weight of the colossus to the south. As the US chief negotiator, Peter Murphy, said to reporter Marci McDonald shortly before he died in 1994, "We didn't enter the agreement over tariffs. The Canadian agreement is a political one—to make sure you don't go back to those policies like the National Energy Policy."[7]

That suited the Tories, too. The government was jubilant at the conclusion of the FTA negotiations and, as so often seemed to be the case in the Mulroney years, self-congratulation was the order of the day for the Prime Minister. Around the country, commentators did their best to interpret the new trade pact, and the public struggled to understand its implications. On January 2, 1988, Mulroney and Reagan signed the agreement in separate ceremonies amid yet more mutual praise. The government soon realized, however, that explaining the actual deal, which in its ultimate form ran into hundreds of pages of dense legalistic prose, was no easy task. On the other hand, the FTA's critics now had a clear target, and they took dead aim at it.

* * *

"It will be a fight to the death," the *Toronto Star* predicted on October 11, 1987, as the first details of the deal were emerging. After two years of relative calm, "a historic debate on free trade [was] searing the nation's consciousness." The FTA was "a massive giveaway of this country," one opposition MP insisted. As the rhetoric slowly but surely heightened, the ghost of Sam Slick, the sly and rapacious Yankee trader, gulling the unsophisticated rubes to their north was revived and once again thrown into battle: "Fears grow the US will siphon off our water," screamed one *Toronto Star* headline. The Mulroney trade deal, Magna International chairman Frank Stronach, one of the few major business leaders to oppose the FTA, said in a speech in April 1988, would slowly erase Canada's unique identity. It would eventually cost Canadians their treasured social programs and, he feared, few Canadian business leaders would go out of their way to stop the FTA, since they headed what were in essence American branch plants. "[I]n due course," he concluded, "we will adopt the American way of life and the American political system." That was a common enough fear, for the FTA's terms stepped up the pace of "harmonization" in the continental market place. The Canadian state no longer had unfettered opportunity to adopt its own industrial strategy; in its purchases, it could no longer follow a policy of giving Canadian firms preference over American; nor could there be a Foreign Investment Review Agency or a National Energy Program. American firms henceforth were entitled to the same treatment offered Canadian companies, and in any future energy crisis the United States was guaranteed "proportional access" to Canadian supplies of oil and gas. Most critics of the FTA returned again and again to these issues as 1988 wore on, constantly underlining the potential costs to Canadian sovereignty and the national way of life.

Yet as the debate grew in intensity, it was increasingly evident that many critics were afraid of appearing to be too anti-American. Blaming the United States too much could backfire. After all, in Canada in 1988, there were as many, and probably more, columnists, media stars, parliamentarians, and academics ready to denounce those who were openly anti-American as there were to call Mulroney and his business supporters the Americans' patsies.

A collection of Canadian nationalists, mostly on the left and with most associated with the universities and the arts, nonetheless took their case against the deal to the public very quickly. In newspaper articles, on television, and in books, they expressed heartfelt but often bitter feelings about the new direction in which Mulroney's government was taking the country. The Prime Minister, already remarkably unpopular and enjoying little credibility with the public, took most of the heat, enough that he felt obliged to promise (but never deliver) an adjustment program for workers who might be hard hit by the FTA. But US domination, Canada's tragic destiny should the deal be approved, was also omnipresent in the critics' campaign. The FTA was a sellout, a surrender to the United States orchestrated by the pro-American Mulroney and the Americanized business élite who were his supporters. In Brian Mulroney, James Laxer wrote, "Canada has had a prime minister who believed in the American way of life and who was committed to bestowing its full blessings on his fellow citizens."[8] As Maude Barlow of the Council of Canadians put it, "Corporate Canada has, in all practical senses, voluntarily merged its interests with those of corporate America."[9] Mel Hurtig added his two cents worth: "Goodbye distinct Canadian values, hello American."[10] Among those American values was a distinctly weaker commitment than in Canada to equity, social welfare, and the idea that all people were entitled to a basic minimum standard of living that included unemployment insurance, medicare, and the other social programs

Canadians had come to take for granted Harmonization, the FTA's professed goal, or "a level playing field" as it was frequently expressed, was widely interpreted by FTA opponents to mean that Canada's social programs—UI and medicare were the most frequently cited—would be lowered to the American standard.

AGAINST FREE TRADE	FOR FREE TRADE
- RAY.	- ANDREW.
- LIBERAL-LEFT.	- TORY.
- PROFESSIONAL.	- BUSINESSMAN.
- ETHNIC BACKGROUND.	- WASP.
- MASTERCARD.	- AMERICAN EXPRESS.
- MAZDA.	- BUICK.
- C.B.C.	- C.T.V.
- MACLEAN'S.	- FINANCIAL POST.
- EXPOS.	- BLUE JAYS.
- SCOTCH or WINE (WHITE).	- RYE AND DIET PEPSI.
- JANE FONDA.	- DOLLY PARTON.
- PASTA.	- BEEF.
- WORRIED THAT FREE TRADE MIGHT ELIMINATE HIS JOB.	- ISN'T WORRIED ABOUT FREE TRADE ELIMINATING RAY'S JOB.

Aislin/The Gazette

Predictably hovering over the arguments of the anti-FTA camp was the spectre of annexation: first the FTA, then a move towards a customs union, a monetary union, free movement of labour across the border, and finally political union. Brian Fawcett in the *Canadian Forum* put the consequences as graphically as any commentator: "Think about your children being drafted for military duty in Central America. Think about not having medicare, and having our streets filled with the poor, the crazy and the elderly. If we become Americans we will be a hinterland. We will be poor, living out of shopping carts spiritually and perhaps literally."

Margaret Atwood, testifying before the House of Commons Standing Committee on External Affairs and International Trade, was as blunt but much funnier in her comments on "the great star-spangled Them." As a separate country, she said, Canada "has done about as well under the US as women world-wide have done under men. About the only position they have ever adopted toward us, country to country, has been the missionary position and we were not on top. I guess," she added to the evident puzzlement of many of the assembled MPs, "that is why the national wisdom vis-à-vis Them has so often taken the form of lying still, keeping your mouth shut, and pretending you like it." The supporters of the FTA, she went on, argued that Canada would get the best of both worlds: "Canadian stability and a more caring society, and American markets; but what if instead we get their crime rate, health programs, and gun laws, and they get our markets—or what is left of them?" To Fawcett, Atwood, and others on the cultural left, the FTA was simply another and the biggest step in the intellectual, cultural, and political destruction of Canada.[11]

In the House of Commons, opposition MPs ripped into the deal when, early in the summer of 1988, enabling legislation was introduced under tight time limits for debate. In a speech that definitively cut his and his party's ties to business, John Turner left no doubt where he stood on June 29:

> Mr Speaker, we are here today to discuss one of the most devastating pieces of legislation ever brought before the House of Commons. We are here to debate a Bill which will finish Canada as we know it and replace it with a Canada that will become nothing more than a colony of the United States.
>
> So urgent and compelling is the impatience of the Prime Minister (Mr Mulroney) to pack up this country and ship it south that we are going to debate this Bill for only a few hours. It took 121 years for Canadians to build this Confederation. The Government is proposing to undo that in less than half that number of hours.

In the Liberal leader's view, Brian Mulroney may have been the sinister one, but the United States was the real threat. Other MPs made similarly impassioned attacks on the deal and, as the debate continued, the opposition began to attack the United States systematically as the best route in which to attack the FTA. Americans had always wanted full control of North American energy supplies, front-bench Liberal Lloyd Axworthy claimed. The United States was the place "where the rich get richer and the poor even poorer," NDP leader Ed Broadbent reminded the House. NDP member Lynn McDonald said Canadians "do not want American crime rates," a certainty, to be sure, though what relevance crime had to the FTA was unclear. "Don't you think they sucked us in?" asked John Parry of the NDP.

Conservative ministers mostly skipped the venomous debate, but government backbenchers who responded to the onslaught were quick to accuse the opposition of anti-Americanism. Theirs was a clever tactic, and its effectiveness indicated just how discredited old-style anti-Americanism had become. Opposition MPs always took great care to refute the charge, and, in doing so, found themselves forced to tone down their most inflammatory anti-FTA rhetoric. Steven Langdon of the NDP said in June 1988 that his party's denunciations of the FTA were "in no way motivated by anti-American considerations." In demanding major amendments to the deal, Liberal Sergio Marchi made the defensive, if awkward, assertion that the Liberals were "not suggesting that we take the Americans to the cleaners or to be anti-American." Howard McCurdy, NDP member for Windsor, Ontario, trod the thin line best: "My wife is an American. Let us not engage in allegations that because we stand for the preservation of a Canada that we love that we are anti-American." Yet later in his speech he admitted, "I do not want the cities of Canada to look like Detroit, New York, or Chicago." McCurdy's was a variant on the classic "some of my best friends are American, but I wouldn't want my daughter to marry one" routine.

All compelling stuff, to be sure, but hardly full of suspense. The massive Conservative majority in the Commons guaranteed easy passage of the free trade legislation. Opposition leader Turner did have one ace up his well-tailored sleeve, however, and on July 20, 1988, he played it. With grave solemnity, Turner announced that he had ordered the Liberal-dominated Senate to delay passage of the FTA until the deal had been approved in a national election. "Let the people decide," quickly became the Liberal mantra, an argument based on the expectation that Canadians would surely see that their interests were not those of big corporations. Though dozens of newspapers agreed that a vote was necessary, Turner's was a risky strategy: he was flouting the will of the democratically-elected Commons and giving the Conservatives a made-to-order excuse to dissolve Parliament and go to the people. After several weeks, Mulroney did just that and called a general election for November 21. "Free trade will very much be the centrepiece of the campaign," Mulroney told reporters after making the official announcement.

*   *   *

The government, the opposition, and the media agreed on at least one thing as the 1988 election campaign began: Canadians faced a historic decision at the polls in November. The three major parties and a host of special interest groups all made it clear that free trade was the issue, and no one doubted that the electoral decision was certain to have enormous consequences for the nation.

The campaign, as a result, was a passionate one, the most exciting election in decades. Families divided on the issue, and long-time friends, their voices raised and their fists shaking, stopped speaking, so heated did the arguments become. Some people actually boasted about having read every clause in the FTA, a herculean feat, though no one (the negotiators possibly aside) could claim to understand what it all might mean. Dinner parties regularly turned into shouting matches, the news shows on television and the phone-in hours on radio featured emotional debate about genuinely important issues, and whole forests fell to provide the newsprint for election flyers and an incredible number of opinion pieces in every newspaper in the land. Hammered by the arguments and counter-arguments, the men and women in the cities and small towns became confused, their views swinging wildly. Opinion polls showed enormous volatility, support for all parties seemed constantly in flux, and gains and losses of 10 percent in the polls in a few days came to seem almost normal.

With the stakes so high, the results so uncertain, each party's campaign became a barrage of competing claims about which one was the most truly Canadian. That desperation also brought about high-profile intervention from groups in Canadian society, most notably the business groups supporting the FTA which had traditionally operated best behind closed doors and eschewed a public profile. Finally, the campaign placed the United

States at centre stage in the campaign and brought Canadian attitudes to their neighbour into full relief. Free trade may have been the central issue, but the provisions of the FTA were so complicated that few were able to understand them in detail. In essence, then, for the vast majority of the electorate, the issue boiled down to a referendum on attitudes to the United States. Voters were offered two competing visions of their country: a separate Canada as independent as it could remain in an increasingly interdependent world versus a North American nation integrated into a continental economy directed from Washington. Could Canada survive on its own? Could the Americans be trusted? That was the choice.

The election began as a three-way race. Polls taken just before the campaign began showed the Conservatives leading with 37 percent of decided voters, and the Liberals and the NDP trailing, with 33 and 27 percent, respectively. The opposition did its best in the early weeks of the campaign to grab headlines. To no one's surprise, the Liberals and the NDP both believed that the FTA had left the government open to attack, though, thanks to some inexplicably stupid campaign strategizing, the NDP largely permitted the Liberals to make the running. Ordinarily a wooden, stumbling speaker, Turner could become genuinely aroused when he spoke about the FTA. He suggested to one crowd that the United States had always dreamed of controlling all of North America's natural resources. "I tell you," Turner said, "Brian Mulroney allowed President Reagan to realize that American dream." A few days later, recalling the trade negotiations, the Liberal leader cracked that Mulroney had acted like the chief waiter at the White House. The differences in the two nations were clear, Turner added: "I'm glad I live in a country where you go to a hospital and they don't check your credit card before they check your pulse." The next week, NDP leader Broadbent suggested that not only was the FTA a bad deal for Canadians but Mulroney was "altogether too chummy" with Reagan. Linking the Prime Minister with the United States at every opportunity was clearly a strategy that the opposition parties shared, though the Liberals played the theme more often and much more skilfully.

From the outset of the campaign, the Liberal's pro-Canadian pitch was aided immeasurably by the host of cultural and social organizations geared up for an assault on the FTA. All believed the trade deal threatened to harm Canadian social programs. For a business in Brampton to be able to engage in a fair fight for market share with a company in Tuscaloosa, it would need lower corporate taxes—and lower taxes, in turn, would require lower social welfare costs. Opinion essays in news-papers, interviews on television programs, and public demonstrations kept the free trade critics in the news. Mel Hurtig became a household name fighting for the cause, his statistics-laden articles appearing in the press and his speeches attracting good-sized audiences. Joined together as the Pro-Canada Network, a large number of ordinarily left-wing orga-nizations—including the Canadian Union of Postal Workers, the Canadian Auto Workers, the National Action Committee on the Status of Women, the National Farmers Union, and several church groups—published a superbly done and colourful pamphlet that was distributed to every household in Canada, the single best piece of election propa-ganda issued in Canada since 1911. Carefully non-partisan in tone (as between the Liberals and the NDP), the pamphlet was nonetheless an impassioned attack on everything in the FTA and a call for action: "The Mulroney government has already decided. But it's not up to them. It's not their country. It's our country." Although its text was more anti-"Brian Mulroney and the gang" than explicitly anti-American, *What's the Big Deal?* was illustrated by the nation's leading political cartoonist, the Montreal *Gazette*'s Aislin, whose acid-tipped pen produced cartoons that were the most memorable of the campaign. Aislin left no doubt where the threat to Canadian sovereignty originated: he drew Cabinet minister Pat Carney singing "God Bless America," John Crosbie as a ludicrous mock Thomas Jefferson, and Brian Mulroney as a lawn orna-ment decorating the front of the White House and pledging allegiance to the Stars and Stripes. Throughout the campaign, in fact, political car-toonists were best able to reflect symbolically the widespread Canadian anxiety about the FTA. The genuine contempt for and fear of American power were represented better visually. To the many political figures and commentators opposed to the FTA, it appeared to be almost dangerous to utter such thoughts in print or on television.

Despite the assistance from the anti-FTA groups, most of which leaned naturally to the NDP, in any case, the Liberal campaign faltered badly at the start. An apparently unbroken string of Liberal gaffes in the first three weeks of the campaign dropped the traditional "government party" to third place in the polls. Turner fumbled a childcare policy announcement and stunned Liberal candidates with a controversial statement on abor-tion, thereby raising serious doubts about his capacity. Behind the scenes, the party's top backroom strategists reportedly hatched a plot to dump him as leader in the middle of the campaign, a plan that was promptly leaked to the CBC and broadcast nationwide.

Meanwhile, a relaxed Brian Mulroney, insulated by his handlers from contact with the media except in carefully arranged circumstances and protected by security men from angry protesters, dismissed his anti-FTA foes as people who were afraid of the future. A poll released on October 21 showed the Tories steady at 43 percent of decided voters, the NDP second at 30, and the Liberals falling off the scale at 25 percent.

Despite the passion animating the converted, anti-free trade rhetoric simply did not seem to be having much impact on average voters. Still, the potential for a voter shift seemed to be there: a Gallup poll showed that by mid-October more Canadians opposed the deal than favoured it. More than half those polled thought the FTA would make Canada too American, and almost as many thought free trade would threaten cultural sovereignty.

Without much hope of capitalizing on the public mood, the reeling opposition parties pinned their hopes on the leaders' debates, scheduled for October 24 and 25. Turner took an especially long time off from the campaign trail to prepare for the showdown. The Liberals knew that the debates would be their last opportunity and, with nothing to lose, Turner planned to come out swinging. For the thousands of Canadians who had already spent more than a year fighting the FTA, this was the final chance to turn back the onrushing tide of Americanization.

The French language debate was first, but the opposition scored few points in the one province that seemed solidly in favour of the FTA. Turner and Broadbent made pointed attacks on the prime minister for jeopardizing Canadian sovereignty, but Mulroney's superior facility in French, his *joual* so good that many francophones believed he was a *Québécois de souche*, allowed few direct hits. The English debate the next evening also started slowly. But with an hour left in the two-day six-hour marathon, Turner took a gamble. When he was asked about the FTA, Turner argued passionately that "the political ability of the country to sustain the influence of the United States, to remain as an independent nation—that has gone forever, and that is the issue of this election." Professing astonishment that anyone could believe ill of his motives, Mulroney defended the deal in what came to be known as his "Log Cabin" speech: "I, today, sir, as a Canadian, believe genuinely in what I am doing. I believe it is right for Canada, I believe in my own modest way that I am nation-building because I believe this benefits Canada, and I love Canada." (Mulroney was also always ready to refer to his hard-working late father and his pensioner mother.) The Prime Minister had raised the stakes, and Turner rose to the challenge:

> We are just as Canadian as you are, Mr Mulroney, but I will tell you this. You mentioned one hundred and twenty years of history. We built a country east and west and north. We built it on an infra-structure that deliberately resisted the continental pressure of the United States. For one hundred and twenty years, we have done it. With one signature of a pen, you've reversed that, thrown us into the north-south influence of the United States . . . and will reduce us, I am sure, to a colony of the United States, because when the economic levers go, the political independence is sure to follow.

Turner had made his point strongly, and Mulroney retreated. "Mr Turner, it is a document that is cancellable on six months' notice. Be serious." His voice raised, Turner asked incredulously, "Cancellable? You are talking about our relationship with the United States." "A commercial document that is cancellable on six months' notice," Mulroney said, the hint of desperation beginning to sound in his unctuous voice. "Mr Turner, please be serious." "Well, I am serious, and I have never been more serious in my life!" the Liberal leader shouted.

Turner had said little in the exchange that he had not been saying for nearly a year. This time, he said it before the entire nation, staking his reputation and his party's campaign on a platform of resistance to the American way of life. In the heated atmosphere of the debate, his accusation that Mulroney had sold out Canada to the Americans made for riveting television. The clip was on every newscast that evening and the next day. While Broadbent seemed weak and halting, and Mulroney had been forced onto the defensive and looked nothing so much as a man watching for a banana peel and unerringly finding it with his foot, Turner had appeared firm and genuine in his anger. A stunning 71 percent of those polled believed Turner won the debate, while 66 percent of the hitherto undecided gave the Liberal leader the nod. The media pundits also scored the debate a convincing victory for the Liberal leader. Overnight, the mood changed, and the gloom among the anti–FTA forces began to lift with astonishing rapidity.

The timing seemed perfect. The Liberal campaign commercial featuring the erasure of the international boundary aired the night before the French-language debates. Its effect was immediate. "In terms of impact, I have one word: Pow!" said a participant in a televised forum on the parties' advertising. The Liberal campaign message—anti–free trade and, yes, openly anti-American—was finally gaining momentum.

The proof was in the polls. Less than a week after the climactic television exchange, the Liberals had leapt into first place in public opinion surveys. They stole support from the Conservatives and the NDP, and, by November 7, a Liberal majority seemed within Turner's grasp if the party's 43 percent of decided voters could be held. "Opponents of the free trade agreement with the United States have played on the classic Canadian neurosis, fear of domination by the United States," the Vancouver *Sun* observed on November 2. "They talk about the threat to Canadian culture, its social programs, and its sovereignty. Evidently, they have struck a chord." Turner's gamble seemed to be paying off, and, at the beginning of November, Canada's voters were poised to reject continentalism.

For the Liberals, however, what went up could well come down. There were still three weeks before voting day, and it began to look as if their campaign had peaked too soon. As the front-runners, they were suddenly the targets, and they were now irretrievably committed to their single-issue campaign. And, critically, the Liberals had to be able to resist the open intervention of a new player: big business.

* * *

"On all sides," historian Frank Underhill observed in the *Canadian Forum* in April 1929, "there are signs to be seen that the same interests are preparing to wave the old flag and to make their own private profit, political and economic, by saving us once more from the United States." Anti-Americanism, he decided, was a "congenital weakness" of Canadians, and particularly so because "there have always been interests in Canada able and willing to exploit it and make profit out of it." The distinguished historian was thinking about the influence Canadian business had exercised in its past efforts to sustain the National Policy of high tariffs; what happened in the middle of the 1988 election campaign would have surprised him. Suddenly, those who a few generations back had desperately struggled to keep the Americans out were now ready, indeed eager, to open the borders.

Canadian business had been a crucial, if mostly background, player in the free trade debate before the 1988 election. In 1981 the five-year-old

Business Council on National Issues, the influential organization formed by the country's 150 largest banks, financial institutions, and manufacturing corporations with total assets of $700 billion, considered free trade with the United States for the first time. By 1983, pushed and prodded by its well-connected president, Tom d'Aquino, it had become firmly attached to the idea. Growing American protectionism and worldwide recession were the reasons the BCNI offered for its changed position. At the same time, the Canadian Manufacturers Association, traditionally the bulwark of protectionist sentiment in small business Canada, was also changing its tune. In 1982 the CMA endorsed free trade with the United States for the first time.

What had not changed since Underhill wrote was that big business in Canada could still exercise enormous influence on the political system. More than one business group discussed free trade with federal bureaucrats, with politicians, and with American business and political representatives in 1983 and 1984. When Brian Mulroney's Conservatives were elected in 1984, business leaders pressed their case for a trade deal with the United States again. Mulroney was sympathetic. With his acute political antennae, he had sensed the change in the national mood, and he had moved his party to the political right. Open markets and reduced government intervention fit well with the Conservatives' new direction. The Prime Minister also could relate personally to the business leaders—after all, he had come to politics directly from the Canadian head office of a large American multinational, Iron Ore Co.

Once formal negotiations with the United States were underway, Canadian business was content to let the government defend free trade. When the 1988 election was finally called, business made generous contributions to the Tories but, at least initially, let the government—cruising along in first place in the polls—explain the benefits of the FTA to Canadians. After the leaders' debates, however, what had seemed a sure thing was suddenly in doubt and, in an attempt to stop the Grits, business pulled out its chequebook and entered the campaign to defend its interests.

The result was an unprecedented flood of advertising and propaganda. At Toronto subway stations, fashionably dressed women passed out pro–free trade pamphlets. Through its trade associations, business bought acres of newspaper space, corporation presidents gave speeches, and the mails groaned under the weight of propaganda pamphlets. The "sheer tonnage was astonishing," wrote Graham Fraser in his fine account of the campaign.[12] A new organization created for campaign purposes, the Canadian Alliance for Trade and Job Opportunities, the 1988 version of 1911's Canadian Home Manufacturers Association, quickly won a major profile for itself, with much of its support coming from multinational firms such as IBM, General Motors, Dow Chemicals, and Shell Oil. From the left, there were even suggestions that the Canadian Alliance had been established at the urging of American corporate leaders. Behind the scenes, too, efforts were also intense. To give but two examples of dozens: when Crown Life Insurance called a meeting for four hundred of its workers to discuss the trade deal, it turned quickly into a pro–FTA lecture from a company vice-president; and Loblaws grocery stores sent each of its thousands of Ontario employees a letter supporting the deal.

With their cause trailing in the polls, business groups showed no hesitation in turning their message into a threatening one: Canada needed this deal, they suggested, or else. That "or else" could be global—Canada might lose international respect; or it could be national—the Canadian economy could again slump into recession. It could even be local: some companies bluntly told their employees they would lose their jobs if the FTA was not approved. Business stole a leaf from the anti–FTA campaign and resorted to cartoons to get its position across. One paid advertisement published on November 19 showed Canada sinking in stormy seas, ready to be swallowed by trade barriers and protectionism, while Japan, the European Community, and an Asian trade bloc looked on impassively. The lifeboat, naturally, was a Canada–US trading zone. This negative message was reinforced when the Canadian dollar dropped dramatically and the Toronto Stock Exchange dipped in response to the polls showing the Liberals ahead.

Canadian business had closed ranks and acted decisively and effectively. It had the advantage of deep pockets and, more important, as an outsider in the campaign, it faced none of the restrictions on spending that limited the money the political parties could spend. Estimates of business contributions to the pro–FTA campaign ranged from $2 to $10 million; it might even have been more. The business expenditures were added to the Tories' advertising budget, and the official information was widely distributed by government.

* * *

Most important, business support for the FTA was helping to reverse the anti-Tory, anti–FTA tide. Between November 11 and 14, three separate rational polls showed the Liberals and the Conservatives in a dead heat. Turner was starting to feel the pressure. Against the judgment of his top advisers, he kept the Liberal campaign focused almost exclusively on the trade deal. The Conservatives, following the lead provided by business, went on the attack. On the one hand, Mulroney stressed that his government intended to enact transitional measures to ensure workers an easy adjustment to the FTA. On the other, a Conservative Party news release published on November 3 suggested that by threatening to rip up the FTA, the opposition was "playing Russian roulette with the livelihoods of over two million Canadian families." The Tories also made an issue of the Liberals' anti-American approach. Mulroney crony Roy McMurtry, recently retired from his patronage appointment as High Commissioner to Britain, published an essay in the *Toronto Star* (of all places) suggesting that the British were surprised by the "latent and gratuitous anti-Americanism" of Canadians, which they found "bordering on paranoia." On November 14 Mulroney himself accused Turner of "fanning the fires of anti-Americanism." The Liberal leader was "on quite a destructive campaign, and anti-Americanism is part and parcel of everything he is trying to do. . . . I think he's going to find out that negativism and destructiveness is [sic] not what Canadians want." The government was now on the attack, and its campaign was regaining momentum. Significantly, a major element in it was to attack the anti-Americanism of the anti–FTA campaigners. In one southwestern Ontario constituency, reeling under the assault, a Liberal candidate watched his support melt by one percentage point a day.

Turner was committed to his approach, however, and as voting day drew near, he hammered home his contention that the government had sold Canada out. The United States and all things American continued to be the focus of his attack. On November 12 Turner accused Mulroney of using "American-style" campaign tactics, a reference apparently directed as much at the effectiveness of Tory advertisements as at their glib slickness and tough language. But the Liberals were no slouches when it came to TV advertising. In response to a Conservative commercial that showed the international border being redrawn on the now famous map, the Liberals produced a new one featuring Mulroney appearing to salute the American flag. Yet at the same time, reeling more than a little under the charges that his campaign was motivated by anti-Americanism, Turner also thought it necessary to clarify some of his attacks on the prime minister. "I haven't challenged the prime minister's patriotism," he told reporters with patent insincerity on November 16. "I just challenged his bad judgment."

The Liberals were making their last, desperate attempt to regain their momentum, but new polls released on November 19 showed the Conservatives back in the lead. The last few days of the campaign threw the electorate headlong into a storm of advertising as the Liberals, the government, and business groups pulled out all the stops. In a last-ditch strategy, the Liberals shouted out the obvious: big business and its American supporters were buying the Conservatives the election.

Only business and the decided anti–free trade voters appeared to hear, and only business had the unlimited resources to strike back. The vice-president of the Business Council on National Issues, Jack Fraser of Winnipeg's Federal Industries, called the Liberal leader "a mad dog—it's one thing to want to be elected, but to screw your country in order to win, that's just disgusting." The head of Noranda Inc., Alf Powis, pronounced Turner "dead wrong" and cried that it would be a "national tragedy" if the FTA was defeated. There had not been an election since 1911 in which corporate Canada had been so involved, so united in its support for one side, and so determined to get what it wanted.[13] The voters seemed to get the message, some deciding that the FTA couldn't be so bad if business liked it, while others began to have their suspicions reinforced that John Turner was not really the best man to have as prime minister.

When Canadians finally headed to the ballot boxes on November 21, the choice seemed clear. Polls showed that nearly 80 percent saw the FTA as the most important issue, and the Liberals and Tories had conspicuously different policies on the deal; the NDP also opposed the agreement, but its disastrous campaign had effectively marginalized the social democrats. The issue was ostensibly trade, but in essence it was largely psychological. Could Canada continue to survive as an independent nation if it shared an open border with the United States? Would social programs such as medicare and unemployment insurance and programs designed to support industry in high unemployment areas be able to withstand the desire of business for its vaunted level playing field? Would the barrier constituted by tariffs, even the low tariffs that had been created by trade agreements in the 1930s and successive reductions in customs duties put in place through the General Agreement on Tariffs and Trade since the Second World War, be displaced by an open border? The absence of free trade before the FTA, in other words, was one of the few things that let Canadians remember that they were different from their powerful neighbours. And if free trade came into effect? That was the question at issue on November 21.

When the ballots were counted, the Conservatives' 43 percent of the vote and 169 seats gave them a solid majority and, under the rules of parliamentary government, a firm endorsement of their trade policy. Turner's Liberals had captured 32 percent of the electorate and 83 seats, a better showing than in 1984, but nowhere near enough to block the FTA. The NDP had dropped in the polls and almost out of public view after the leaders' debates, but Ed Broadbent's social democrats still received 20 percent of the vote and 43 seats. That meant that more than half of voting Canadians had chosen to support parties that were strongly against free trade. Incredibly, despite the election campaign (or, perhaps, because of the confusion generated by the blizzard of claims and counter-claims), opinion polls also showed that more than three-quarters of Canadians did not feel sufficiently informed on the FTA to make an evaluation of it. Nonetheless, the Tories and the FTA had won, and the psychological barrier that constituted the international border had suddenly become much more permeable.

Like most of those who had fought against the FTA with crusading zeal, John Turner was not particularly gracious in defeat. He told his MPs a few weeks later that big business support for the Conservatives was "nothing short of the Americanization of politics, as the Government wants to Americanize everything else in this country." The Prime Minister had won "a tarnished mandate, a sullied victory," Turner added, as if the Liberal Party had never been the beneficiary of large contributions from corporate supporters during its long tenure of power in the twentieth century. Nonetheless, there was some truth in the Liberal leader's heated words. In 1891 and 1911 the politicians had set the agenda, assisted by business. In 1988 big business had not only set it, but had virtually taken over the campaign when the Tories and their leader flubbed their roles.

The opposition, however, made no further attempts in Parliament to stop the Canada–United States Free Trade Agreement, and it came into effect on January 1, 1989. The extent to which the fears of the doomsayers would be confirmed, the extent to which free trade would hasten the Americanization of Canada, remained to be seen.

The Liberals' gamble on a pro-Canadian, anti-American campaign had failed. Facing an incumbent government, the massive intervention of Canadian business, and an anti–free trade vote split with the NDP, the

Liberals could not hold together a coalition broad enough to unseat the Conservatives. Despite the odds, however, the anti-FTA, anti-American appeal had been surprisingly effective: support from women's groups, labour, the left, and the arts was overwhelming. There was one part of the country, however, where the appeal had meant almost nothing. It was in Quebec, as in so many elections in the past, that the battle of 1988 was won.

*   *   *

Quebec's attitudes to the United States before, during, and after the election showed just as many contradictory elements as those in any other region of the country. In April 1985 federal Trade Minister James Kelleher had been warned by his department "to expect a protectionist front" in Quebec. Quebec businesses, especially sectors such as textiles that remained heavily dependent on tariffs to protect their markets, were expected to line up against the idea, but Kelleher was soon to be pleasantly surprised. Business representatives in the province who met the minister were enthusiastic about Ottawa's trade agenda. Clearly, there had been a collective decision that the future lay in free trade with the United States.

In many ways, this was surprising. Protectionism had been an article of faith for Quebec industry and agriculture and the province's nationalists for at least a century. In the 1960s and 1970s, under both Liberal and separatist governments, *nationaliste* economic and cultural policies aimed directly at checking growing American economic control in Quebec. Those policies lasted until the early 1980s, when a new nationalism, at once anti-statist and pro-capitalist, began to take root. By 1985, with the return to office of Robert Bourassa's Liberals, the transformation was complete. A generation of *nationaliste* economic, linguistic, and cultural policies had created a new, powerful francophone business class that was ready to express Quebec's cultural distinctiveness internationally. That class, dubbed "Quebec's New Quiet Revolutionaries" by historian Ramsay Cook, was in power. Brimming with self-confidence, convinced that it could compete with anyone, anywhere, Quebec business was ready to embrace all the opportunities that the FTA might offer.

Many of the men and women at the top of Quebec's new economy remained dedicated *nationalistes*, and some were outright separatists. For the *indépendantistes*, and for many hitherto federalist business leaders, the FTA offered a rare opportunity for the province to lessen its dependence on

English Canada's markets and, moreover, to deal the central government's powers a smashing blow. Incredibly, American cultural domination and the prospect of more US investment was viewed as less threatening to Quebec than English-Canadian political interference. This was the ultimate irony of the anti-FTA campaign in English Canada: any weakening of Canadian sovereignty seemed sure to aid Quebec's historic claim to independence. The more the Liberals put their message across, the more separatist Quebeckers wanted to vote for the Conservatives (who had, in any case, cultivated the separatists assiduously in Mulroney's years in power). In this context, the huge US market was an opportunity, not a threat. Even for Québécois committed to Canada, no embedded tradition of anti-Americanism truly remained, or at least not enough to create any reluctance to take advantage of this economic opportunity. English-Canadian nationalists, many of whom had spent years trying to strike links based on their common left-wing ideology with Quebec separatists, had long assumed that the province's cultural nationalism would automatically make French Canadians share their own fear of closer ties with the United States. They were dead wrong. Polls showed an absolute majority of Québécois in support of free trade when it was offered for endorsement in the election of 1988—and there was outright shock and anger among anti-FTA crusaders in Canada.

In the election of 1988, Quebec gave its votes to Mulroney's Tories and to the Free Trade Agreement. The vote was for tighter links with the United States. Quebeckers rushed to embrace the continental economic vision of the "boy from Baie-Comeau," as Mulroney reminded Quebeckers that he, Premier Bourassa, and Parti Québécois leader Jacques Parizeau all supported the deal. Bourassa's government published an analysis of the FTA before the election which concluded that the deal "est décidément un pas en avant important pour le Québec." In the end, there was little dissent, and, astonishingly enough, as the separatist academic/journalist Daniel Latouche put it correctly, "the free trade debate passed almost unnoticed in Québec," so strong was the support for the FTA. Mulroney swept 63 of the 75 seats and increased his percentage of the vote over 1984.

In the process, English Canada's nationalists, desperately fighting against the FTA, felt betrayed as never before by their compatriots in Quebec. The split was complete, and the resurgence of separatism after the failure of the Meech Lake accord and the defeat of the Charlottetown constitutional package in a national plebiscite would be received with marked coolness in left-wing English-Canadian intellectual circles. Quebec had turned towards the "paradise" of *les États*, and the separatists, men and women who had never read or understood their André Laurendeau, naively aimed to set course for independence and to the south.

Philip Resnick, a political scientist at the University of British Columbia and a veteran of many English-Canadian nationalist battles, could not understand or accept Quebec's decision to embrace free trade. Soon after the 1988 election he accused Quebeckers of voting "with supreme indifference to the issues of both Canadian identity and appropriate models of society so clearly posed in the rest of Canada."[14] Resnick was right in commenting on the francophone failure to pay much attention to the debate over the FTA that had torn Canada apart, but he was also wrong. He was right because the debate over free trade was not really about free trade. Rather, it was about whether Canadians would take the symbolic and psychological step towards closer integration with the United States. Symbols dominated discussion about the FTA in English Canada: Mulroney as the "traitor" who wanted to follow the "American way" towards further "Americanization" had little to do with the specifics of a complicated international trade agreement. But symbolic phrases did have everything to do with how Canadians viewed themselves and their future.

At the same time, Resnick was wrong because, despite Quebec's apparent "supreme indifference," the province had deliberately and massively supported the winning side in the free trade election. Quebec's political and economic élites had worked side by side with their English-Canadian counterparts to get the deal approved. Despite fears in the rest of Canada about the price of closer American integration, Quebec's "*moi* first" approach simply led the rest of the nation down the garden path towards a form of sovereignty-association between Canada and the United States.[15]

More and more, Canadians and Québécois alike recognized that New York, Los Angeles, and Washington had become Canada's "imperial centre." Both assumed they could deal with the United States; Québécois, however, believed that their linguistic uniqueness could protect them from the worst effects of Americanization. One thing was beyond doubt in both Canada and Quebec: the simplistic, reflexive anti-Americanism that had so long dominated Canadian thinking was no longer triumphant.

Even so, there were still traces of anti-Americanism in Quebec, enough that, in 1993, Mario Roy, the entertainment writer of *La Presse*, could publish *Pour en finir avec l'anti-américanisme*, an attack on what he perceived as the continuing and irrational strength of anti-Americanism in francophone circles. Roy hit out at the daily press and its condemnation of the United States as a sick society and a mercenary state with totalitarian public opinion. To Roy, fascinated by American culture, anti-Americanism was nothing less than a turning away from the dominant modes of expression of the modern era. The response of Quebec intellectuals was predictably harsh, but also more than slightly puzzled.[16]

Far more typical were the responses to the United States of all those who yearned for an independent Quebec. Latouche talked of the Parti Québéccis' "deep admiration" for the United States, and other writers pointed (wrongly, if Roy was to be believed) to the "total absence" in Quebec of the anti-Americanism that "poisons the activities of the international left." No leftist, René Lévesque had always claimed to have few, if any, Canadian feelings. In 1969 he acknowledged: "I've always had an incredibly strong sense of being North American. The place where I'm most at home outside Quebec is the United States."[17] The comments of Lucien Bouchard, at the time of the 1988 election a new Conservative Cabinet minister and not yet the leader of the separatist Bloc Québécois, thus seemed entirely typical. Soon to marry an American, Bouchard waxed lyrical about the United States: "That was paradise. America. Ah, *les États*. We had a few people in our family who lived there. My great-uncle spent his life in the States, and he would come back in the summer with candy bars and cigarettes. He was the rich man in the family. What he said about *les États* was always marvellous."[18] Again, Bouchard said, "I think Quebeckers are more like the Americans, more republican than English-Canadians . . . every man for himself. What I love about Americans is their sense of liberty."[19] If he is unlucky enough to lead Quebec to independence, Premier Bouchard may have the responsibility of discovering just how much liberty the United States will permit his new country. Every man for himself, indeed.

*   *   *

The election defeat of 1988 obliged John Turner to return to an unwelcoming private sector that would not quickly forget his heretical opposition to the FTA, and the Liberal Party replaced him with Jean Chrétien in 1990. By that time, there were heavy job losses and rising unemployment rates, especially in manufacturing industries that were quick to seize the opportunity provided by the FTA to relocate to the south—in the Greater Toronto area 150 businesses, mainly food processing and auto parts, moved to Michigan in the first five years of the 1990s. Trade disputes with the United States continued unabated, though the dispute resolution process in the FTA provided a means of dealing with them. In most, Canada won its case. There was also a recession that seemed to confirm the worst fears of the FTA's critics.

What was most surprising was that the debate over free trade all but disappeared from the Canadian political agenda, however much unions and the Council of Canadians continued to denounce it. In part, this relative calm was the product of booming trade—exports accounting, for example, for 33 percent of the Gross Domestic Product in 1994 (or $249 billion), up from 27 percent in 1981, and for 60 percent of the country's manufacturing production, up from 25 percent a decade before. Once the FTA came into effect, exports to the south increased by 77 percent in dollar value, and each year the growth continued. By 1996 an incredible 80 percent of all Canadian exports were going to the United States, an increase from 66 percent just twenty years before. The lines of trade now ran north and south, and trade with the United States greatly exceeded interprovincial trade. Canada had definitively become part of a much larger American economy.

In December 1992 the Mulroney government concluded an agreement with the United States and Mexico that turned the FTA into a larger still North American Free Trade Agreement. The Americans had initiated the discussions with Mexico City, and Canada came to the negotiating table only when it saw its own interests at stake. Protests over NAFTA in Canada began from the predictable quarters, what Tory strategists (with the delicacy that was soon to mark their election campaign advertising in the 1993 election that reduced them to two seats in the House of Commons) labelled "that old left-wing, crypto-communist, anti-free trade, NDP-Liberal con group."[20] Labour, social welfare agencies, cultural nationalists, and artists all claimed that what was left of Canadian sovereignty was once again in jeopardy. There were demonstrations, angry letters to editors, and sympathetic support from the NDP, a virtually leaderless party apparently on the road to extinction. What was missing was any genuine passion. Canadians clearly had no burning desire for NAFTA, but after the 1988 battle, the sense that nothing could be done was all-pervasive.

The Chrétien Liberals read the public mood correctly—there would be no more desperate campaigns attacking American influence in mainstream

Canadian politics. Chrétien refused to make NAFTA a major issue in the general election of 1993, instead promising only "side deals" to improve deficient parts of the trade agreement. When the Liberals formed a majority government after the vote, no significant changes in government trade policy were expected, and predictably none were offered, although NAFTA notably failed to live up to its proponents' expectations. When the Joint House-Senate Committee on Foreign Affairs held hearings in 1994 on where Canada should be going abroad, of 506 presentations, Richard Gwyn noted in the *Toronto Star*, only *one* "sounded the old cries about protectionism and Canadian content." As Senator Allan MacEachen, a one-time nationalist Liberal put it, "People have absorbed free trade. It, and the global economy, are now taken for granted." Indeed, some had taken to referring to Canada as a nation of "cross-border consumers" rather than citizens. For all practical purposes, then, Canadian anti-Americanism seemed as dead as the dodo, and Canada, it seemed, had at last accepted its North American destiny. In any case, so inextricably intertwined had industry on both sides of the border become that disentangling Canada from the United States was now utterly impractical. The die was cast—for better or for worse.

Anti-Americanism once had defined the way Canadians thought of themselves, and from the mid-1950s through to the late 1980s, Canada had experienced an unusually prolonged period of nationalism, characterized as usual by pronounced outbursts of anti-Americanism. But as the 1988 election made clear, however much John Turner and the FTA's critics on the left had tried to crank it up for one last hurrah, anti-Americanism ultimately proved not to have legs. Its force had been diluted by events and the passage of time, and it retained its effectiveness only in the editorials of the *Toronto Star*,[21] on the political left, with cultural groups, and with a few intellectuals. Anti-Americanism had been marginalized, by-passed, and overtaken by events.

CONCLUSION

THE END OF ANTI-AMERICANISM

Aislin/The Gazette

The *New York Times* headline on December 17, 1995, was bubbling: "Yankee Come Back: American Money Makes the Whole World Sing." The days of "Yankee Go Home" anti-Americanism around the globe were over, the newspaper said. In Vietnam, for a time until the government cracked down, the signs in the airport proclaimed "Coke welcomes you to Hanoi." So much for the world's fear of Coca-colonization that seemed so strong in the years from the 1950s to the 1980s.

Every day, in every way, Canada, like the world, becomes outwardly more American. American television is all-pervasive in the country, its generally mindless culture completely familiar to Canadians who under-stand all the allusions. The brand names in the stores are the same (often Japanese!), and the stores themselves are increasingly American-owned. The Wal-Mart mega-store style is mirrored in giant emporia selling every-thing from office supplies to foodstuffs and computers. Even the beer stores, once 100 percent Canadian, have been selling American beer for years, sometimes imported but more usually bottled under licence in Canada, with the standard 5 percent alcohol content. The hosers article of faith—that American beer was pee—seemed to have disappeared under the blizzard of Budweiser and Coors advertisements.

The influence of the United States has naturally extended via television into the big business of sport. The Montreal Expos and the Toronto Blue Jays brought major league baseball to Canada, and the latter team, with its two World Series victories, has been an enormous success in spreading the "American" game's popularity. That baseball was a hundred and fifty years old in Canada scarcely mattered, for the way the modern game is played is as American as apple pie. Mild anti-Americanism arises only when Americans forget that the Canadian teams are in a different country or when a US Marine Corps colour guard carried the Canadian flag upside down at a World Series game in Atlanta. The Blue Jays' shrewd management defused the incident and turned boos into cheers by having the Marines carry the Canadian flag, right side up, at the next game in Toronto while a Canadian colour guard carried the Stars and Stripes. Still, as philosopher Mark Kingwell observes, the Blue Jays' victories "chal-lenged American dominance" by demonstrating that a team from outside the United States could be the best in the game.[1] Toronto's Americans and Dominicans were better than theirs!

Even Canada's national sport has been co-opted. The National Hockey League with its minority of Canadian teams irrevocably dances to the tune of the big market cities in the United States, and Canadian influence over "our game," declining for decades, has greatly diminished. The sale of the Quebec Nordiques and the Winnipeg Jets to the United States suggests that "small market" teams wherever located are no longer viable in these circumstances. When professional basketball came to Vancouver and Toronto in 1995, it threatened to divide the winter sport market in those cities with hockey, further weakening the Canadian pres-ence in the NHL. The Canadian Football League, its game different from the National Football League's and arguably better, tried to save itself by expanding into the United States, with completely predictable results. The American teams lost money and in 1996 they all withdrew, even though Baltimore had won the Grey Cup in 1995. Scarcely anyone noticed. The Grey Cup game, once a powerful nationalizing force, had become an unwatched bore sandwiched between American sports broadcasts. According to a devastating *Maclean's* poll in April 1996, few fans seemed to care if the CFL was or was not Americanized, most clearly wishing that NFL teams would come to Canada. Brian Williams, a CBC sports commentator, lamented: "It's so typically Canadian. We have something over 100 years old and it's got a wonderful tradition. We've got to get out of this mindset that if it's not American, it's not good."[2] Unfortunately, the CFL had stopped being good years before.

In a continental market dominated by television and media dollars, there seems little way to resist the trend of Americanization. Indeed, the Canadian team owners, visions of big bucks dancing in their heads, seem eagerly to accept it. Strikingly, even in the area of sport, overt anti-Americanism no longer seems viable. Most football fans clearly prefer the NFL over the CFL and, while hockey fans bemoan the decline in quality brought on by expansion, they do not seem to connect it to the Americanization of the game. Even Winnipeg, which gamely rallied in the vain attempt to save its team, did not resort to stone-throwing as the Jets slipped away to the south. It was money that had won, not the Americans.

Sport continues to bring out the differences between Canadians and Americans very sharply. When a Canadian junior hockey team beat the United States at the World tourney, Canadian chests swelled. When Ben Johnson won the 100 metres at the Seoul Olympics over American Carl Lewis, there was enormous exultation in Canada. Lewis presented himself as a boastful braggart, a showboating grandstander, and Johnson's win stirred cheers from the most phlegmatic. In that moment of victory, Johnson symbolized a triumph of quiet over noise, of civility over hype, of Canada over an ugly America. It was all turned to dust when the doping scandal broke and the Olympic Committee removed Johnson's medal. Of course, the whole sad episode was attributable to the malign influence exercised by America on sport, where winning at any cost is all that matters.

Rodewalt/*Calgary Herald*

*   *   *

Canadians live with the realities of a prolonged recession and the effects of globalization. Governments in virtually every provincial capital and in Ottawa are hacking and slashing at programs and budgets, following the global agenda as defined in the Republican-dominated Congress in Washington. The Liberal government's Trade Minister (along with the Prime Minister, the Premiers, and a Team Canada of industrialists) continue to travel the world touting free trade and expanded trade, and American investment is avidly sought. The days of Yankee Go Home, such as they were in Canada, are over. Here too it's Yankee Come Back— and bring money. After the Free Trade Agreement of 1988 and the election of that year, and despite a continuing series of trade disputes characterized by American bully-boy tactics, anti-Americanism is weaker in Canada now than ever before.

The current situation mirrors that described by historian Frank Underhill in 1950, just as the Cold War began to threaten to turn into a major war. The University of Toronto scholar said, a shade over-optimistically, "only the Communists and a diehard remnant of the Tories go about talking of 'American Imperialism.'" Then, he corrected himself. "Well, no, this isn't quite correct. There are also those academic intellectuals in our universities who are still thinking up nasty wisecracks about American imperialism regardless of the fact that most of their own pet research projects are apt to be financed by money from Rockefeller or Carnegie or Guggenheim."[3] As usual, Underhill had it fundamentally right and, almost a half-century later, little (other than the granting agencies he mentioned and the all-but-total demise of the Tory Party) has changed. In the late 1990s a small number of professors in the universities remain at the centre of anti-Americanism, joined by the leadership of a few national trade unions, a part of what is left of the New Democratic Party, and some low-circulation magazines. Anti-Americanism as ideology is confined to the left of the political spectrum— the bloodied remnants of the democratic left and the unreconstructed irredentists on the Marxist left. Many of these are the people who never could see the faults in Soviet Communism, but who dwelled on those of American (and Canadian) capitalism. They were free to hold such views only because their liberal democracy cherished the idea of free speech, but this scarcely crossed their minds. The American defence umbrella—which permitted Canada its virtually free ride on defence for most of the Cold War— protected them from the consequences of their beliefs, but few noticed or cared. George Orwell wrote in 1945 that "if you are jealous of the wealth and power of America . . . you cannot get rid of these feelings simply by taking thought. But you can at least recognize that you have them, and prevent them from contaminating your mental processes."[4] Many anti-Americans who remain at large cannot make that effort.

The left, the last repository of militant anti-Americanism, today is a broken reed. The New Democratic Party is on the verge of extinction in federal politics, and its survival in the provincial capitals is probably limited to the time Saskatchewan's Roy Romanow and British Columbia's Glen Clark remain active politicians. The Marxist left, never strong outside the universities, tried to play the anti-American card in the 1950s, but its leadership was clumsy and amateur. More recently, it has been completely discredited by the collapse of the Soviet Union and the "democratic" revival in Eastern Europe. The trade unions that led the fight against the FTA and NAFTA are now devoting all their efforts to the vain attempt to preserve their members' jobs in the face of government and corporate budget-cutters. This may not be a permanent condition, of course, but today it seems unlikely that a newly vibrant left will ever muster the popular support to lead Canada out of the FTA, the NAFTA, and the American empire—and into impoverished independence in a world divided among competing trade blocs.

*   *   *

There are, nonetheless, a host of differences that remain between Canada and the United States. Canada has entrenched multiculturalism in an effort to stop the melting pot bragged about in the United States from doing its work. Social democracy, however attenuated today, has thrived in the past and continues to struggle onward in Canada; in the United States, socialism has no past and less of a future. Unions remain stronger in Canada than in the United States, and the influence of religion is less. Canada's welfare state, its policies of equalization, and its medicare system still provide a measure of important differentiation. And Canadians truly are, just as their forebears claimed in the nineteenth century, more law-abiding than their gun-happy, litigious southern neighbours. What seems clear, however, is that the differences are eroding under the pressures of economic and cultural harmonization. Just as Canada's independent capacity to act in the world has become constrained by the continental relationship, so too has the ability of Canadians to lead lives that differ in their essentials from those of Americans.[5] The decline of anti-Americanism surely is a recognition of the truth that Canadians are, every day, more like Americans.

At the same time, it is important to recognize that Canadians most definitely do not want to be part of the United States. There is a popular belief that Canada is the best of all nations in which to live, much as the United Nations has proclaimed with great regularity. As columnist Dalton Camp put it when he heard a news broadcast in 1995 announcing Canada's first-place global ranking, "We already knew that"—and every Canadian, even the disgruntled separatist in Quebec, does too. Robertson Davies said much the same thing in a 1989 *Harper's* article: "Americans are precisely what we are not and what we don't want to be." That probably overstated matters on both counts, but there is undoubtedly a widespread Canadian understanding that the United States, however rich and powerful, is not necessarily a better place to be. Nor is it automatically a benign force on

Canada's border. Washington and Wall Street have clear aims, and those aims might drastically affect Canada and Canadians. Still, Davies would have been more correct if he had said that "United Statesians" are precisely what we are not and what we don't want to be. Canadians are Americans who clearly do not want to be US citizens. Opinion polls show strong nationalism in every part of the nation, even polls in Quebec, and there is so little support for Canada becoming part of the United States that it is usually below the margin of error.

But what about Quebec, traditionally much less anti-American than English Canada? If Quebec goes its own way, the slippage to the south could accelerate. Whether the United States would want all the provinces or whether it would cherry-pick the richest is unclear. The United States has its own serious problems, and the adhesion of new states could disrupt the delicate balance that uneasily binds north and south, east and west.

Ironically, if Quebec secedes, one major genuine difference that still remains between Canada and the United States will disappear. Bilingualism and biculturalism have not been popular ideas in any part of Canada, but there is no doubt that the French fact—the distinct society that exists in life if not in constitutional law—has made Canada unlike its great neighbour. In the 1890s, anti-Americanism and the idea that Canada was part of the British Empire existed strongly enough for a credible propaganda case to be made that the two societies were genuinely unique. In the 1990s, anti-Americanism is feeble and the British Empire is in the dustbin of history. Some wistfully point to the monarchy as a key element of Canadian distinctiveness, but this is surely a bad joke: the monarchy has discredited itself beyond any possibility of redemption. Canadians are now on their own against the force of Americanization, with or without Quebec. The one certainty is that it will be harder to preserve a separate Canadian nation in North America if Quebec goes its own way, not least because of geography. It is also certain that a separate Quebec will be more exposed to the assimilationist forces of continentalism than it is as part of Canada.

Perhaps, some suggest with more hope than sense, Canadian anti-Americanism will have a great resurgence. For all the reasons adduced in this book, this is extremely unlikely. Before the Second World War, Canadian business and finance had a vested interest in preserving Canada as a protected market, and they employed anti-Americanism as a weapon to this end. But the Great War, the Second World War, and the Cold War, coupled with Britain's disappearance as a great power, drove Canada to the south.

Business and finance gave up the ghost of economic independence with scarcely a whimper, trading in their pounds sterling and British ideals for American dollars and acceptance on Wall Street. From being a proponent of anti-Americanism, Canadian business became its opponent.

The Liberals, Walter Gordon's nationalist efforts notwithstanding, were the first to understand and accept this shift in Bay Street's attitudes. The Conservatives took longer, but John Diefenbaker discredited anti-Americanism in his party so thoroughly that his successors had not the slightest desire to use it; indeed, the Tories after Diefenbaker embraced continentalism with wholehearted zeal. The simple fact that the Conservative Party fought and won the 1988 election on free trade and that their Liberal successors accepted and expanded the concept demonstrates that the business class is now wholly absorbed by American finance. Business will never again finance campaigns against the United States as it did in 1891 and 1911.

When I was a child in the 1940s, the Loyal Orange Order's parades in Toronto were massive demonstrations of Protestant power and solidarity— Up with King Billy and To Hell with the Pope! Today, the Orange Order has been reduced to a minor sectarian group of no consequence, so dispirited that it can find no one to ride King Billy's white horse, if it can even borrow a horse. In many ways, the same transformation has occurred in the power of Canadian anti-Americanism in this century. A generation from now, the Free Trade election of 1988 will, I suspect, be widely recognized as the last gasp of a once powerful motivating force.

Even so, anti-Americanism will likely continue in an attenuated, powerless form as a useful and instinctive device that Canadians will employ to differentiate themselves from their neighbours. Canadian writer Michael Ignatieff, speaking from his base in London, noted that, "viewed from the US, the differences between Americans and Canadians may seem very minor. Viewed from Canada," however, he added, "they form the crux of an identity." With luck, the Canadian desire to preserve those minor differences will be based on a rational desire to avoid absorption into the United States; today and in the future, perhaps, the arguments will also be more rational than they often have been in the past.

And if Canada has no luck? Then, increasingly, Canadian anti-Americanism will simply be a North American regional variant. Just as people in the Deep South of the United States will continue to look askance at Northerners, and Midwesterners will always wonder about the goings-on in New York and Los Angeles, so too will Canadians puzzle over and carp at the Americans and continue to compare their accents, their "ehs" and their "aboots," to the nasal American tones. Pierre Berton put this neatly: "My belief was that we might still end up with a country called Canada—but that it would be *de facto*, if not *de jure*, an American state. We were pretending to be an independent nation in spite of the Americanization of our economy, our politics, and our culture."[6]

Canada may well ultimately be absorbed by the United States. If this happens, it will not be because the President ordered the Marines into Canada to seize the country by force (presumably carrying the Maple Leaf flag upside down as they cross the border). The American people, however bellicose they may be at times, simply would not stand for any such action. "If Canadians lose their independence," the diplomat Arthur Andrew wrote, "it will be because they themselves have willed it. No amount of diplomacy can save those who have lost their desire to be different."[7]

This is surely true. With all its hatred, bias, and deliberately contrived fearmongering, anti-Americanism was once the Canadian way of being different. Now it has faded away, and good riddance to it. Anti-Americanism never was and never could become the basis for any rational national identity. Canadians are fortunate enough to live in God's country, the best of all places on earth, a land graced with North America's bounty and few of the United States' worst problems. Yet we somehow cannot lift our eyes off the depressing news in the daily paper to realize our great good fortune.

There are Canadian virtues—grit, tolerance, opportunity, civility, compassion, and equality—and they should be part of any definition of national character. So should our love of the land, our shared history, our forms of governance, our common love of hockey, and those policies that bind us together like medicare and equalization. Somehow we seem on the verge of forgetting the transcendent importance of these attributes and of eliminating these programs, forgetting how important they are as props of our self-definition as Canadians. If we do forget them, if we continue our internecine federal-provincial bickering and the dismantling of the institutions—not least the national government—that have differentiated us more sharply than we realize from our neighbours, then, tragically, Canada's fate will be all too obvious. Self-inflicted wounds can be every bit as fatal as any other.

What lies beyond anti-Americanism? Only when Canadians begin to understand their land and their origins, when they can assess their national history of truly great achievements without a search for politically correct victims, and when they become confident of their own worth and their limitless future, only then will the Canadian identity become truly defined without resort to glib, mindless prejudice. Like other peoples in a world of global corporations and giant trading alliances, Canadians are searching for ways to preserve a national identity in the McWorld that threatens to swamp them. This is no easy task in North America, to be sure, but the one certainty is that anti-Americanism is not the vehicle of choice to achieve it.

Two hundred years after the Loyalists came to British North America, we are finally outgrowing our reflexive anti-Americanism. It will be a tragedy if we cannot use our new maturity to resolve our domestic problems. The real challenge for Canada, something vitally important for our survival as the other North Americans, will be to continue to resist absorption, formal or informal, into the American empire that threatens to engulf us. A healthy Canadian nationalism—in the best sense the desire to preserve an independent but interdependent nation—remains as necessary as ever in the past.

NOTES

INTRODUCTION

1 A.Z. Rubinstein and D.E. Smith, "Anti-Americanism: Anatomy of a Phenomenon," in Rubinstein and Smith, eds., *Anti-Americanism in the Third World: Implications for U.S. Foreign Policy* (New York 1985), 1–5.

2 Paul Hollander, *Anti-Americanism: Critiques at Home and Abroad, 1965–1990* (New York 1992), viii; Paul Johnson as quoted in James Simmons, *Americans: The View from Abroad* (New York 1990), 209. Henry Fairlie noted the strength of anti-Americanism—anti-*Amerika* even—in the intellectual life of the United States during the Vietnam War. Perceptively, he observed that "anti-Americanism in America . . . is in some of its aspects a reflection of Americanism. It is as agitated by the symbols and myths and metaphors of the 'American experience' as others . . . are consoled by them." "Anti-Americanism at Home and Abroad," *Commentary* (December 1975): 30.

3 A.Z. Rubinstein and D.E. Smith, "Anti-Americanism in the Third World," *Annals*, no. 497 (May 1988): 35.

4 Kenneth Minogue, "Anti-Americanism: A View from London," *National Interest*, no. 3 (Spring 1986): 48. British anti-Americanism is now said to be weak, and especially so among those of highest social class. See Hugh Brogan, "The Cost of Absurdity," *Times Literary Supplement* (October 5–11, 1990): 1076–8; United States Information Agency, *Opinion Research Memorandum*, May 11, 1993.

5 J. Van Houten, "Europe," *Wall Street Journal*, August 3, 1983, 19.

6 Erwin Scheuch, "Hating America—the World's Favorite Pastime," *Atlas*, 19 (September 1970): 19–20; Fairlie, "Anti-Americanism," 38.

7 Quoted in Simmons, *Americans*, 208.

8 "This is the meaning of anti-Americanism in Canada—opposition to the Americanization of Canada whether in economic, social, cultural or political terms." W.M. Baker, "The Anti-American Ingredient in Canadian History," *Dalhousie Review*, 53 (Spring 1973): 58.

9 Hugh MacLennan, "How We Differ from Americans," *Maclean's* (December 15, 1946): 9.

10 Rick Salutin, *Living in a Dark Age* (Toronto 1991), 25.

11 On French anti-Americanism, see Tony Judt, *Past Imperfect: French Intellectuals, 1944–1956* (Berkeley, Cal., 1992); D. Lacorne et al., eds., *The Rise and Fall of French Anti-Americanism* (London 1990); David Strauss, *Menace in the West: The Rise of French Anti-Americanism in Modern Times* (Westport, Conn., 1978); and Richard Kuisel, *Seducing the French: The Dilemma of Americanization* (Berkeley, Cal., 1993).

12 P.E. Corbett, "Anti-Americanism," *Dalhousie Review*, 10 (October 1930): 295.

13 Charles Doran and J.Sewell, "Anti-Americanism in Canada?" *Annals*, no. 497 (May 1988): 106.

14 Harry Johnson, "Unlovely Canadianism," in William Kilbourn, ed., *A Guide to the Peaceable Kingdom* (Toronto 1970), 208–9.

1: BLIND HATRED?

1 Douglas Glover, *The Life and Times of Captain N.* (Toronto 1993), 24, 41–2, 108, 131.

2 S.F. Wise, "The Place of the Loyalists in Ontario and Canadian History," in S.F. Wise et al., eds., *"None Was Ever Better . . ." The Loyalist Settlement of Ontario* (Proceedings of the Annual Meeting of the Ontario Historical Society 1984), xii–xiii. Compare W.A. Deacon, "The Bogey of Annexation," in his *Poteen: A Pot-Pourri of Canadian Essays* (Ottawa 1926), 9.

3 Quoted in Jane Errington, "Loyalists in Upper Canada: A British American Community," in Wise et al., *None Was Ever Better*, 35.

4 Ibid., 59.

5 *Dictionary of Canadian Biography*, vol. 9 (Toronto 1976), 754; Jane Errington, *The Lion, the Eagle, and Upper Canada* (Montreal 1987), 44–5.

6 Charles Humphries, "The Capture of York," in M. Zaslow, ed., *The Defended Border* (Toronto 1964), 261.

7 J.L.H. Henderson, ed., *John Strachan: Documents and Opinions* (Toronto 1969), 32ff. A more realistic view of the "Cool Calculators" in the militia can be found in George Sheppard, *Plunder, Profit, and Paroles: A Social History of the War of 1812 in Upper Canada* (Montreal 1994), 40ff.

8 S.F. Wise and R.C. Brown, *Canada Views the United States* (Seattle 1967), 29–30; Fernand Ouellet, "Québec et les Etats-Unis (1760–1850)," *First Canadian-American*

Institute . . . 1967 (Plattsburgh 1967), 46ff. Of course, all Canadians did look to and largely accepted American models. W.B. Munro noted in 1929 that "In the government and politics of Canada most of what is superimposed is British; but most of what works its way in from the bottom is American." Cited in F.H.U., "O Canada," *Canadian Forum*, 10 (February 1930): 115.

9 Quoted in Fred Landon, *Western Ontario and the American Frontier* (New York 1941), 156.

10 David Mills, *The Idea of Loyalty in Upper Canada, 1784–1850* (Montreal 1988), 79.

11 Wise and Brown, *Canada Views the United States*, 33.

12 Peter Burroughs, ed., *The Colonial Reformers and Canada, 1830–1849* (Toronto 1969), 189. See Allan Greer, *The Patriots and the People: The Rebellion of 1837 in Rural Lower Canada* (Toronto 1993).

13 Catherine Parr Traill, *The Backwoods of Canada* (Toronto 1929), 335, 338.

14 Norman Knowles, "Inventing the Loyalists: The Ontario Loyalist Tradition and the Creation of a Usable Past, 1784–1924" (PhD thesis, York University, 1992), 392.

15 Quoted in D.V.J. Bell, "The Loyalist Tradition in Canada," *Journal of Canadian Studies* 5 (May 1970): 23–4.

16 Archives of Ontario, Brock Monument Papers, III, Proceedings of Public Meeting, June 17, 1840; ibid., Resolutions of Brock's Monument Committee, nd.

17 Stephen Otto, "Brock's Two Monuments," *Cuesta* (1991–92): 15–17.

18 J.W. Kendall, "Blueprint Defiance of Manifest Destiny: Anti-Americanism and Anti-Republicanism in Canada West, 1858–1867" (MA thesis, McGill University, 1969), 6.

19 Murray Barkley, "The Loyalist Tradition in New Brunswick," *Acadiensis*, 4 (Spring 1975): 27.

20 Alphaeus Todd, "Is Canadian Loyalty a Sentiment or a Principle?" *Rose-Belford's Canadian Monthly and National Review* (November 1881): 528.

21 United Empire Loyalist Centennial Committee, *The Centennial of the Settlement of Upper Canada by the United Empire Loyalists* (reprint; Boston 1972), 20–2.

22 Norman Knowles, "Shall We Not Raise There Again. . . . The Loyalist Tradition and the Adolphustown Centennial Celebrations of 1884," *Ontario History* 80 (March 1988): 18ff. Knowles finds rather more ambivalence in the Adolphustown speeches than I do.

23 F.H.U[nderhill], "O Canada," *Canadian Forum* 10 (January 1930): 79.

2: UNDER WHICH FLAG?

1 *The Mail and Empire* (Toronto), February 20, 1911.

2 Quoted in Carl Berger, *The Sense of Power* (Toronto 1970), 161–2, 166.

3 J.S. Willison, *Laurier and the Liberal Party*, vol. 2 (Toronto 1903), 120.

4 G.T. Denison, *The Struggle for Imperial Unity* (Toronto 1909), Chap. 12.

Denison's account of the Commercial Union movement he fought was widely reprinted in 1911.

5 Sir Joseph Pope, ed., *Correspondence of Sir John Macdonald* (Toronto nd), 478.

6 Quoted in P.B. Waite, *Canada 1874–1896: Arduous Destiny* (Toronto 1971), 223.

7 Lawrence Martin, *The Presidents and the Prime Ministers* (Toronto 1982), 48.

8 Quoted in Patricia K. Wood, "'Under Which Flag, Canadian?' Anti-Americanism and the Election of 1891" (MA thesis, Queen's University 1991), 63.

9 K.A. MacKirdy, "The Loyalty Issue in the 1891 Federal Election," *Ontario History* 55 (1963): 143ff.

10 Waite, *Canada 1874–1896*, 225.

11 O.D. Skelton, *The Life and Letters of Sir Wilfrid Laurier* (Toronto 1921), vol. 1, 418.

12 National Archives of Canada (NA), G.R. Parkin Papers, vol. 69, Mss, 23 February 1899, ff. 21765ff.

13 Quoted in Berger, *The Sense of Power*, 172.

14 J.L. Granatstein and Norman Hillmer, *For Better or for Worse: Canada and the United States to the 1990s* (Toronto 1991), 34. On the response in Canada, see J.A. Munro, "English-Canadianism and the Demand for Canadian Autonomy: Ontario's Response to the Alaska Boundary Decision, 1903," *Ontario History*, 57 (December 1965): 189ff.

15 Quoted in A.D. Gilbert, "'On the Road to New York': The Protective Impulse and the English-Canadian Cultural Identity, 1896–1914," *Dalhousie Review*, 58 (Autumn 1978): 409.

16 PEI-born physician and author Andrew MacPhail, one of the leading critics of reciprocity, wrote in a book published in 1909 that life "is safer in a Yukon dance hall than in Madison Square Gardens." Quoted in ibid., 410.

17 K.A. Clements, "Manifest Destiny and Canadian Reciprocity in 1911," *Pacific Historical Review*, 42 (1973): 39.

18 Quoted in Robert Bothwell, *Loring Christie: The Failure of Bureaucratic Imperialism* (New York 1988), 54; Robert Bothwell and John Kirton, "'A Sweet Little Country': American Attitudes Towards Canada, 1925 to 1963," *Queen's Quarterly* 90 (Winter 1983): 1080. Professor Bothwell reminded me of these wonderful quotations.

19 Quoted in Granatstein and Hillmer, *For Better or for Worse*, 50. On Grey's view of the pact, see Gordon Stewart, *The American Response to Canada* (East Lansing, Mich. 1992), 127.

20 Quoted ibid., 121.

3: ON THE AMERICAN ROAD

1 George Grant, *Technology and Empire: Perspectives on North America* (Toronto 1969), 69–71.

NOTES

2 United States National Archives, Treasury Department Records, box 24, White to McAdoo, June 21, 1917.

3 J.L. Granatstein and Norman Hillmer, *For Better or For Worse: Canada and the United States to the 1990s* (Toronto 1991), 58.

4 Archives of Ontario, W.T. Gregory, "Who Won the War?," Mss Misc. Collection MU2131–1919 no. 1.

5 Beckles Willson, *Redemption: A Novel* (New York 1924), 275; Macnaughton address to the Canadian Club of Montreal, March 1919, in Toronto Metro Reference Library, History, Mf. B6275, reel 3, no. 14 I am indebted to Dr Jonathan Vance for these two references.

6 NA, R.L. Borden Papers, Connaught to Borden May 15, 1916, f. 36377.

7 Will R. Bird, *And We Go On* (Toronto 1930), 283. I am again indebted to Dr Vance for this reference.

8 Quoted in Mary Vipond, "National Consciousness in English-Speaking Canada in the 1920s: Seven Case Studies" (PhD dissertation, University of Toronto, 1974), 147–8.

9 Hugh Keenleyside, *Canada and the United States* (New York 1929, 1952), 353–4.

10 B.K. Sandwell, "The Annexation of Our Stage," in Don Rubin, ed., *Canadian Theatre History: Selected Readings* (Toronto 1996), 16ff; A.G. Bailey, "Literature and Nationalism after Confederation," *University of Toronto Quarterly* 25 (1955–56): 411.

11 *Canadian Annual Review, 1922* (Toronto 1923), 71.

12 Quoted in John Weaver, "Canadians Confront American Mass Culture, 1918–1930" (unpublished paper, nd), 25; Mary Vipond, "Canadian Nationalism and the Plight of Canadian Magazines in the 1920s," *Canadian Historical Review* 58 (March 1977): 43.

13 Quoted in Ramsay Cook, "Landscape Painting and National Consciousness in Canada," *Historical Reflections* 1 (Winter 1974): 279–80.

14 Gustave Lanctot, ed., *Les Canadiens français et leurs voisins du sud* (Montréal 1941), 305.

15 Georges Pelletier, "Notre américanisation par le journal," *Notre Américanisation* (Montréal 1937), 188–9.

16 D.J. Horton, *André Laurendeau: French-Canadian Nationalist, 1912–1968* (Toronto 1992), 80–1, 195–6.

17 NA, W.L. Grant Papers, vol. 5, Hankey file, Grant to Maurice Hankey, November 17, 1921, and vol. 2, Dafoe file, Grant to J.W. Dafoe, December 29, 1927.

18 John T. Saywell, *'Just Call Me Mitch': The Life of Mitchell F. Hepburn* (Toronto 1991), 441–2, 451–2.

19 Douglas Francis, *Frank H. Underhill: Intellectual Provocateur* (Toronto 1986),

115ff.; University of British Columbia Archives, Alan Plaunt Papers, box 4, file 26, Underhill to Plaunt, September 13, 1940 and January 10 and 12, 1941.

20 F.D. Roosevelt Library, Hyde Park, N.Y., F.D. Roosevelt Papers, PSF Canada, Moffat to Sumner Welles, August 14, 1940; Harvard University, J. Pierrepont Moffat Papers, vol. 17, Moffat to C.M. Gauss, August 29, 1940.

21 NA, R.B. Hanson Papers, file S-175-M-1, Meighen to Hanson, August 19, 1940.

22 Quoted in James Eayrs, *In Defence of Canada*, vol. 3: *Peacemaking and Deterrence* (Toronto 1972), 349–50.

23 J.L. Granatstein, *How Britain's Weakness Forced Canada into the Arms of the United States* (Toronto 1989), 49.

24 Donald Creighton, *Canada's First Century* (Toronto 1970), 352–3.

25 Donald Creighton, *Towards the Discovery of Canada* (Toronto 1972), 169, 273, 279–81.

26 Charles Taylor, *Radical Tories: The Conservative Tradition in Canada* (Toronto 1982), 23. See also Creighton's article "Watching the Sun Quietly Set on Canada," *Maclean's*, November 1971, 29ff.

27 Morton review in *Canadian Historical Review* 45 (December 1964): 320–1.

28 *Ottawa Citizen*, December 18, 1974, quoted in Norman Hillmer, "From Bosom to Bony Lap," *Acadiensis* 11 (Autumn 1981): 172.

4: WITCH-HUNTS AND FELLOW-TRAVELLERS

1 *Foreign Relations of the United States 1952–54*, vol. 6 (Washington 1986), 2054.

2 Reg Whitaker and Gary Marcuse, *Cold War Canada* (Toronto 1995), 365. The conclusions of this book may have to be revised when the Soviet archives are searched for Canadian material.

3 Stephen Endicott, *James G. Endicott: Rebel Out of China* (Toronto 1980), 272. The one-time Moderator of the United Church, J.R. Mutchmor, flatly described Endicott as a communist leader in the United Church. See *Mutchmor: The Memoirs of James Ralph Mutchmor* (Toronto 1965), 177.

4 NA, James Endicott Papers, vol. 1, Peace Movement file, "Keynote Address to the Canadian Peace Congress," 6 May 1949. I am most grateful to Professor Stephen Endicott for granting me access to his father's papers.

5 See Sergei Goncharev et al., *Uncertain Partners: Stalin, Mao and the Korean War* (Stanford 1994), 136ff.

6 Endicott Papers, vol. 40, file 871, "An Investigation of American Germ War in Korea," nd.

7 Ibid., W.H. Brittain to M. Jennison, May 30, 1952.

8 Ibid., file 874, "My Investigation of American Germ War in China," April 26, 1952.

9 Ibid., vol. 36, file 709, "The Attack on My Character," May 1952; Endicott, *James G. Endicott*, 296–8.

10 John English, *The Worldly Years: The Life of Lester Pearson 1949–1972* (Toronto 1992), 164, 171.

11 James Eayrs, *Canada in World Affairs October 1955 to June 1957* (Toronto 1959), 99–100. There were frequent articles in the early 1950s on McCarthyism in *Maclean's, Liberty, Saturday Night,* and other publications, and the Canadian Institute of Public Opinion reported on July 3, 1954, that of the 64 percent of Canadians who had heard of McCarthy and understood what he was about, 25 percent disapproved of him and 14 percent approved. Disapproval increased from east to west across the land.

12 H.S. Ferns, "Return to the Record: The Contribution of Herbert Norman," *Canadian Forum,* November 1986, 9.

13 Quoted in Joseph Barber, *Good Fences Make Good Neighbors* (Toronto 1958), 20.

14 NA, Arnold Heeney Papers, vol. 2., Diary, April 4, 1957, ff. A year earlier, however, on March 27, 1956, Prime Minister St Laurent had told Eisenhower that he was expecting "a nationalistic type of attack would be made by the opposition and many relatively minor points of criticism involving the United States would be exaggerated. It would also be alleged that they had become subservient to the United States." *Foreign Relations of the United States, 1955–1957,* vol. 27 (Washington 1992), 863.

15 Quoted in Roger Bowen, *Innocence Is Not Enough* (Vancouver 1986), 325

5: TOO CLOSE FOR COMFORT

1 See Denis Smith, *Rogue Tory: The Life and Legend of John G. Diefenbaker* (Toronto 1995) 20ff.

2 United States Treasury Department, Washington, Accession 68A5918, box 87, file Can/9/30, Scope and Objectives Paper for Meeting of United States–Canada Ministerial Committee on Joint Defense, November 8–9, 1959.

3 NA, Arnold Heeney Papers, vol. 2, Memoirs 1959 file, Diary, March 29, 1959; vol. 1, Memoranda of Conversations, August 30, 31, 1960.

4 J.F. Kennedy Library, POF, box 113, Canada Security 1961 file, Memorandum for the President, February 17, 1961.

5 Ibid., Canada Security—Trip to Ottawa (B) file, Scope Paper, May 2, 1961.

6 H. Basil Robinson, *Diefenbaker's World* (Toronto 1989), 268–9.

7 The most recent account, especially useful on naval questions, is Peter Haydon, *The 1962 Cuban Missile Crisis: Canadian Involvement Reconsidered* (Toronto 1993).

8 United States Declassified Documents, (78)301E, Colonel Burris to the Vice-President, February 6, 1963; Smith, *Rogue Tory,* 496–7.

9 George C. Marshall Library, Virginia Military Institute, W.W. Butterworth Papers, box 2, file 25, letter of January 14, 1963, and attached envelope addressed to *Ottawa Journal.*

10 Donald Fleming, *So Very Near: The Political Memoirs of the Honourable Donald M. Fleming,* vol. 2: *The Summit Years* (Toronto 1985), 627–8.

11 Butterworth Papers, box 2, file 25, telegram, Butterworth to State Department, April 23, 1963.

12 Ibid., R.Z. Smith Memorandum of Conversation, April 6, 1963.

13 Ibid., Butterworth to State Department, May 24, 1963.

14 Ibid., Vought memo, June 30, 1967. Dalton Camp, effectively running the Conservative campaign, has been quoted as saying, "We all knew it was a forgery. We all said 'Don't use it!'" Knowlton Nash, *Kennedy and Diefenbaker* (Toronto 1990), 286.

15 Butterworth Papers, box 2, file 25, Butterworth to Department of State, April 15, 1963. Butterworth's line was not uncommon in Canada. See, for example, John Saywell in *Financial Times*, March 11, 1963: "It will be interesting to see if [anti-Americanism as an electoral device] works. Its failure will be one measure of our maturity. Its success could be soul destroying."

16 Heather Robertson, *Igor: A Novel of Intrigue*, vol. 3: *The King Years* (Toronto 1989), 11–12.

17 Graeme Gibson, *Gentleman Death* (Toronto 1993), 216–17.

6: CLASS TRAITOR

1 Donald Creighton, "Presidential Address," Canadian Historical Association *Annual Report* 1957, 8ff.

2 United States Treasury Department, Washington, Acc 68A5918, box 85, file Can/0/25, Ottawa to State Department, February 12, 1957.

3 Queen's University Archives, J.J. Deutsch Papers, vol. 3, Deutsch to T. Kent, January 16, 1957. Deutsch had spoken warmly of US investment in a Vancouver address before the *Preliminary Report* appeared. See US Treasury Department, Acc 68A5918, box 87, file Can/6/2, US Consulate-General Vancouver to State Department, November 8, 1956.

4 *Winnipeg Free Press*, January 24, 1957.

5 US Treasury Department, Acc. 68A5918, box 87, file Can/6/2, Ottawa to State Department, February 12, 1957.

6 Queen's University Archives, J.M. Macdonnell Papers, vol. 45, file 37, Research Report no. 69, April 11, 1957.

7 J.L. Granatstein, *Canada 1957–1967: The Years of Uncertainty and Innovation* (Toronto 1986), 70ff.

8 Walter Gordon Papers (Toronto), L.B. Pearson file, Gordon to Pearson, March 9, 1960.

9 Walter Gordon, *A Political Memoir* (Toronto 1977), 81.

10 In MacLennan's untitled chapter in D.L.B. Hamlin, *The Price of Being Canadian* (Toronto 1961), 35.

11 Bank of Canada Archives, Louis Rasminsky Papers, file LR76–549, "Some Comments on the Budget," May 31, 1963.

12 J.F. Kennedy Library, J.F. Kennedy Papers, box 19, National Security Files, "Discriminatory Measures in Canadian Budget," June 28, 1963.

13 Ibid., NSF, box 17, Canada General file, "Canadian Reaction to Proposed U.S. Balance of Payments Measures," July 19, 1963.

14 Rasminsky Papers, file LR76–5630–1, "Meeting . . . August 18, 1963."

15 Denis Smith, *Gentle Patriot: A Political Biography of Walter Gordon* (Edmonton 1973), 231.

16 NA, Abraham Rotstein Papers, vol. 4, Newman to Rotstein, May 18, 1965.

17 Mitchell Sharp, *Which Reminds Me . . . : A Memoir* (Toronto 1994), 147.

18 Gordon Papers (Toronto), docs on Pearson file, December 22, 29, 1966. Opinion polls did not suggest Gordon's issue had broad support. On March 23, 1968, the Canadian Institute of Public Opinion reported that 56 percent wanted to encourage US investment, as against 26 percent who wanted to stop it.

19 Cited in Blair Fraser, "The Sharp/Gordon Debate," *Maclean's*, July 23, 1966, 9.

20 Gordon Papers (Toronto), docs on Gordon Papers, Pearson file. Sharp's view of this struggle is quite dissimilar. Sharp, *Which Reminds Me*, 143–5.

21 NA, Gordon Papers, vol. 37, "Canadian–American Relations," September 22, 1960.

22 Gordon Papers (Toronto), Pearson file, memo, February 20, 1968.

23 Glen Frankfurter, *Baneful Domination* (Toronto 1971), 196–7.

24 J.L. Granatstein and Robert Bothwell, *Pirouette: Pierre Trudeau and Canadian Foreign Policy* (Toronto 1990), chapter 6.

25 NA, Gordon Papers, vol. 4, Gordon to Mrs A. Jarvis, October 18, 1966.

7: THE ANTI-AMERICAN AMERICANS

1 Heather Robertson, *Igor: A Novel of Intrigue*, vol. 3: *The King Years* (Toronto 1989), 40–1.

2 Quoted in F.H. Epp, "American Causes of World War III," in J.H. Redekop, ed., *The Star-Spangled Beaver* (Toronto 1971), 118.

3 Lawrence Martin, *The Presidents and the Prime Ministers* (Toronto 1982), 226–7. Press reports at the time offered a radically different interpretation. See Blair Fraser, "Backstage at Camp David," *Maclean's*, May 1, 1965, 3. On April 26, however, Canada was advised that Johnson was "giving most careful consideration" to a bombing pause. NA, Paul Martin Papers, vol. 227, C.S.A. Ritchie to Martin, April 26, 1965.

4 Martin, *The Presidents and the Prime Ministers*, 227.

5 Quoted in Blair Fraser, "Backstage at Ottawa," *Maclean's*, February 19, 1966, 1.

6 Dennis Lee, *Civil Elegies and Other Poems* (Toronto 1972), 44ff. "Civil Elegies" was written in 1968. See Stan Dragland, "On Civil Elegies" in K. Mulhallen et al., eds., *Tasks of Passion: Dennis Lee at Mid-Career* (Toronto 1982), 172, 184.

7 In Jim Christy, ed., *The New Refugees: American Voices in Canada* (Toronto 1972), 16.

8 Douglas Fetherling, *Travels by Night* (Toronto 1994), 99, 113. Fetherling's characterization of the kinds of Americans who came to Canada is different from the one used here. See 145–6.

9 For example, House of Commons, *Debates*, December 2, 1966, 10666–7. On FBI-RCMP cooperation, however, see editorial in *Maclean's*, September 17, 1966, 4.

10 For example, House of Commons, *Debates*, March 30, 1966, 3616 and February 1, 1967, 12523.

11 Robert Bothwell, *Canada and the United States: The Politics of Partnership* (Toronto 1992), 98. NA, Records of the Immigration Branch, vol. 725, Military Personnel file, contains substantial correspondence both for and against admission of resisters. The quoted phrase is from J.M. Cameron to Allan MacEachen, May 3, 1969.

12 In Christy, *The New Refugees*, 125.

13 Cited in Renée Kasinsky, *Refugees from Militarism: Draft-Age Americans in Canada* (New Brunswick, NJ, 1976), 156.

14 John Sandman in Christy, *The New Refugees*, 108.

15 Ibid., 109.

16 *Toronto Star*, December 17, 1970.

17 Quoted in J.H. Thompson and S. Randall, *Canada and the United States: Ambivalent Allies* (Montreal 1994), 247–8.

18 In *America, Love It or Leave It*, video recording by Alioli and Associates Ltd., Toronto, 1990.

8: ANTI-YANKVILLE

1 Mathews's letters to author, December 6, 24, 1994.

2 R. Mathews and J. Steele, *The Struggle for Canadian Universities* (Toronto 1969), 47–8.

3 I am indebted to Sarah McKinnon of the University of Winnipeg for reminding me of this fact, which remains unchanged to this day.

4 NA, Robin Mathews Papers, vol. 4, MacLennan to Mathews, February 2, 1971. MacLennan had been speaking out against the Americanization of Canada for some years. See Elspeth Cameron, *Hugh MacLennan: A Writer's Life* (Toronto 1981), 312.

5 Patricia Welbourn, "Made in U.S.A.," *Weekend Magazine*, March 22, 1969, 4.

6 Letter, Mathews to Granatstein, April 17, 1995.

7 Ibid., December 24, 1994.

8 See Robin Mathews, *Treason of the Intellectuals: English Canada in the Post-Modern World* (Prescott, Ont., 1995), 109. The chapter in Mathews's book on which this reference is based is, among other things, an attack on the author of this book.

Wrong-headed, to be sure, but as always provocative and difficult to counter!

9 Mathews Papers, vol. 7, Lee to Mathews, February 21, 1972, and reply March 2, 1972.

10 Ibid., Mathews to Lee, March 4, 1972.

11 Ibid., vol. 20, Lower to Mathews, January 30, 1972.

12 Letter, Paul Grayson to author, March 14, 1995.

13 University of Waterloo Archives, Jack Brown Secretariat Records, file 53, "Mathews' Report on Decanadianization of the Universities," William Davis to Mathews, August 8, 1969, A80-0031. I am indebted to Frank Clarke for this document.

14 J. Paul Grayson Papers (Toronto), clippings (especially *Globe and Mail*, February 1, 1973, *London Free Press*, February 2, 1973), submissions to Select Committee, January 1973, and Grayson letter, nd.

15 Letter, Mathews to author, February 12, 1995.

16 Mathews Papers, vol. 2, Mathews to Brian Fawcett, April 5, 1985.

9: IMAGINING CANADA

1 John Metcalf, *Freedom from Culture: Selected Essays, 1982–92* (Toronto 1994), 116–17. Grant's comment on Mowat is in his "Fate of the Willing," *Books in Canada* (January–February 1988): 19.

2 *Lament for a Nation: The Defeat of Canadian Nationalism* (Toronto 1965). Quotations below are from the 1965 edition. The review of Grant's book by Kenneth McNaught in *Saturday Night* (August 1965), 7–9, was especially useful. The tart appraisal of *Lament* is from Mordecai Richler's review in the *Sunday Herald Tribune*, Book Week, October 31, 1965, 2.

3 William Christian, *George Grant: A Biography* (Toronto 1993), 247–8. In an article by Judy Steed in the *Globe and Mail*, July 9, 1983, Grant said that "Dief was such a maniac in many ways but he stood firm against the Kennedys when it mattered."

4 Christian, *Grant*, 263.

5 Ibid., 250.

6 Ibid., 251.

7 Ibid.

8 George Grant, "Nationalism and Rationality," *Canadian Forum*, 50 (January 1971): 337.

9 Northrop Frye, "Sharing the Continent," in his *Divisions on a Ground* (Toronto 1982), 57ff.

10 Margaret Atwood, *Survival: A Thematic Guide to Canadian Literature* (Toronto 1972), 35–6, 238ff. See Atwood's comments on *Survival* in her *Second Words: Selected Critical Prose* (Toronto 1982), 385ff. See also Laurence Steven, "Margaret

Atwood's 'Polarities' and George Grant's Polemics," *American Review of Canadian Studies* 18 (1988): 443ff.

11 David Staines, "Moving Away from Disbelief: The Rise of a Canadian Reading Public," *American Review of Canadian Studies* 14 (1984): 359–60.

12 Quoted in Jamie Portman, "Not by Bread Alone: The Battle over Canadian Culture," in David Thomas, ed., *Canada and the United States: Differences That Count* (Peterborough, Ont., 1993), 360–1.

13 Robert Fulford, *Best Seat in the House* (Toronto 1988), 196–7.

14 Kate Fillion, "Travels by Night a Bleak Road," *Globe and Mail*, April 25, 1994.

15 Farley Mowat, "Letter to My Son," in A.W. Purdy, ed., *The New Romans* (Edmonton 1969), 2–3.

16 Farley Mowat, *My Discovery of America* (Toronto 1985), 47, 53ff. Mowat's account of "Buster" Brown's views and career is only marginally correct.

17 Robert Fulford, "Canada's Restive Nationalism," *Art News* 76 (April 1977): 76.

18 Greg Curnoe, "Amendments to Continental Refusal/Refus Continental," *20 Cents Magazine* 4 (April 1970). Curnoe's amendments were to his friend and fellow artist John Boyle's "Continental Refusal," ibid.

19 Joe Hermer, "Handlebar Mustache," *Literary Review of Canada*, December 1994, 12.

20 Barrie Hale, "Talking Pictures," *Canadian Magazine*, July 17, 1976, 12.

21 Dennis Reid, *Greg Curnoe: Canada. Xe Biennale. Sao Paolo. 1969* (np, nd), 47–9; Barry Lord, *The History of Painting in Canada: Towards a People's Art* (Toronto 1974), 231.

22 Fulford, *Best Seat*, 78.

23 Ibid., 77.

24 Hermer, "Handlebar Mustache," 13.

25 Robert Fulford, "General Perspectives on Canadian Culture," *American Review of Canadian Studies* 3 (Spring 1973): 119.

26 Tom Wayman, *A Country Not Considered: Canada, Culture, Work* (Concord, Ont., 1993), 33, 83.

27 Fulford, *Best Seat*, 195.

28 *Globe and Mail*, January 23, 1996.

29 *Time*, March 1, 1971, 7.

30 Fulford, *Best Seat*, 199.

31 *Globe and Mail*, March 10, 1995. Since proportionately more Canadians than Americans had cable TV, colour TVs, VCRs, and CD players, the exposure to American media was enormous (*New York Times*, November 7, 1993).

32 Susan M. Crean, *Who's Afraid of Canadian Culture?* (Toronto 1976), 275–7.

10: LAST GASP ANTI-AMERICANISM

1 Peter C. Newman, *The Canadian Revolution 1985–1995: From Deference to Defiance* (Toronto 1995).

2 *The Gallup Report*, November 11, 1985.

3 *Globe and Mail*, October 7, 1985.

4 Sam Gindin, "Breaking Away: The Formation of the Canadian Auto Workers," *Studies in Political Economy* 29 (Summer 1989): 84.

5 David Orchard, *The Fight for Canada* (Toronto 1993), 258; Hurtig in Duncan Cameron, ed., *The Free Trade Papers* (Toronto 1986), 200.

6 Michael Hart et al., *Decision at Midnight: Inside the Canada–U.S. Free Trade Negotiations* (Vancouver 1994), 311.

7 Marci McDonald, *Yankee Doodle Dandy: Brian Mulroney and the American Agenda* (Toronto 1995), 227.

8 James Laxer, *False God: How the Globalization Myth has Impoverished Canada* (Toronto 1993), 2.

9 Maude Barlow, *Parcel of Rogues: How Free Trade is Failing Canada* (Toronto 1990), 20.

10 Mel Hurtig in *Canada Not For Sale: The Case Against Free Trade* (Toronto 1987), 7.

11 Brian Fawcett, "Big Deal," *Canadian Forum* (July–August, 1994), 18; Atwood quoted in Robert Mason Lee, *One Hundred Monkeys* (Toronto 1989), 50ff; Michael Dufresne, "Anti-Americanism in English-Canadian Political Thought: The 1988 Free Trade Agreement" (MA thesis, Carleton University, 1994), 34. I am greatly indebted to Mr Dufresne's work.

12 Graham Fraser, *Playing for Keeps* (Toronto 1989), 325.

13 Newman, *The Canadian Revolution*, 275.

14 Philip Resnick, *Letters to a Québécois Friend* (Montreal 1990), 57.

15 This is Richard Gwyn's phrase in his able *Nationalism Without Walls: The Unbearable Lightness of Being Canadian* (Toronto 1995), 43.

16 See Paul Chamberland, "Le retour du père Ubu," *Le Devoir*, décembre 18–19, 1993; Montreal *Gazette*, December 24, 1993.

17 Robert Chodos and Eric Hamovitch, *Quebec and the American Dream* (Toronto 1991), 225.

18 Quoted in Jeffery Simpson, *Faultlines* (Toronto 1993), 281.

19 *Maclean's*, November 29, 1993, 15.

20 McDonald, *Yankee Doodle Dandy*, 53.

21 *Toronto Star*, September 23, 1994; January 8, 1995.

CONCLUSION

1 Mark Kingwell, "Colonialism, Civility, and the National Team," in William

Humber and John St James, eds., *All I Thought About Was Baseball: Writings on a Canadian Pastime* (Toronto 1996), 169.

2 *Globe and Mail*, November 16, 1995.

3 Quoted in Kenneth McNaught, "Frank Underhill: A Personal Interpretation," *Queen's Quarterly* 79 (Summer 1972): 134–5.

4 George Orwell, "Notes on Nationalism," in S. Orwell and I. Angus, eds., *The Collected Essays, Journalism and Letters of George Orwell* (London 1968), vol. 3, 380.

5 Seymour Martin Lipset, *Continental Divide* (New York 1990), is a useful indicator of the differences.

6 Pierre Berton, *My Times: Living with History 1947–1995* (Toronto 1995), 390.

7 Arthur Andrew, *The Rise and Fall of a Middle Power* (Toronto 1993), 64.

BIBLIOGRAPHY

INTRODUCTION

While there is a varied international literature on anti-Americanism as a world phenomenon, the quantity is not especially impressive. As might be expected, most of what exists is by Americans. The United States Information Agency's polls, published as *Opinion Research Memoranda,* are suggestive guides to attitudes around the world as they ebb and flow. Among the books I have found particularly helpful are Tony Judt, *Past Imperfect: French Intellectuals, 1944–1956* (Berkeley 1992); D. Lacorne et al., eds., *The Rise and Fall of French Anti-Americanism* (London 1990); Richard Kuisel, *Seducing the French: The Dilemma of Americanization* (Berkeley 1993); Reinhold Wagnleitner, *Coca-Colonization and the Cold War: The Cultural Mission of the United States in Austria After the Second World War* (Chapel Hill 1994); and R. Lunden and Erik Asard, eds., *Networks of Americanization: Aspects of the American Influence on Sweden* (Uppsala 1992). The sole Canadian book of a general nature that treats the subject is Alan Smith's collection of essays, *Canada: An American Nation?* (Montreal 1994), although Claude Savary, dir., *Les rapports culturels entre le Québec et les États Unis* (Québec 1984) is useful on Quebec attitudes.

1: BLIND HATRED?

Primary sources employed in this chapter include the W.L. Mackenzie clippings and the Brock Monument Papers in the Archives of Ontario, J.J. Talman's *Loyalist Narratives from Upper Canada* (Toronto 1946), J.L.H. Henderson, ed., *John Strachan: Documents and Opinions* (Toronto 1969), and the very useful Champlain

Society Ontario Series volume edited by Colin Read and R.J. Stagg, *The Rebellion of 1837 in Upper Canada* (Toronto 1985).

The writings of S.F. Wise are the best starting point for study of the impact of Loyalist attitudes on Canadian thinking. Many of his essays are collected in his *God's Peculiar Peoples* (Ottawa 1993), and in his book with R.C. Brown, *Canada Views the United States* (Seattle 1967). The book by Mills, T*he Idea of Loyalty in Upper Canada, 1784–1850*, cited in the notes to this chapter, is also an important contribution, as are the Jane Errington volume, *The Lion, the Eagle, and Upper Canada* (Montreal 1987), and Neil MacKinnon's book *This Unfriendly Soul: The Loyalist Experience in Nova Scotia 1783–1791* (Montreal 1986). On the Loyalists' travails, Christopher Moore's *The Loyalists* (Toronto 1994) is a model of popular history. Good studies from an American point of view include Gordon Stewart, *The American Response to Canada since 1776* (East Lansing 1992) and R.C. Stuart, *United States Expansionism and British North America, 1775–1871* (Chapel Hill 1988).

The creation of the Loyalist myth is splendidly explored in Murray Barkley's articles on New Brunswick in *Acadiensis* (Spring 1975) and on the Canadas in S.F. Wise et al., eds., *"None Was Ever Better . . .": The Loyalist Settlement of Ontario* (Toronto 1984), and in Norman Knowles's PhD dissertation, "Inventing the Loyalists: The Ontario Loyalist Tradition and the Creation of a Usable Past, 1784–1924" (York University, 1992). Carl Berger's *The Sense of Power* (Toronto 1970) remains important as an examination of Canadian imperialist/nationalist thinking in the nineteenth century.

Susanna Moodie's *Roughing It In The Bush* (Ottawa 1988), Catherine Parr Traill's *Backwoods of Canada* (Toronto 1966), and Anna Jameson's *Winter Studies and Summer Rambles in Canada* (Toronto 1965), offer the British immigrants' perspective, while T.C. Haliburton's tart and funny *Sam Slick* (Toronto 1923) is an important literary source from early nineteenth-century Nova Scotia.

2: UNDER WHICH FLAG?

Primary sources employed include the Sir John A. Macdonald, Sir George Parkin, Sir Robert Borden, Sir George Foster, and Sir Wilfrid Laurier Papers at the National Archives of Canada, as well as the Department of External Affairs Records held there. Joseph Pope's *Correspondence of Sir John Macdonald* (Toronto nd) is more than a century old but still useful.

Indispensable books include Donald Creighton's two-volume life of *John A. Macdonald* (Toronto 1952, 1955) and O.D. Skelton's *Life and Letters of Sir Wilfrid Laurier* (Toronto 1921), C.C. Tansill's *Canadian–American Relations, 1875–1911* (New Haven 1943), G.T. Denison's *The Struggle for Imperial Unity* (Toronto 1909), Goldwin Smith's *Canada and the Canadian Question* (Toronto 1891), and Samuel Moffett, *The Americanization of Canada* (1907; reprinted Toronto 1972). Peter Waite, *Canada, 1874–1896* (Toronto 1971) is a must read, as is R.C. Brown and Ramsay Cook, *Canada, 1896–1921* (Toronto 1974). P. Stevens, ed., *The 1911 General Election: A Study in Canadian Politics* (Toronto 1970), collects most of the important documents. One critically useful article is Robert Cuff's analysis of "The Toronto Eighteen and the Election of 1911," *Ontario History* (December 1965).

For a brief survey of the trade issue from its nineteenth-century beginnings to the Free Trade Agreement of 1988, see my "Free Trade between Canada and the United States: The Issue That Will Not Go Away," in D. Stairs and G. Winham, eds., *The Politics of Canada's Economic Relationship with the United States* (Toronto 1985). Sara Jeannette Duncan's *The Imperialist* (reprinted, Toronto 1961) remains the definitive fictional description of turn-of-the-century Canadian attitudes to trade questions, far superior to the discussion of the 1911 reciprocity election in Ralph Connor's *The Major* (Toronto 1927).

3: ON THE AMERICAN ROAD

Primary sources used in this chapter include the Sir Robert Borden, Mackenzie King, W.L. Grant, R.B. Hanson, and Arthur Meighen Papers in the National Archives of Canada, the F.D. Roosevelt Papers at Hyde Park, NY, and US Treasury Department Records at the United States National Archives in Washington. J.W. Pickersgill's *Mackenzie King Record* (Toronto 1960–70) is invaluable in presenting an edited version of King's huge diary from 1939 to 1948.

Much of my own writing has been concentrated on this era. See *How Britain's Weakness Forced Canada into the Arms of the United States* (Toronto 1989); (with Robert Cuff), *Ties That Bind: Canadian–American Relations from the Great War to the Cold War* (Toronto 1977); *Canada's War: The Politics of the Mackenzie King Government, 1939–1945* (Toronto 1974); *A Man of Influence: Norman A. Robertson and Canadian Statecraft, 1929–1968* (Ottawa 1981); and "Mackenzie King and Canada at Ogdensburg, August 1940," in J.J. Sokolsky and J.T. Jockel, eds., *Fifty Years of Canada–United States Defense Cooperation* (Lewiston 1992). All treat Canadian–American relations and attitudes in substantial detail.

Very helpful sources include all volumes of James Eayrs, *In Defence of Canada* (Toronto 1962–83); Carl Berger, *The Writing of Canadian History* (Toronto 1986); Charles Taylor, *Six Journeys: A Canadian Pattern* (Toronto 1977); and Lawrence Martin, *The Presidents and the Prime Ministers* (Toronto 1982). Donald Creighton's *Forked Road: Canada 1939–1957* (Toronto 1976) is not his best-researched book, but it, like George Grant's *Lament for a Nation* (Toronto 1965), does at least present a coherent anti-American view of Canadian history. Ramsay Cook's article, "Imagining a North American Garden," *Canadian Literature* (March 1984), was also very suggestive.

4: WITCH-HUNTS AND FELLOW-TRAVELLERS

Primary sources used include the James Endicott, L.B. Pearson, and John G. Diefenbaker Papers and the Department of External Affairs Records, all at the National Archives in Ottawa, and the debates of the House of Commons. American documents from the enormous array of *Foreign Relations of the United States* volumes for the period were also used. I have made use herein, and in subsequent chapters of opinion polls undertaken by the Gallup Poll of Canada.

Basic books for the period include the autobiographies of Pearson, *Mike* (Toronto 1972–75), and Diefenbaker, *One Canada* (Toronto 1975–77); the very fine biography of Pearson by John English, *The Worldly Years: The Life of Lester Pearson,*

1949–1972 (Toronto 1992); Stephen Endicott's biography of his father, *James G. Endicott: Rebel Out of China* (Toronto 1980); John Hilliker and Donald Barry, *Canada's Department of External Affairs*, vol. 2: *Coming of Age, 1946–1968* (Montreal 1995); James Eayrs, *Canada in World Affairs, October 1955 to June 1957* (Toronto 1959); and J.L. Granatstein and David Stafford, *Spy Wars: Espionage and Canada from Gouzenko to Glasnost* (Toronto, 1990). Charles Taylor's *Six Journeys* examines Norman sympathetically, but it has been superseded by the two biographies: Roger Bowen, *Innocence Is Not Enough* (Vancouver 1986), which is extraordinarily pro-Norman, and James Barros, *No Sense of Evil* (Toronto 1986), which is not.

On the germ-warfare charges during the Korean War, see especially Mark Taylor, *Chinese Attitudes toward Nuclear Weapons: China and the United States During the Korean War* (New York 1989); on the Korean–Soviet–Chinese planning for Korea, Sergei Goncharev et al., *Uncertain Partners: Stalin, Mao and the Korean War* (Stanford 1994) is indispensable.

5: TOO CLOSE FOR COMFORT

Primary sources used in this chapter include the John G. Diefenbaker, L.B. Pearson, Howard Green, J.M. Minifie, A.D.P. Heeney, and Douglas Harkness Papers, as well as the records of the Department of External Affairs, all at the National Archives, Ottawa; the Gordon Churchill Papers, which I saw on Vancouver Island; the John F. Kennedy Papers at the J.F. Kennedy Library in Boston, Mass; the W.W. Butterworth Papers at the G.C. Marshall Library, Lexington, Va; and records of the Departments of State and Treasury at the US National Archives, Washington.

Basic published sources include the Diefenbaker memoirs, which are almost completely unreliable, and Denis Smith's good biography, *Rogue Tory* (Toronto 1995). H. Basil Robinson's *Diefenbaker's World* (Toronto 1989), a study of Dief and foreign policy by his External Affairs' aide, is excellent, as is Peyton Lyon, *Canada in World Affairs, 1961–1963* (Toronto 1968). Donald Fleming's memoir is a treasure trove: see the two volumes of *So Very Near: The Political Memoirs of the Hon. Donald M. Fleming* (Toronto 1985). Lawrence Martin's *The Presidents and the Prime Ministers* is good on this period. *Kennedy and Diefenbaker: Fear and Loathing Across the Undefended Border* (Toronto 1990), by Knowlton Nash, is one book whose title says it all. Finally, see my *Canada 1957–1967: The Years of Uncertainty and Innovation* (Toronto 1986).

6: CLASS TRAITOR

Manuscript sources used include the Walter Gordon Papers, which were in Gordon's office when I first saw them, but are now in the National Archives in Ottawa; the L.B. Pearson, F.H. Underhill, and the Abraham Rotstein Papers also there; Louis Rasminsky's Papers at the Bank of Canada Archives; the John Deutsch and J.M. Macdonnell Papers at the Queen's University Archives; the J.F. Kennedy Papers at the Kennedy Library, Boston; and US Treasury Department records at the Treasury Department, Washington.

Gordon's own *A Political Memoir* (Toronto 1977) and Denis Smith's *Gentle Patriot* (Edmonton 1973) are essential sources, as are the several books that Gordon wrote from 1960 onwards on policy questions, always including the problem of American investment. The Pearson memoirs and John English's biography offer Pearson's viewpoint on the collapse of his relations with Gordon, while Mitchell Sharp, *Which Reminds Me . . . : A Memoir* (Toronto 1994), presents that of Gordon's antagonist in Cabinet. The literature on foreign investment is massive, ranging from scholarly studies (relatively few) to polemics (a huge number). The basic text on the history of Canadian business is Michael Bliss, *Northern Enterprise* (Toronto 1987).

7: THE ANTI-AMERICAN AMERICANS

Primary sources used in this chapter include the Paul Martin and the L.B. Pearson Papers, and the Department of External Affairs Records at the National Archives; the National Security Files in the Lyndon B. Johnson Papers at the L.B. Johnson Library, Austin, Texas; and the debates of the House of Commons.

Lawrence Martin's *The Presidents and the Prime Ministers* is at its best on the Pearson-Johnson relationship. James Eayrs's *In Defence of Canada*, vol. 5: *Indochina: Roots of Complicity* (Toronto 1983) is another book whose title gives its thesis, as is Robert Bothwell's *Canada and the United States: The Politics of Partnership* (Toronto 1992). On American draft resisters in Canada, see Renée Kasinsky, *Refugees from Militarism* (New Brunswick, NJ 1976); Jim Christy, ed., *The New Refugees* (Toronto 1972); Roger Williams, *The New Exiles* (New York 1971); and James Laxer, "The Americanization of the Canadian Student Movement," in I. Lumsden. ed., *Close the 49th Parallel, etc.: The Americanization of Canada* (Toronto. 1970). Regrettably, Alan Haig-Brown's *Hell No, We Won't Go* (Vancouver 1996) was published too late to be used in this chapter.

8: ANTI-YANKVILLE

Primary sources employed include the Robin Mathews and Walter Gordon Papers at the National Archives, university records in the University of Waterloo Archives, and Paul Grayson's papers in his possession. Professor Mathews's letters to me have also been most helpful.

The literature on the Canadianization of universities is voluminous. Much of the best article literature can be located in the *Journal of Canadian Studies* from 1970 onwards, in the histories of universities (e.g., J. Gwynne-Timothy, *Western's First Century,* London 1978) or the memoirs of university administrators (e.g., Claude Bissell, *Halfway Up Parnassus,* Toronto 1974). Additional sources, among a multitude, include essays in Ian Lumsden, ed., *Close the 49th Parallel, etc.,* Alan Cairns, "Political Science in Canada and the Americanization Issue," *Canadian Journal of Political Science* (June 1975), S.D. Clark, "The American Takeover of Canadian Sociology: Myth or Reality?" in his *Canadian Society in Historical Perspective* (Toronto 1976), and Ramsay Cook, "Nationalism in Canada or *Portnoy's Complaint* Revisited," *South Atlantic Quarterly* (Winter 1970). Symons's report is *To Know Ourselves: The Report of the Commission on Canadian Studies* (Ottawa 1975).

9: IMAGINING CANADA

This chapter draws on a wide range of sources, most of an ephemeral kind. Exceptions include Mary Vipond's able PhD dissertation, "National Consciousness in English-Speaking Canada in the 1920s" (University of Toronto 1974), John Weaver's equally good dissertation, "Imperilled Dreams: Canadian Opposition to the American Empire, 1918–30" (Duke University 1973), Robert Fulford's *Best Seat in the House: Memoirs of a Lucky Man* (Toronto 1988), Charles Taylor's *Radical Tories: The Conservative Tradition in Canada* (Toronto 1982), W.L. Morton's *The Canadian Identity* (Toronto 1961), George Grant's *Lament for a Nation* (Toronto 1965), and William Christian's *George Grant: A Biography* (Toronto 1993) which, while an able study, must be the worst proofread book ever published by a Canadian university press. Paul Audley produced a very useful guide, *Canada's Cultural Industries* (Toronto 1983).

The Margaret Atwood writings used include *Survival* (Toronto 1972), *Second Words* (Toronto 1982), "Backdrop Addresses Cowboy," in A.W. Purdy, ed., *The New Romans* (Edmonton 1968), *The Robber Bride* (Toronto 1993), and *The Handmaid's Tale* (Toronto 1985). The Mowat material includes "Letter to My Son" in Purdy, ed., *The New Romans,* and *My Discovery of America* (Toronto 1985).

The material on Greg Curnoe comes from, among other sources, Barry Lord, *The History of Painting in Canada: Towards A People's Art* (Toronto, 1974); Pierre Théberge, *Greg Curnoe: Retrospective* (Ottawa 1982); Dennis Reid, *Greg Curnoe. Canada. Xe Bienniale. Sao Paolo. 1969* (np, nd); and Curnoe's articles in *Canadian Forum, Fuse,* and *20 Cents Magazine.*

10: LAST GASP ANTI-AMERICANISM

The 1988 election, the Free Trade Agreement, and NAFTA produced a substantial literature, much of it polemical. On the last Trudeau years, Christina McCall and Stephen Clarkson, *Trudeau and Our Times,* vol. 2: *The Heroic Delusion* (Toronto 1994) is good. Useful studies of the 1988 election include Richard Johnston et al., *Letting the People Decide: Dynamics of a Canadian Election* (Montreal 1992); Graham Fraser, *Playing for Keeps* (Toronto 1989); and Robert Mason Lee, *One Hundred Monkeys* (Toronto, 1989). The best examination of the FTA negotiations is Michael Hart et al., *Decision at Midnight: Inside the Canada–U.S. Free Trade Negotiations* (Vancouver 1994). Examples of the polemical literature include David Orchard, *The Fight for Canada: Four Centuries of Resistance to American Expansionism* (Toronto 1993), and Stephen McBride and John Shields, *Dismantling a Nation: Canada and the New World Order* (Halifax 1993). On attitudes in and to Quebec, see Jeffrey Simpson, *Faultlines* (Toronto 1993); Robert Chodos and Eric Hamovitch, *Quebec and the American Dream* (Toronto 1991); and Philip Resnick, *Letters to a Québécois Friend* (Montreal 1990).

INDEX

C